Colin

All about Selling

All about Selling

Alan Williams

McGRAW-HILL Book Company (UK) Limited

London · New York · St Louis · San Francisco · Auckland · Bogotá
Guatemala · Hamburg · Johannesburg · Lisbon · Madrid · Mexico
Montreal · New Delhi · Panama · Paris · San Juan · São Paulo
Singapore · Sydney · Tokyo · Toronto

Published by
McGRAW-HILL Book Company (UK) Limited
MAIDENHEAD · BERKSHIRE · ENGLAND

British Library Cataloguing in Publication Data

Williams, Alan
  All about selling
  1. Selling
  I. Title
  658.8'5   HF5438.25

  ISBN 0–07–084593–X

Library of Congress Cataloging in Publication Data

Williams, Alan.
  All about selling.

  Includes index.
  1. Selling. I. Title.
HF5438.25.W525   1983   658.8'5   82–25877
ISBN 0–07–084593–X

12345   MoC   86543

Typeset by Phoenix Photosetting, Chatham
Printed and bound in Great Britain by Mackays of Chatham Ltd

To Margaret
the librarian in my life

Contents

Preface   xi

Acknowledgements   xiii

1. The fundamentals of selling   1

    What is selling?   1
    What is salesmanship?   2
    The qualities of a professional salesman   4
    Why do people buy?   5
    Selling as a career   8

2. Product and applications knowledge   15

    The importance of knowing your product   15
    What is product knowledge?   16
    Sources of knowledge   20

3. Prospecting   25

    Sources of prospective users   26
    Using the telephone   29
    Dealing with management   35
    Sales enquiries   38
    Prospect qualification   39
    Spotting tomorrow's successes and failures   41

4. Territory management   44

    Every salesman should be a farmer   44
    Time management   46
    Organization and documentation   48

5. Communications   56

    The basis of communications   56
    Obstacles to communication   58
    The veil of mystique   61
    There is more than one way of making a point   62
    Fuelling the fire of annoyance   62
    Demonstrations   64
    Presentations and visual aids   65
    Sales sensitivity   67
    What makes people tick?   69
    Don't send a memo   69

6. Initiating the sale   72

    Preparing the sales call   72
    The structure of the sales call   75
    Opening the interview   77
    The sales presentation   79
    Sales benefits and advantages   81
    The qualifications of sales benefits   82

7. Disciplines of the sales negotiation   85

    Selling solutions   85
    Situation evaluation   87
    Evaluating the competition   88
    Feasibility studies   91
    The sales proposal   93
    Don't sell futures   94
    Reference selling   95
    Attacking the competition   97

8. Overcoming sales resistance   99

    The nature of sales objections   99
    The importance of being flexible   100
    Apathy and inertia   100
    Emotional considerations   101
    Sources and kinds of sales resistance   102
    Basic types of sales objections   103
    The importance of good timing   108
    Essential disciplines   109
    Dealing with sales objections   112
    Summary   123

9. Closing the sale   125

    Basic principles   125
    Disciplines and objectives   131
    Closing methods   151
    After the close   171

10. Final stages of the sale   174

    Attempting to close the wrong person   174
    No order is ever absolutely secure   176
    Proposal follow-up   177
    Contracts and agreements   178
    Delivery promises   180
    The lost sale postmortem   182
    'No' does not always mean 'goodbye'   184
    Handling mistakes   185

11. Political and emotional forces   188

    Selling in times of economic recession   188
    Company politics   189
    Always get the story right   190
    Always locate the actual decision-maker   192
    The organization within the organization   193
    Types of buyer   195
    Steering committees   197

12. Some financial aspects of selling   199

    Prospecting and company cashflow   199
    The implications of discounts   200
    Overdue accounts   201
    Profitable selling   201
    Is the price too high?   203

13. Personal disciplines   205

    Personal appearance   205
    Mental and physical fitness   206
    Working in the office   208
    Workload priorities   209
    The effective use of selling time   210
    Positive thinking   211
    Public conversations   211
    Routine calls   212

Consequential thinking   213
Familiarity breeds contempt   214
Consistency   215
New Year resolutions   216
Company cars   218
A code of practice for professional salespeople   221

Index   224

Preface

'There is no subject so old that nothing new can be said about it.'
Feodor Dostoievsky 1821–81

Most people get into writing books about selling as a natural extension of their everyday activity, usually sales training. It is a very useful and sensible way of documenting their skills and experience, as well as being an acceptable public relations exercise. My decision to write this book came about not so much from an urgent desire to teach, but rather that of being a salesman who enjoys writing. For many years I have been involved in composing music and writing for the theatre as well as in some journalistic activity related to computers and selling. This work is merely an extension of these pursuits. It is not intended to be a comprehensive textbook for sales training, it is rather a source of leisurely self-education. It is not so much the way to do it, but more the way I have done it, having made a lot of mistakes and learned a lot of lessons on the way. As Oscar Wilde once said, 'Experience is the name everyone gives to their mistakes.'

Someone once described selling as 'the art of giving people your own way'. Certainly, it is an indisputable fact that truly understanding people and being able to persuade them to your point of view is a substantial quality for the pursuit of success, not only in selling, but in any role where achievement is ultimately dependent on the actions of others. One only has to read the newspapers any day of the week to see how ineffectual the average manager, politician, husband or wife can be when it comes to truly understanding the problems and motivations of those around them.

This book is not just for salespeople, it is for anyone who is involved with selling anything, whether it be products, ideas, philosophies or themselves. It is about persuading others. It is about self-organization and motivation. It is about winning in the game of social and self-survival.

I cannot finish this introduction without mentioning what might appear to be a piece of blatant male chauvinism. Throughout this book I have referred to all salespeople in the male gender. Normally, I would not run the risk of demeaning the many successful women in selling by even raising the topic; but unfortunately there is a prejudice against women in selling and I would not wish to perpetuate it by any misconception my writing might give. In every instance that I have used the term 'salesman', 'saleswoman' could equally apply. However, I have to say I hate the word 'salesperson'; like 'chairperson', and similar words, it is a patronizing nonsense that is, in my opinion, a greater insult than chauvinism itself.

I hope you will enjoy reading this book whether you approach it as a 'novel' or a reference document. Whatever your motivations, I wish you all the sales success you deserve.

Alan Williams

Acknowledgements

Writing this book has not been without its problems. Had it not been for the help of many good friends I guess it would never have happened.

I would like to declare my thanks and appreciation to Malcolm Peltu for starting me out with 'The Sales Bit', Dorothy Fincham for her patience and encouragement when things were getting rough, my colleagues at Sales and Marketing Recruiters for their support and confidence where I really needed it, Sue Arnold my diligent typist who became a Tupperware saleswoman as a result of her interest, and my wife, Margaret, for tolerating my highs and lows. I hope they all think it was worth while!

I would also like to record the fact that some of the items in this book are based on articles that first appeared in *Computer Weekly*, an IPC publication.

1.

The fundamentals of selling

'Everyone lives by selling something.'

Robert Louis Stevenson 1850–94

This book is likely to be read by a wide range of people covering many levels of sales experience; sales managers, senior, junior and trainee salespeople, experienced business people considering a move into a selling role, or even young people about to leave an academic environment. In order to assist the inexperienced and provide a reminder to those already established in the selling profession, let us start out with some thoughts on what the selling process is about.

What is selling?

There are no slick or simple answers to this question. Selling embraces too many horizons and interpretations to be explained away merely in terms of technique, emotion, philosophy or business function. Many definitions have been put forward over the years, but none appear to fully embrace the total power and significance of the selling process. Such explanations are usually limited to the confines of its main component, salesmanship. Clearly, salesmanship is the skill that enables products to be sold and salespeople to achieve success. But the salesman's role within the scheme of things cannot be effective unless he has a positive understanding of the total mechanism in which his activity is the principal function. Selling must be fully appreciated in its broadest context as both the cornerstone of individual company success and the key to national prosperity and economic expansion.

In its fundamental context, selling is the active element of marketing. It is an inseparable ally, upon which the ultimate success of marketing depends. It is the initiation of a 'domino effect' that concludes in the satisfaction of the buyer's need, having pursued a route that inevitably embraces the creation, maintenance and expansion of employment, and the prosperity of employer and employee alike. In other words, the company mechanism cannot logically operate until somebody sells something. Selling is the purveyor of the new, despite the suspicion and protestations

1

of those who are secure in the comfort of the old. It is a positive agent for change, innovation, and new ideas; a key factor in the expansion of a progressive society. Selling is a bridge between the maker and the user; it is a justification and outlet for the product of a business enterprise in its ability to persuade potential consumers to try, buy, and use. Selling is the process on which the health, growth, and survival of a commercial business ultimately depends. It is the sustaining force of free enterprise. To describe it merely as the transfer of goods, services or ideas from one party to another in exchange for money is a serious understatement.

Ralph Waldo Emerson once said, 'If a man can write a better book, preach a better sermon, or make a better mouse-trap than his neighbour, tho' he build his house in the woods, the world will make a beaten path to his door.' Sadly, the world is not like that. The 'better mouse-trap' syndrome is self-deception at its worst; the kind of naïvety and blind optimism that has brought about the decline and fall of many otherwise admirable business enterprises. The story goes that in order to prove the inability of the average citizen to identify and accept a bargain when he sees one, a man once stood in the street offering pound notes for sale at a penny each. He didn't make a sale all day! This, perhaps predictable, outcome was not simply an example of public suspicion and the vendor's credibility, it simply points out that no matter how good your products, and how attractive the deal may be, you still have to sell it. A bargain is not a bargain unless you believe you need or want it. That is where the art of salesmanship begins.

What is salesmanship?

There are many truisms related to the subject of salesmanship. For example:

Salesmanship is 90 per cent people and 10 per cent things.

Salesmen make orders, clerks take orders.

Salesmanship is 10 per cent inspiration and 90 per cent perspiration.

However, none of them actually provides a fundamental understanding of the salesman's role in the process of 'providing goods that don't come back to customers who do come back'.

Salesmanship is a skill of many elements, but its predominant function is persuasion, for which the dictionary definition is 'to convince'. This is the salesman's role; to convince the potential buyer that his product represents the best solution to the problem and the best value for money within the circumstances that prevail. The salesman is the negotiator of a fair exchange that benefits both the buyer and the seller within an arena that can always be revisited.

2

Salesmanship is a process of infinite varieties. It could be seen simply as the application of a predictable technique, but in reality it is manifest in as many different forms as there are individual salesmen. Learning the skill is a long-term heuristic process where being a 'born salesman' is no more than a short cut and every day teaches a new lesson. Sales success is as much dependent on intelligence and sensitivity as it is on hard work and expertise. Salesmanship is a highly professional skill where the most ignominious form of failure is to sell the wrong product for the job, whether knowingly or not. In its best form it is a creative and conceptual pursuit that reaches beyond the face-value of the client's apparent problem and preconceived ideas. It is primarily a people- rather than a product-orientated process where good service is second nature. Salesmanship is based on effective two-way communications and the analysis of human motivations. It is above all a skill where product knowledge, industry, and personal integrity are merely a beginning, and the scope of problems and opportunities are endless.

The 'toe-in-the door', 'Hello Sunshine, have I got a deal for you!' image of salesmanship has been promoted by the ignorant and uninformed for many a year and no doubt this misconception will continue to be offered to those who are liable to believe anything. Salesmanship is not a confidence trick where fat rewards await the fast-talking, smart guy who only needs to work a couple of days a week to achieve untold riches. Like any other job, success results from the effective application of professional skills and hard work. Salesmanship is neither a high pressure technique nor the application of some magic formula or special device for tricking the reluctant buyer into submission. It is not order-taking or the exploitation of a blatant marketing edge or merely the serving of a booming economy devoid of competition. It is not simply a matter of being able to get on well with people. 'Everybody sells' is a well-intentioned marketing expression that has led to an unfortunate misconception among people on the periphery of selling. The implication is that any untrained person can sell. Nothing could be further from the truth. Certainly everyone within a company environment is able, by virtue of their personal attitude and awareness, to reduce or improve the success of their salespeople. However, salesmanship is significantly more than merely keeping existing clients happy. One could be forgiven for witnessing an inadequate salesman at work and deciding one could, at worst, do significantly better. Unfortunately, that is no yardstick to measure by. Perhaps the slogan ought to be: 'Everyone in a business enterprise is responsible for maintaining an environment that is conducive to sales success'.

In this broader context it is also important for people in any kind of business role to realize the importance of salesmanship and its ability to affect individual career progress. How often have you witnessed the failure of talented artists, brilliant technicians, creative designers and the like,

3

simply because they could not sell their ideas or themselves?

A reasonable synopsis of the power of salesmanship is that the best salesman in town, armed with the worst product, will usually outsell the worst salesman in town with the best product.

The qualities of a professional salesman

To many people outside the selling arena, a salesman is a peripheral employee who intersperses the indulgence of expense account living with the pleasure of articulate deception. They are ruthless exploiters of the uninformed and slow witted and are motivated only by sales commission. They are brash, arrogant, insensitive, and are born survivors. They are overpaid and underworked, a speculation, an unfortunate necessity.

In contrast, salespeople may see themselves as unappreciated pioneers at the 'sharp end' of a company, which must expand or die; solitary travellers who must balance the insatiable demand for revenue growth with the frustrations of client dissatisfaction and an inadequate product portfolio. Unlike their non-sales colleagues, their day-to-day performance is constantly measured: sales targets, competitions, product quotas, sales plans, commission structures, call reporting systems, are all designed to control and identify the winners and the losers. They must keep a level head despite the financial and emotional boost of success and the deprivation and humiliation of failure—whilst the product, it seems, goes on forever. At best they are yesterday's heroes.

Both of these descriptions are, of course, emotional and extreme, but they do serve to highlight some of the human qualities that are necessary for survival in a selling role and also some of the attitudes which prevail.

Assuming that such a thing as a perfect person can exist, what human qualities should the ideal professional salesman have?

Sensitivity	Creativity	Objectivity
Perception	Diligence	Prudence
Determination	Discipline	Self-motivation
Awareness	Control	Self-organization
Articulation	Empathy	Intuition
Common sense	Initiative	Tenacity
Courage	Ambition	Integrity
Confidence	Intelligence	Physical fitness

That is a very demanding list, but one way or another these qualities are regularly demanded of the salesman. So, you can understand the indignation of salespeople at even the slightest suggestion that there might be anything 'down market' about their profession. However, there are many companies and individuals who, for reasons best known to themselves, give the impression that they believe selling is something the neighbours

4

didn't ought to know about. Some, apparently, even adopt pseudonyms in order to hide their real identity. These fall into two categories, the 'embarrassed' and the 'ashamed'. The first is the salesman who admits to being involved in selling, but feels the need to augment his job title in order to give it an aura of respectability. The second is a complete 'cover job' in case friends and neighbours get to know what he does during the day.

For these readers who are still subject to this kind of insecurity, here is a simple system for instant generation of socially acceptable and totally misleading job titles to be used instead of the word 'salesman'. Just select any one word from the 'Disciplines' column and follow it with one of the 'Functions'.

Disciplines	Functions
Sales	Executive
Marketing	Consultant
Accounts	Engineer
Technical	Representative
Commercial	Co-ordinator
Applications	Manager

The point I am wishing to make, is that someone who comes to sell you something is 'a salesman'. When a buyer meets a salesman he expects that person to try and sell him something. After all, his very job depends on the existence of sales people. Whom else is he going to buy from? He is the last person to be impressed by meaningless titles—he might even take exception to them!

This may sound like a digression from the qualities required of a salesman, but, as far as I am concerned, it is not. Selling is a skill with demands which far outstretch the range of most other professional occupations, and for that reason the title 'salesman' or 'saleswoman' is a name to wear with pride.

Why do people buy?

People buy in order to fulfil a conscious or subconscious need or desire. The actual product or service they obtain is not in itself the prime motivation for the transaction, it is merely the means whereby that requirement is satisfied. They do not buy the object for what it is, they buy its implications, or the idea it promotes. In a business environment the need usually takes the form of a problem that has to be solved. Whether or not the party concerned is actually aware of the problem is something else. A company might, for instance, have problems related to warehousing and distribution. The fact that their deliberations on the subject result in the installation of a computer is almost irrelevant. What they have really bought is the means of achieving a higher level of customer service, fewer stock shortages and redundancies, faster delivery and reduced capital investment. These are the real benefits of buying. If the same results could have been achieved by purchasing a new coffee-vending machine they could just as easily have acquired one of those instead.

In other words, their requirement was not for an electronic machine with flashing lights. They simply needed to solve a specific business problem and gain the benefits of doing so. Other factors such as prestige, insecurity and political gain might have come into the action, and might even have been the deciding factor in a balanced competitive situation, but the primary reason for buying was to satisfy the need to have more effective warehouse control in order to achieve increased revenues and greater profits.

Similarly, the insurance salesman is not really selling insurance policies, he is providing the potential policy holder with the security of knowing that if an unforeseen tragedy occurred his family would be provided for. What would be the motivations for buying in this case? Anxiety, affection, health, insecurity? It's up to the salesman to find out.

The person who buys a particular make of new car could be motivated by a variety of different influences. It could be personal prestige, financial investment, physical security, economy, social status, excitement, tax avoidance, or even a desire to travel, but not simply the prospect of exchanging his hard-earned income for a metal box on wheels.

The conclusion of this thesis is simple. A product should not be sold merely on the strength of its appearance and specification, but rather on the ensuing benefits that the purchase will bring about. In other words, sell the profit not the investment.

This leads to another aspect of why people buy. Different customers will select the same item for different reasons, because of their varying individual motivational forces. People cannot be positively categorized in terms of what is likely to turn them on or off. To assume usually results in being mistaken. It is, therefore, essential that salespeople develop the skill to identify these emotional 'hot buttons', for without this level of understanding it is not possible to present the reasons for buying that the buyer wishes to hear. There is no point in trying to persuade a chief engineer that the principal justification for buying a particular generator is its economy, just because that was the main justification used by previous purchasers, when all he is interested in is reliability and mobility. On the other hand, the managing director of the same company may see economy as the only consideration. 'One man's meat is another man's poison.'

For instance, the salesman might state that the telephone monitoring system he is selling is able to handle complete management control of individual telephone usage by providing details of all incoming and outgoing calls for every extension in the building. If the prospect reacts very positively at that stage, it may well be that his prime motivation is a desire to

6

feed his inherent megalomania. However, further questioning may reveal that his principal requirement is to reduce his escalating telephone costs, or even catch the person who calls his aunt in Brisbane every other lunchtime. One thing for sure, it won't be because the machine looks seductive or has a racy technical specification!

The identification of these individual motivations demands a variety of skills and personal attributes, particularly an effective questioning technique, sensitivity, perception, and the ability to listen as opposed to hear. Very often the truth can be perceived in little more than innuendo.

You may think this all sounds rather obvious We all know that one buys an umbrella to keep off the rain, rather than for the thrill of owning a fabric-covered, collapsible metal frame with a handle. Yet, in selling practice, this simple truth, no more profound than common sense, is often overlooked. Like the man said, 'I know you know it, but do you do it?'

Let us look at some of the emotional forces that motivate people to buy:

Sustenance	Anxiety	Insecurity
Prestige	Comfort	Affection
Sex	Health	Curiosity
Politics	Taste	Inertia
Pride	Avarice	Megalomania
Malice	Credibility	Acceptance
Impulse	Popularity	Self-expression

There are others, of course. All the salesman has to do is identify those which are most likely to influence the final decision.

Another concept of the buying process is its apparent two-level structure that equally applies whatever the product might be. It is as applicable to fork lift trucks as it is to a pair of stockings. I call it the 'technical/emotional split'.

It is a common occurrence for a salesman to achieve the position of favourite contender on the short-list, only to lose the business to an inferior, competitive product. More often than not, this is because he has not appreciated the switch from technical to emotional decision criteria that often occurs in the final stages of negotiation.

The buyer has first to ask himself which products can do the job at a price his company can afford. This produces the well-known short list, which normally consists of several contenders. Having reached this point, the technical evaluation is virtually over, and the buyer has greater scope for exposing his own emotional needs. 'I know all the products on the short-list will do the job at a price we can afford,' the buyer thinks, 'so why don't I choose this one?' Because:

'The supplier makes me feel important.' (*ego*)

'It will please the managing director.' (*politics*)

7

'The supplier is a large and progressive company.' (*security*)

'It might not be the best, but it will require the least effort from me.' (*inertia*)

'The salesman might just make a special delivery to my home.' (*avarice*)

'It matches the wallpaper!' (*impulse*)

The reason why so many salespeople are able to 'snatch defeat from the jaws of victory' is because they relax when they reach the point of price/ performance superiority. They fail to appreciate that the selling process becomes more critical between the short-list and final decision stages, primarily because the situation not only moves from the technical to the emotional, but very often from the logical to the illogical.

Selling as a career

The myth still prevails that salespeople are born and not made. Conversely, the rumour persists that anyone with the appropriate training can be a salesman. If we pursue the source of the latter we are likely to come across a whole bunch of partisan sales-trainers. Whilst there is considerably less truth in the former, both are misleading. Providing the individual has sufficient intellect, industry, dedication and training, any career is possible, but it isn't as simple as that. There is such a thing as vocational compatibility.

There is no point in being a salesman if your basic talents are not suited to it. I spend a lot of my time in the recruitment business, specializing in the placement of salespeople, and I am continually confronted by people who shouldn't really be in the job. Being a salesman has a lot of attractions; a high level of independence, above average income, expense account, company car, and so on. For many people these are the sole reasons why they started the job rather than the satisfaction of a vocational urge or a real liking for it. I wouldn't suggest for a moment that becoming a salesman should be the result of 'divine revelation', but it is essential that people considering the sales profession first spend some time evaluating their human characteristics and motivations. Is there any point in taking up a job simply because it looks attractive, particularly where the chances are that at best one is likely to be an average performer? For some people the answer might still be yes, if only through force of circumstances. Nevertheless, the question must be asked and the personal evaluation carried out.

All the selling books will tell you that salesmanship is a skill that can be learned, just like any other occupational skill. And who am I to disagree with that? The point I wish to make is that simply learning a trade, or even achieving success in it, is not necessarily a reliable recipe for everlasting job satisfaction. Before deciding upon the profession of selling as a career one must consider all the options available having first established a reasonable understanding of one's personal strengths and weaknesses. To be objective about oneself is a desperately difficult task, but with the help of a well-informed onlooker, such as a vocational guidance consultant, it can be done. In the words of the poet Robert Burns, 'God gi' us the strength to see ourselves as others see us.'

Probably the worst people to ask about the merits of a career in selling are salesmen. Like any other people who are committed to a profession, their response is likely to be too partisan. The additional risk of asking salespeople about their occupation is that they are likely to have the additional skill to 'sell' the idea. For my own part, I will try to avoid the temptation!

Assuming that one has the right human characteristics for the job, a career in selling has many benefits to offer. One of the biggest attractions is the existence of commission, which usually comprises part or even all of the salesman's income. This means that for the greater part, earnings are a direct function of the amount of time and effort put into the job.

Unlike almost any other occupation, selling offers the possibility of achieving high earnings irrespective of age, sex, or race. A very special feature indeed. For some aspiring salespeople this will be a very attractive feature, for others the implied insecurity may be too much to even contemplate. It is perfectly true that some companies do not pay commission at all, but performance-related income is a reflection of free enterprise in general and selling in particular, where achievement is usually measured by the skill and endeavour of the individual. Those who feel this to be a risk rather than an opportunity are unlikely to succeed in selling.

Another very significant benefit of pursuing a career in selling is the high contribution it can make to subsequent career advancement. An overwhelming proportion of senior executives within the more progressive major corporations come from a selling background. This is because the basic skills of salesmanship rely on the ability to persuade people. Long gone are the autocratic days when people were motivated by intimidation. You may remember from your childhood days Aesop's fable *The North Wind and the Sun*. When the wind and the sun competed to discover which of them was the most powerful it was not the power of the wind that made the man remove the sack from his back, it was the persuasive warmth of the sun. Likewise, the managers who make it to the top are those who have the persuasive skills to sell their own ideas and motivate their subordinates into carrying them out.

The virtually independent lifestyle of salespeople is also a very attractive career feature. While the performance of the individual is continually measured by way of sales targets, incentive schemes, and the level of billing; day-to-day activity is usually free of any form of supervision. By and large, salespeople are left to achieve their objectives in the best way

9

they can, and the more successful they are the less help/interference they get. This also implies a high level of trust and responsibility. The opportunity of investing prime selling time in leisure pursuits rather than exploiting selling opportunities is always there. Forget those stories about all the big deals that are tied up on golf courses. The salespeople who usually come out top, time after time, are the ones who are always prepared to make that extra sales call and who don't switch off the moment they have achieved their sales target.

These benefits apart, a career in selling must eventually give the individual a healthier attitude towards living. Salespeople are typically optimists, but they are not blind. They have the strength to see opportunities where others see problems and they instinctively seek solutions. They are activists and participants who understand that communications is a two-way street. They find satisfaction in providing service and have an altruistic interest in people. With such attitudes they are well equipped for both a positive role in society and the achievement of personal satisfaction.

From outside looking in, it is easy to make the mistake of regarding selling as a singular occupation. Nothing could be further from the truth. While the basic skills are essentially the same, the variations of industry, product, territory, outlet, value, and duration of the sale are virtually infinite. Here are some examples:

Suppliers
Manufacturers
Agents
Wholesalers
Retailers

Products

Tangibles	Intangibles
Business equipment	Insurance
Foodstuffs	Advertising
Electrical goods	Consultancy
Industrial supplies	Maintenance

Territories
National
International
County
Postal district
Nominated organizations
Specified industry

Outlets
Company
Institution
Government department
Wholesaler
Retailer
General public

Values
Fire extinguisher—say, £60
Small business computer system—say, £20,000
Chemical process plant—say, £50 million

Duration of sale
Fire extinguisher—one call
Small business computer system—up to six months
Chemical process plant—up to two years

There is a distinct relationship between the value of a product and the length of time normally involved in selling it. That is a fairly obvious conclusion. A salesman is hardly likely to pop into his friendly neighbourhood government department with the salutation 'Hi! Do you want any battleships today?' Whereas he might just get away with it if he were selling paper bags to a well-established retail customer. However, there is an aspect of value/duration that might not be quite as apparent to the inexperienced. The process of winning sales, and even losing them, is a motivational force in itself. To win is to have the confidence to succeed again. To lose is to learn and create the challenge to do better next time. If this is a regular event the salesman's interest and motivation is continually regenerated. Those who sell very high-value products subject to extended periods of negotiation do not enjoy this benefit. They must have the tenacity, patience, and understanding that comes not only from having the appropriate human characteristics, but also the knowledge and skills that come from extensive exposure to the product, the market place, and strategic selling at a variety of levels from the boardroom to the shopfloor. Consequently, the selling of such products is an area that salespeople must graduate towards rather than considering it as a starting point!

There is also a variety of modes in which the salespeople may operate. The essence of salesmanship is the 'new account salesman'. He is a pioneer; a 'hunter' rather than a 'skinner'. His job is to sell his company's products to people who have not bought them before, and without the salesman's actions are unlikely ever to do so. He, more than any other salesperson, is the bringer of new ideas and the identifier of unsolved problems while being exposed to the most prejudice and resistance. This kind of role demands a high level of self-motivation, 'bridled' aggression, and imagination.

Then we have the 'existing account salesman' whose job is to both protect and expand established business. While there is perhaps less need for drive and agression in this kind of job, there is a considerable need for persistence, enthusiasm and the ability to maintain empathy in the relationship with the client. The sphere of responsibility could range from a large number of different companies, with a wide distribution of locations, to one organization with a single contact point.

However, the dividing line between new and established account selling does not exist in most cases. Salespeople are usually expected both to maintain existing accounts and generate new ones within the bounds of their individual sales territories.

Merchandisers are a familiar feature of selling to the retail trade. Their primary function is promotion as opposed to the direct selling of the product. In some cases they are responsible for ensuring that the product is freely available for purchase by the general public. This could entail inventory checking and order taking at the retail shop level, as well as the creation of product displays, perhaps tied up with television, radio and press promotion. They may also advise the shopkeeper on ways of maximizing sales as well as handling any problems he may have in terms of faulty products, overdue shipments, etc. In other trades, like the pharmaceutical business, they advise on new products and their application by a variety of means including film-shows, lectures and the presentation of technical literature. This can be an excellent grounding for sales trainees before they are exposed to the rigours of direct selling to large department stores, shopping groups, and wholesalers.

Door-to-door selling is an occupation which by and large the general public misguidedly sees as the total scope of selling as a career. Make no mistake, it is a job which demands considerable skill, particularly when it comes to identifying needs and overcoming objections. Products for this activity include double-glazing, encyclopaedias, insurance, cosmetics, brushes and fire extinguishers. Price tends to be a very important factor in this kind of selling, and the sales negotiation is generally limited to a single call. Contrary to popular prejudice, the ethical standards of door-to-door salespeople are, in my opinion, no less than for most other professions.

Retail selling has significantly less credibility as a career in Britain than it has in other countries, particularly North America. The fact that in this country people are called shop assistants as opposed to salespeople is some measure of the attitude that generally prevails. Rewards for retail salespeople are often unattractive, and therefore generally unappealing to the calibre of people who might enjoy a successful career in that industry. Sales training in the retail industry is a relatively unusual occurrence and salespeople are usually left to their own devices. This is a sad state of affairs, for in an environment where the buyer is prepared to travel to the product, selling can be a delight. This arena offers many opportunities for people with sensitivity, imagination, and basic selling skills, where more often than not the customer's problem is not whether to buy but what to choose.

These, then, are the principal areas of a *modus operandi* for salespeople, but it is not as simple as that. Each category of role can be applied to a wide variety of products and industries. A new account salesman could be selling anything from soft drinks to complex computer systems. A salesman responsible for existing accounts could be calling on retail stores or even major airlines. Door-to-door selling could demand sufficient product knowledge to sell a handbrush or a sophisticated home security system. Retailing could demand an appreciation of underwear or sufficient knowledge to advise on the right specification of air-conditioning. The permutations are as endless as the potential challenges and opportunites for the ambitious individual.

Deciding on the most suitable aspect of selling is only part of getting one's career started on the right footing. There is then the matter of choosing the right employer. This is not always as easy as it sounds, particularly in times of economic recession. Nevertheless, one has to start out with the right ideal, and, in selling, the important thing is to work for a major marketing-orientated company early on in one's career. The bigger the name the better. Such companies have not only the resources to invest in comprehensive training but their names also look good on one's *curriculum vitae* at a later stage. To have spent a few years with such companies as *Rank Xerox, British Olivetti, IBM, Proctor and Gamble, Burroughs, Kalamazoo, Unilever,* and the like, gives a lot of extra credibility to subsequent applications for employment.

One essential qualification for success in a sales career is personal mobility. This is not simply the willingness to travel around in pursuit of one's daily occupation, but also to relocate one's home to anywhere in order to take up opportunities for career advancement. It is absolutely reasonable for people to decide to stay put rather than leave behind people and places they love; but this almost certainly implies waving goodbye to future prospects of significant promotion. Another aspect of location in terms of career advancement is the 'head office' syndrome. Despite the wish to be fair in all things, top management will more often than not go for familiar faces than qualifications when it comes to advancing people into significant job opportunities. For this reason it can often be of considerable advantage to the individual to work a sales territory close to head office. That way, one becomes not only a name with a good performance but also a familiar personality with some knowledge of how things work at the 'seat of power'.

Finally, there are two dangers to be wary of in pursuit of a sales career. One is the frequency of changing jobs, and the other 'career cul-de-sacs'.

13

Never leave a job before sufficient time has passed for the initial task to be completed. When asked what has been achieved in a previous job, the applicant must always be able to prove beyond a shadow of doubt that at least he kept his side of the bargain. As a basic guide, potential employers are likely to be suspicious about an applicant who has lasted less than three years in a job. Changing jobs is always risky, and like my mother once told me, 'You don't know people until you live with them.' A job change must have a reason greater than whim or the grass being greener. There needs to be a real continuity of career development that is implied by the sequence of employers and job functions, and a clear indication that each move was well considered—redundancy and such things apart.

The career cul-de-sac is something that most often happens later in one's working life, but can, in fact, happen at any stage. This is simply taking an apparently attractive job, which, due to the size of a company, its organization, or its performance, can offer no real possibility of further advancement within that company should the initial job not work out. These situations are best avoided no matter how attractive the apparent rewards, unless, of course, you believe you have reached your ceiling of competence or are contemplating retirement as your next occupation.

2.

Product and applications knowledge

'Integrity without knowledge is weak and useless, and knowledge without integrity is dangerous and dreadful.'

Samuel Johnson 1709–84

Selling is, to all intents and purposes, the process of satisfying the buyer's needs; or more accurately, perhaps, the solution of his problem. However, the apparent problem is not always the real one, not because the buyer is in any way trying to mislead the salesman, but probably because he is experiencing a problem he has never had before. Yet, the salesman's task is not only to identify the real problem, but also to find the best possible solution to it. The only way this can be achieved is by having fluency in the buyer's own business language, and a broad knowledge of the product being sold and the best ways of putting it to use. Without such comprehensive knowledge the salesman has little chance of sustained success, whether his product be nuclear reactors or plastic cups.

The importance of knowing your product

It is completely unsatisfactory for all concerned if the salesman is continually saying 'I'm sorry, I don't know. I'll try and find out and come back to you.' It reduces the client's confidence in both the salesman and his product and also makes the salesman feel inadequate.

There are many reasons why familiarity with one's product and its applications is important and none more so than the self confidence that it generates. There is no point in taking up any job if one cannot feel 100 per cent committed to it; and it is not really feasible to enjoy a job without having the confidence of knowing what it's all about. Knowledge is a great professional strength that quickly earns not only the respect and admiration of both clients and colleagues, but also makes sales success so much easier. I know many salespeople who are successful, despite the fact that they are not particularly good at selling. Their secret is that they know so much about their product, and the ways in which it can be used, that people virtually give them the business because they feel assured that someone so familiar with the subject will get the solution right and will be a pillar of strength in times of trouble. Competitors who could apparently 'sell them under the table' fail to get into the final reckoning because they do not have the skills to discover the real problem and the best solution.

It is easy to identify salespeople who have complete product and applications knowledge. They have an unshakable self-confidence that is quite apart from arrogance. They exude a quality of assurance that inspires those around them with confidence; they think and act with only success in mind.

As you will read in Chapter 8, overcoming sales resistance is a very significant factor in the business of selling. You will also be presented with the proposition that objections are best dealt with by regarding them for what they really are, that is, demands for information. Many salespeople are very apprehensive about such situations as they have a real fear of being unable to come up with the right answer. The ignominy and intimidation is a terrible prospect for them. Yet all they really lack is sufficient knowledge to come up with the appropriate answer. The satisfactory rebuttal of sales objections does not demand a quick-footed liar, it requires a knowledgeable person who has immediate access to the truth. Salespeople who have complete fluency in their product and its application virtually welcome sales objections for it presents them with an additional opportunity to demonstrate their knowledge and skill and thus strengthen their case for securing the order. They also have absolute faith in the validity of whatever sales proposition they are putting forward, because the process of getting to know their product has also given them confidence in its capability. If it hadn't, they would have moved to some other company where their confidence could be justified.

As I have already mentioned, the principal value of product and applications fluency is its facility for enabling the salesman to identify the real problem and the best solution. Very often the buyer will not be absolutely clear about his needs. Of course, he knows he has a problem, otherwise he wouldn't be discussing the matter. However, that doesn't mean to say he knows precisely what the problem is. The salesman who can specifically identify it for him, and also come up with the most effective and imaginative solution, must surely be well ahead of his competitors.

What is product knowledge?

Most books on the subject of selling, as well as many comprehensive sales training courses, talk about the importance of product knowledge. In my experience basic product knowledge alone is often of little value. What is more important is really knowing about the nature of the client's business and the way in which the product could be put to use in his particular case. It is most important to make a clear distinction between product and applications knowledge. First there is the basic product itself.

Basic product knowledge
The product could be a piece of equipment, a consumable item, a service, or one of many other tangible or intangible items. Yet it is not the product alone that is being sold, for implicit in its provision are a variety of integral components. Firstly, there is the company and its reputation, experience, stability, history, policy, performance, and so on. Secondly, are the supporting facilities: maintenance, delivery, technical advice, design, production, and so on, which are as much a part of the product as a widget or a washer. Without complete familiarity with each of these areas, the salesman's product knowledge is incomplete.

Applications and industry knowledge
Along with basic product knowledge, and perhaps more importantly, there is applications and industry knowledge. Whatever the nature of the product, it is purchased for a specific use. That is what is meant by its application. For example, one prospective customer may want to overcome a shortage of warehouse space, another may want to produce conveyor belts for use in special glass manufacture, whilst a third may want to know his production costs in order to get his selling price right. Without a proper understanding of the client's business and the markets he is selling into (i.e., what his customers want from him), it is very difficult for a salesman to have a clear understanding of his problem. In the first case, the absence of a proper understanding about warehousing, and the needs of access and maximum space usage, is an obstacle in itself. Having no repertoire of possible solutions is another. Therefore, even though the salesman's company could supply a high-reach, fork-lift truck with a given load capacity and dimensions, supplying the right product would be difficult unless the potential buyer specified his precise need. There is a world of difference in the strength of the salesman's position when he is able to advise the buyer what he ought to have, rather than be told what is required. In the second case, knowledge of conveyor belt manufacture and the demands of its users is obviously desirable. Yet, knowing that the product in question must be of woven wire construction, and that a particular quality and tensile strength is standard for this kind of work, makes the fact that the salesman works for a wire manufacturer virtually incidental. Merely knowing that his company can supply a particular kind of wire is, once again, likely to limit his sales potential to supplying only what the user is able to specify himself. The third case is well illustrated by telling a story against myself.

Back in the 'sixties I was working as a junior salesman for *IBM*, based in the Midlands. One day a prospective buyer telephoned the office to say he was interested in buying a computer. My job? Go and sell him one! The interested company was in the Black Country and it was in the metal casting business. Frankly, I didn't know a thing about that particular industry,

17

but I was prepared to learn. It was the managing director who had made the original call, so in the time-honoured fashion I ensured that my negotiations were focused around him. Job costing I knew about, at least in principle, as it had been one of the subjects covered in depth during my basic training as a systems analyst. So, I was able to talk about the subject with a reasonable amount of fluency. My subsequent excursion into the works was an interesting experience and after a number of conversations with shopfloor management, I felt I had a grip on the situation.

The solution I proposed was simple, yet, I thought, imaginative. I had learned that every casting produced had an accompanying job ticket handed in by the caster on completion of the job. This was already used as a docket for generating piece-work earnings. My scheme was to incorporate both job costing and payroll into the same system, as well as producing the basis for a stock control system, all at little extra cost. So, I put my proposals forward for a fairly modest computer system with full confidence that the business was almost mine. Well, it wasn't. The competition got the business instead! I was very shaken by the outcome and contacted the managing director to find out why I had lost the business. He was very understanding and patiently explained the situation to me.

'Don't blame yourself lad,' he said, 'I suppose it was because you don't know the business. Take this job ticket for instance. You can't go basing a system on them. How would we get on in June and July and running up to Christmas?' I didn't even know what he was talking about. 'They save them up you see; everybody knows that!' (Really?) 'Instead of handing them in they save them up for their holidays; shove 'em in their back pockets, then hand 'em in just before they go away. It's a tradition, always has been!' Terrific! I appeared to be the only person in the Black Country who didn't know about this informal savings scheme. The fact was, I didn't know my client's business and my experience of his particular application was sparse to say the least of it. On the other hand, I could have blown his mind with technical details of my product; access times in milliseconds, processing speeds in nanoseconds, capacity in megabytes, language processors, monolithic architecture, the whole bit. 'Nay lad, don't give me all that computer stuff. Can you do me job costing?'

Competitive knowledge

One of the most important aspects of product knowledge is fluency in everything one's competitors are able to supply. It is not possible for the salesman to sell effectively if he doesn't know what he is selling against, nor is it possible for sales management and marketing people to plan their strategies effectively in isolation from the activities and capabilities of their competitors. Yet many salespeople give little or no attention to the maintenance of detailed records of all products which could affect their own performance. Some go through the motions of establishing such systems, but

18

once faced with the inconvenience of continually collecting up-to-date information, allow this essential source of data to diminish into no more than a file for those competitive brochures that occasionally drift onto their desk.

If one accepts that the salesman is selling a solution to a problem, based on a number of agreed benefits and advantages, then it stands to reason that competitive salesmen are doing the same thing. The only way the salesman can ensure that a particular emphasis is placed on the areas of benefit unique to his company's product is to know what the competition is claiming and their business methods. This in turn depends on acceptance by the salesman that the collection of competitive information in the field is just as much a part of the normal day-to-day operation as prospecting and call reporting. Such information is essential, not only in the establishment of a selling strategy that can exploit market opportunities, based, perhaps, on direct product superiority or gaps in opposing product ranges, but also in order to be able to justify sales support which may be required in the light of competitive activity.

Marketing people also need to have a total knowledge of all aspects of competitive activity, particularly new product developments, from total product ranges to the release of new features, perhaps augmented with the occasional 'market whisper' about forthcoming new products. Whatever their formal procedures might be, there is no form of market research which is as effective for unearthing new product revelations as information gleaned by salespeople in the field. It is not unknown for investment to be made in new products which subsequently fail miserably through lack of prior information on new and/or existing competitive products which for one reason or another prove to be superior. Then afterwards, for at least one salesman to comment, 'I could have told you our new product would fail, the 'XYZ' company has been selling a far superior product on my patch for months!' Who has failed whom? The whole process of 'keeping tabs' on competitors must be a continual team effort, and therefore salespeople must have a real awareness of the sources of information, the means for collecting it and the importance of such input to both personal and company success.

I have always tried to keep an up-to-date file on each significant competitor into which any brochure or piece of information I obtained can be placed. Each is prefaced with a brief write-up on the individual company and its products, providing the following information:

1. Company name.

2. Existing and new products, principal features and benefits.

3. Usual selling policy, strategy, techniques.

4. Name of local salesman and background.

5. Recent special promotions in terms of advertising, prices, trade-ins, etc.

6. Details of significant successes versus own products, and reasons why.

7. Major advantages for, and disadvantages against, own products.

8. Price details.

9. Delivery details.

10. Maintenance facilities, location, response.

11. Types of client and industry in which competition mainly occurring.

12. New announcements anticipated.

13. Primary business targets for sales effort, by product and application.

Sources of knowledge

There is an infinite number of things we do not know; only a fool would claim to know everything about anything. Even the word 'expert' does not imply absolute capability, but rather the possession of a special skill or knowledge. The salesman's responsibility must be to apply himself to learning every day of his selling life, not only by the formal means of education by study and tuition, but also by keeping his eyes and ears open at all times. In the complex and demanding world of selling, there is a considerable need for product and applications knowledge. For this reason most suppliers make a considerable investment in the provision of technical information to clients and employees alike in the form of classroom training, instruction manuals, technical literature, sales brochures, etc. However, the salesman must never make the mistake of assuming that self-education is a passive process. There are many ways in which personal knowledge can be expanded and with it the rewards of more effective selling.

Internal training

The amount of training provided by a company for its employees is usually a reflection of its size. For the larger organizations, formal courses of product training are a recurrent process. Many even have their own training establishments. With others, and I guess this is the greatest proportion of companies, training is usually given when it can be put off no longer, and is often given by people who know, as opposed to those who know how to teach. Some companies never get round to formal training at all, other than the occasional presentation at a sales meeting, usually on the launch of a new product. Unfortunately, the salesman has little control of his company's attitude towards training. All he can do is strive to gain maximum benefit from whatever is provided. What he should never do is make the mistake of regarding a training course as a holiday, a chance for escaping the rigours of the field and living it up with the lads. Anything new that can be learned is likely to pay off in extra earnings sometime later on.

The selling manual

If your company doesn't have a formal selling manual, make one of your own! Most large companies have a tome that contains everything the salesman ever wanted to know about the company and its products, but never dared to ask: product specifications, price and delivery details, model range, peripheral equipment, related supplies, reference users, competitors, and so on. It is a total source of information that should accompany the salesman wherever he goes.

I have only ever worked for two companies with the organizational prowess and foresight to generate such documents, and even these had the continuing problem of keeping them up to date. A particular problem was the fact that their salespeople only got around to reading what circumstances required of them, i.e., client demands. Consequently, their knowledge, relative to all there was to be known, was very limited. Whereas in other companies where I have worked, salespeople have been obliged to construct their own 'flogging book', and by doing so have learned something about everything within it. The point I am trying to make is the importance of having a selling manual and ensuring that its entire contents are studied and understood.

The sales meeting

If you don't have regular sales meetings, you are probably working for the wrong company! Sales meetings are an irreplaceable source of information interchange. Such events will, of course, involve discussions about the past selling period and the prospects for the next, but usually a particular subject will be highlighted by way of a presentation, demonstration, role play, etc. These are very important educational devices, for they are usually based on the field experience of salespeople, as opposed to the, sometimes naïve, suppositions of office-bound executives and technicians.

As one might expect, many sales meetings are devoted to sales statistics, performance analysis, and the like, particularly at the start and end of selling periods. But such meetings do not deny the salesman the opportunity for collecting product knowledge. This is probably the only regular opportunity for meeting with other salespeople who are experiencing the same problems and opportunities as oneself. Few individuals have the depth of collective knowledge that resides within any sales team. The chances are that all the answers to all the salesman's questions exist somewhere within his own selling operation. Very few sales situations are unique. Any problem the salesman may have could well be affecting his colleagues in a similar fashion, some of whom will almost certainly have found the answer. If not, a group interchange of information may well bring about a solution.

'I'm having real trouble getting people to accept our revised terms for leasing. Has anyone else experienced the same problem and, if so, have they been able to get around it?'

'Does anyone know of a client who has used our equipment in a mobile environment using a diesel generator as a power source?'

'I'm using a completely different way of demonstrating the new product and it's really paying dividends. Would anyone like to hear about it?'

The sales manager

Sales managers are a bit like fathers, they usually know more than their sons and there is seldom anything their offspring may be confronted with that they have not experienced already. Yet, typically, the last thing a son will do is ask his father for advice. It is only when he becomes a father himself that he realizes how foolish he was to have neglected such an abundant source of information.

Sales managers usually get to be appointed in their job, not only because they have proven that they can sell, but also due to the breadth of their experience and ability to assist and motivate others. There is no ignominy in asking for a sales manager's advice; that is what he is there for. Any sales manager will get great pleasure from helping his subordinates, it gives real purpose to his existence. Besides which, he can be the salesman's shortcut to knowledge; the means of avoiding expensive mistakes. It is all very well saying, 'We learn by our mistakes', but implicit in this is the expense of putting them right and the cost of losing the order. If that can be avoided by consultation between the salesman and his manager, why do it the hard way?

I am not suggesting that such consultation should always be one-way traffic. Any truly effective sales manager will have regular counselling and appraisal sessions in the field, with individual members of his sales team. Such occasions should be exploited to the full, rather than being regarded as unnecessary and tedious interruptions of precious selling time. This kind of one-to-one training method is a very valuable opportunity, not only to obtain advice on selling techniques, product and applications knowledge, and specific client situations, but also to get someone else involved in real-life selling in order to gain an immediate critique of the strengths and weakness of one's particular selling skills. The distillation of information that ensues from the conversations between the salesman and his sales manager whilst travelling between calls can also be extremely useful.

The sales supporter

As well as sales managers, people in technical support, warehousing, maintenance, delivery or administrative roles, are always delighted to help by providing information to salespeople. They also get real pleasure from the compliment of being asked for advice. It well behoves every salesman to ensure that he has the support of such people and the wisdom to use their skills and knowledge to the full. Only a fool has too much pride to say, 'I do not know.' The person who, in effect says, 'You have the experience and skill to solve my problem, will you help me?', has both increased his knowledge and won himself a friend.

The public library

Maybe it's because my wife is a librarian, but I have always been aware of the considerable amount of commercial information that resides in any public library. There are well-known directories: *Kelly's Kompass, The Stock Exchange Year Book,* and *Dunn and Bradstreet.* However, it doesn't end there. One can also find lists of local companies by type of industry, names of local trade associations, the local electoral role, technical journals for specific pieces of industrial and commercial information, street maps, weekly and monthly journals, the daily newspapers, and a feast of other information that may occasionally be needed by the salesman.

The product manual

As far as the actual product is concerned, the most authoritative source of information must be the comprehensive technical documents created for the guidance of end users and supporting technicians. This, of course, equally applies to competitive equipment as well as to one's own. Unfortunately, most salespeople regard them only as reference documents and often, because of their size and complexity, use them merely for dipping into whenever they are asked for information they cannot bring to mind. 'It's got to be in here somewhere!' This is not smart. It may be a considerable effort, but the salesman who does not carry out the essential task of reading his product manuals from cover to cover, several times over if need be, is guilty of severe dereliction of duty. Okay, some product manuals are so technical in their content that even the supporting technicians are not absolutely familiar with every aspect. Nevertheless even in such circumstances, complete fluency with what is contained where, and a general idea of the likely answer, is important if the salesman is to maintain his credibility with the buyer.

The customer

In my experience, established users always know far more about the salesman's own product, in the context of their own applications area, than the salesman's own technical support people. Customers are not, in the absolute sense, interested in the product manual; they are only interested in what can be done to make the product operate in the most effective manner. In many cases that could be contrary to what it says in the book! While the supplier's attention is devoted to installing as much product as he can, the buyer's efforts are directed towards maximizing its use. Consequently, users often have tricks for getting round faults and schemes for enhancing capacity that remain totally unknown to the supplier. This kind of information can be the source of otherwise unattainable knowledge for future reference.

Ultimately, product knowledge, indeed all knowledge, can only be achieved by way of personal effort. Much of this may be attained from books, lectures, films, etc., but the greatest source of knowledge is there to be tapped simply by having the humility to say, 'I don't know, will you help me please?' In the words of Rudyard Kipling:

I have six honest serving men
They taught me all I know
Their names are What and Why and When
Where and How and Who.

3.

Prospecting

'Nothing great was ever achieved without enthusiasm.'

Ralph Waldo Emerson 1803–82

The most significant measure of a salesman's performance is the amount of business growth he achieves from new accounts. Many apparently successful salespeople can survive for many years on the natural expansion and benevolence of existing accounts or unexpected 'windfalls'. They appear to have the knack of always being in the right place at the right time. Of course, they have no trouble in justifying their performance, and make it clear that there is just as much effort involved in protecting existing clients from the approaches of competition as there is in prospecting, and that expansion by way of introducing new products and applications demands a lot of dedication. As for those who appear to live on an endless diet of 'bluebirds', they will always argue that being in the right place at the right time is not an act of divine providence but the result of well-conceived planning. Nevertheless, I have seen many such people suddenly plummet to the bottom of the sales performance table, by being moved away from account management into new account selling or by simply running out of luck. In other words, as soon as they were asked to become 'hunters' rather than 'skinners' they couldn't 'hack' it, as the task of generating business from cold was either beyond their capability or was a practice too long neglected to be anything other than an obligatory drudge and therefore seldom, if ever, performed.

The amount of prospecting salespeople have to do depends not only on the kind of product, market, and territory, but also on their sales awareness and ambition. Retail salespeople seldom do any. Those in consumer selling, particularly those with the major corporations, have the greater part of their demand created by extensive advertising, whereas the typical salesman in commercial or industrial selling fails or succeeds in direct proportion to the amount of prospecting he carries out.

Whatever the means of generating new revenue, it is reasonable to say that every business entity is ultimately confronted with the possibility of expanding or dying. Standing still in times of inflation and rising costs is in reality but another form of contraction. It must always be remembered that any business, no matter how static, is based on what was at one time new business and that the same diet that brought it into being is necessary for its future sustenance.

Sources of prospective users

One of the principal activities of the company I work for is the recruitment of sales and marketing personnel. One of the questions we always ask candidates is what they most dislike about selling. By far the most common response is 'cold selling', 'prospecting', 'pioneering', and so on. Some are actually afraid or demotivated by the very thought of it. Many regard it as a necessary chore; very few find it the stimulating and rewarding process which it can be. It is merely a matter of doing it properly with a good strategy and common sense.

The most important considerations of effective prospecting are 'vertical marketing' and reliable sources of company information. 'Vertical marketing' is simply the process of confining pioneering activity to a particular application within a specific industry. Prospecting is so much easier and effective when carried out in this fashion. The salesman soon develops a familiarity with the chosen business sector and an appreciation of its problems and opportunities, which in turn gives him greater confidence, and thus more likelihood of success. New business opportunities are numerous, if one cares to seek them in a positive manner. It is all a matter of analysing the business scenario in a constructive manner. Consider the following nine sources:

1. Existing clients
One of the best sources of new business is existing clients. I don't mean 'Please Mr Customer, will you buy some more.' That is a job for account managers and sales support people. It is the process of discovering from satisfied users who else in their particular industry or locality might have a requirement for similar products or services. You will be surprised how well informed your client can be.

2. The press
Press articles and advertisements in both national and trade journals are an excellent source of information. They tend to reveal what a company is doing, its achievements, its markets, its products. If an advertisement appears for pipeline engineers, the chances are they have secured a big contract, and, if you are selling welding gear or ultrasonic testing equipment, they could represent a major business opportunity.

3. Trade associations
Trade associations are regarded by many as a good source of prospects, but

26

in my experience an individual enquiry goes to so many potential suppliers, and takes so long to travel from the enquirer to the supplier, that it is often more trouble than it is worth by the time the salesman receives it.

4. Direct mailing

Mailshots can often be very rewarding, but, like all prospecting, its effectiveness is a direct function of its specialization. It is relatively easy to ensure a good response level by promoting a generalized appeal. However, it is far more important to ensure that respondents are real prospects whose requirements match the clearly defined capabilities of the supplier. A considerable amount of time can be wasted by pursuing people who merely wish to satisfy their curiosity. It is essential to emphasize a particular product for a particular need within a particular industry.

5. Social contacts

Social contacts are thought by some to be a good source of new business prospects. I recommend you to avoid this source at all cost. Friends of friends want special treatment, and they don't expect you to lean on them when they are not doing their share or chase them when their account is overdue.

6. Trade directories

Comprehensive company information is essential for producing a well controlled selling strategy and is usually relatively easy to locate. Unfortunately, many salesmen generally consider this to be unnecessary, or at best a nuisance. In truth, that attitude is as sensible as fighting a war without military intelligence. A potential buyer will always react more favourably to the salesman who has obviously taken the time to research into his company than the one who appears to have telephoned impulsively after dipping into *Yellow Pages*. The salesman has so much more credibility in the eyes of the prospective buyer when he is well informed. If he has gone to the trouble of discovering their size of operation, range of products, markets, and so on, he is the kind of person who is likely to make similar efforts to ensure they are well cared for if they do business together.

Company information is usually available to the general public in trade directories, which can be found in local public libraries, chambers of commerce, and other commercial centres. I have found *Dunn and Bradstreet, Kompass,* and, perhaps most of all, the *Stock Exchange Year Book* to be the most useful in the past. These sources can usually supply information such as:

Correct company name.
Address and telephone number.
Names and titles of directors.

Annual turnover.
Products.
Principal applications.
Markets.
Subsidiaries.
Date of inception.

This kind of background provides a considerable insight to the likely needs of a company and a greater fluency in discussing potential business opportunities.

7. Door-to-door canvassing
Some products require this kind of cold calling. It is a very demanding process that can be both exhausting and discouraging. Many salespeople take a 'black or white' view of this type of prospecting, on the basis that they are either in a type of selling that totally demands or excludes it. In reality, those who believe themselves to be 'above' it are usually guilty of being taken in by their own prejudice, for there are few areas of selling where occasional sorties or one-off cold calls are inappropriate. A tour of an industrial estate or a visit to an interesting company close to an existing client's premises is likely to reveal much more than a telephone call. Do they have the appearance of a successful company? Does the receptionist know who handles your kind of merchandise? Will she be more willing to provide the information you require than to a disembodied voice over the telephone? Does your product demand no significant pre-call preparation? If so, will the buyer see you now?

8. Business colleagues
Salespeople are not the only ones who get out and about. Maintenance engineers, technical support people, delivery people, and the like spend a lot of time in the field meeting users and people of similar disciplines from other suppliers. These are good friends to have around, particularly if the salesman troubles to ask them to keep their eyes and ears open for business opportunities. Who knows, there might even be a 'pint' in it for them!

9. Other salespeople
There are many salespeople who call on the same types of business operation, or even departments who are not in competition with each other. Those selling pharmaceuticals, as opposed to those in medical equipment, may be dealing with the same buyer but are not in contention. Such salespeople regularly come into contact with each other during the course of their selling activity and often become aware of business opportunities outside their own sphere of interest. The creation of relationships with non-competitive salespeople can often be a mutually beneficial process.

Using the telephone

The telephone is a two-edged sword. It can be the means of swift communication when you have an urgent need for information or an irritation when you are busy. If the salesman is to achieve success in his use of the telephone, he must be in complete sympathy with the possible situation at the other end of the line, rather than considering only his ambitions as a caller.

The telephone is an impolite and inconsiderate device. There are no means of assessing the importance of any call until the message has been accepted. Consequently, every communication is usually given top priority, whether it is urgent or trivial. It could be that the next telephone call you receive will be your biggest and best new business prospect; on the other hand, it could be your wife to say the vacuum cleaner has just broken. You won't know until you pick up the receiver and get involved. It is therefore quite understandable that most senior executives regard every call with a degree of suspicion. In most cases they are extremely busy people and don't want, or can't afford, to get involved with anything other than essential matters. As a result, a large proportion of such people have a secretary to filter out the important from the irrelevant telephone calls, therefore protecting the boss from the diversions of strangers and time wasters.

Making appointments

The first rule is to sell the appointment not the product, unless, of course, you are in telesales! If the objective of the call is to arrange a meeting with the buyer, then the process must be limited to that. There is always a temptation for the salesman to be drawn into supplying product information once the buyer has agreed to make an appointment. This has to be avoided, for there is no better way of talking oneself out of the appointment, and therefore out of the business. A considerable factor in the buyer's willingness to meet the salesman is innate curiosity. Once this has been diluted by verbal description, there is a considerable risk of a change of mind. 'Now that I have a clearer appreciation of your product I think it will be better if we leave our meeting until a later date.' Like never!

The second rule is to ensure that every prospect is thoroughly qualified for business potential before the call is made. The facility for this process varies according to the type of product being sold. It is obviously easier to qualify prospective users of aeroplane engines than paper towels. The former virtually dictates the companies and the pertinent contacts, whereas the latter limits the market to people who wash their hands. The criteria for qualification can vary considerably: number of employees, type of industry, etc. Trade directories and other sources of information may be used. But whatever the means, the outcome must be a collection of companies whose nature indicates a clear potential for business. Again, depending on the type of product or the prospective client, a variation of approach may be called for. In some cases a preceding introductory letter giving reasons for the forthcoming call may be appropriate. In others, it may not be feasible to qualify potential demand before the event and therefore qualification within the call itself may be necessary.

I recall an occasion when our office manager had a telephone call from a supplier of photocopier paper. 'Hi Liz!' said the caller. It was the first time we had received a call from the saleswoman concerned, and as Elizabeth had only been with us for one week, they were hardly on Christian name terms. However, Elizabeth ignored the contrived informality and listened politely to the extended presentation on the types of paper available, prices, benefits of the service, and so on. I recall we were very busy at the time and wondered why the call was taking so long. Eventually Elizabeth asked my advice. As she had been with us so briefly she was not aware of our consumption of stationery. 'It's a saleswoman from a photocopier supplier. They have a special offer on orders of ten packs or over for A4 paper. Do you have any idea how much we use?' As it happened, I did, and ten packs was over a year's supply. No attempt had been made to qualify our requirements and therefore everyone's time had been wasted. If only she had qualified the situation first the incident would have been avoided.

The third rule is to have a 'planned presentation' that contains an opening statement that is likely to gain attention, qualifying questions if appropriate, the justification for a subsequent meeting, an accompanying list of answers to likely objections, the actual request for an appointment and a terminating statement. Brevity is the best approach. Once the prospect has agreed to the time and place of the appointment, the call should be concluded immediately.

The fourth rule is to ensure that any telephone prospecting exercise is well organized before it is put into effect. Simply locating a name in a directory is extremely inefficient. Lists should be extracted according to geographic location to allow ease of journey planning. Other information, such as name of contact, telephone number and dialling code, most likely area of product interest, possible application areas, etc., can not only make the exercise much easier to control but also provides a useful list for future reference.

The fifth rule is to remember the purposes for which the telephone should not generally be used. While this section discusses the telephone in the context of sales prospecting, now is as good a place as any to regard it momentarily in a broader context. The telephone can be a useless or even dangerous device in some areas of sales activity. It is such a convenient medium that the salesman often grabs it instinctively without really considering the implications of his actions or how much better the situation might be handled on a face-to-face or written basis. The kinds of situation that spring most readily to mind are:

30

Sorting out problems.
Getting decisions.
Providing explanations.
Delivering technical detail.
Supplying evidence.
Establishing the truth.

The 'planned presentation'

It is worth expanding the topic of the telephone presentation itself. Assuming the 'desk qualification' process has been performed satisfactorily, the basic elements of what is to be said need to be considered very closely. The opening statement is crucial; it cannot be left to impulse. The first few seconds are the most important, for it is during that brief period that the prospect will decide whether or not he wishes to proceed with the communication. In other words, it is the recipient's period of counter qualification. 'Is there any justification for speaking with this person and, if so, shall I or shan't I?' The main objective is to establish immediate rapport, while at the same time stating who you are and where you are from. The greater the prospect's goodwill, the more likely he is to give a positive reaction. This calls for a creative mind and a sympathetic attitude on the part of the salesman.

For some salespeople an unconventional approach may work best, while for others it may be better to aim at an emotional target such as curiosity, pride, avarice, and so on. For others, a sympathetic approach may be most effective; acknowledging the intrusion, the pressures he must already be under, and so on. The main thing is that the salesman uses the approach that works for him in order to establish an acceptable message that says, 'Here I am, this is where I'm from and I'm here to help you.' Failure at this juncture virtually implies that any chances of making a sale are lost. It is therefore essential to get it right, and this cannot be achieved by leaving the process to chance.

Having 'weathered the storm' of the opening statement, the next stage is to carry out any qualification if this is appropriate to the types of product being sold. This must be precise and couched in open-ended questions rather than those which merely invite 'yes' or 'no'. The question, 'Do you use photocopier paper?' is not as good as, 'How much photocopier paper do you use?' This achieves the more important qualification and also stimulates dialogue. There is nothing more sterile than a one-way conversation with a prospective user. Very often such qualification may be inappropriate, as all the necessary analysis was available before the event. In this case the justification for the appointment has to be presented. This is more likely to come from the benefits of the product rather than its description. The statement, 'We have significantly reduced the warehousing costs of several companies similar to your own', is more likely to appeal to a prospective buyer than, 'I'd like to come and talk to you about fork-lift trucks.' An integral part of this benefit statement is, of course, the request for an appointment; one implies the other. This calls for an 'optional close', i.e., the choice of alternative dates rather than a specific time and day. The prospect may not accept any suggested date, but that way he will feel obliged to offer an alternative if he is really interested.

A further device which has worked well for me in the past, is to agree to the duration of the meeting. If the prospect knows the amount of time he is committing himself to, he is more likely to say 'yes', particularly if the requirement is relatively brief.

Telephone disciplines
Using the telephone is not simply a matter of grabbing the receiver and sticking it next to your ear. There are many considerations to take into account. Here are my top ten:

1. Consider the implications of the call before you make it.

2. Plan the presentation.

3. Listen more than you talk.

4. Regard the call from the recipient's point of view.

5. Don't react to the person, only his situation.

6. Take notes as you may forget something important.

7. Don't make any assumptions.

8. Don't interrupt.

9. Ask open-ended questions.

10. Terminate the call as soon as your objectives are achieved.

The telephone operator
Salespeople are often presented with that old selling adage 'start at the top'. However, despite this heart-felt plea, some will often begin their selling cycle at whatever level fate inflicts upon them. In practice, it is certainly best for a salesman to start his actual selling at the chief executive level wherever possible. Nevertheless, it is generally advantageous for the very first telephone contact to be at a much lower level, namely the telephone operator.

I have already stressed the importance of being well prepared for this first contact. The salesman can collect a vast amount of company information from directories and the like, but they can offer no answers to questions like, 'Which is the best day to catch the financial director?' or 'What is the name of the new managing director?' When it comes to information on organization, names, locations, products, and habits of all kinds, a sales-man's best friend is his prospect's telephone operator. The same applies for the correct company name and address, the managing director's correct name and initials, the best times to catch him, and the names of his closest aides. If he is really charming, without being patronizing, the salesman may even be given an outline of the company's primary products and mar-kets. It is important to ask about the company's current involvement with your own particular product or service, for the operator will almost cer-tainly have some idea on the current situation.

In most organizations the telephone operator has the greatest amount of verbal interaction with the largest number of people, and will tend to know more about what is happening within the company at the people level than anyone else, including the managing director. So, not only at the begin-ning of the sales negotiation, but also at many subsequent stages, the tele-phone operator can be the salesman's greatest ally.

An important point to bear in mind is that female telephone operators and secretaries do not generally provide helpful information to salesman as a result of being 'chatted up'. I have often seen salesmen involved in this pursuit, and most efforts have been pathetic. For every Roger Moore employed in selling there are probably a dozen Michael Crawfords. Like most aspects of selling, there is only one reliable approach, and that is based on courtesy, truth, and common sense.

The first step is a simple request for assistance: 'I wonder if you would help me please. I believe you are the person most able to provide the information I need'—or words to that effect. People like to help. It is a com-pliment to be asked, and most people respond altruistically.

The second step is when most salespeople go wrong, as they become devious rather than asking for the information they really need. They seem to lose sight of the fact that they are dealing with an intelligent and percep-tive human being, and that their clumsy attempts to wheedle information are not only very obvious but have the effect of implying much greater significance to the subject than it really deserves, thus creating a greater reluctance to answer than if the same questions had been presented in a straight-forward manner. It is not unethical, improper or impolite to ask for the managing director's name, whether or not the company already uses your kind of equipment, who is responsible for it, who supplied it, and when it was installed. If the operator knows, you will be told. After all, isn't the purpose of your call to initiate a process that will be to the ultimate benefit of the operator's company? If that is not so, you shouldn't be mak-ing the call; if it is, you should feel confident in your entitlement to ask.

The protective secretary
One of the natural hazards of establishing contact with a new business prospect is the protective secretary. The response, 'Mr Prospect is in a

meeting at the moment', must be familiar to many a salesman. The immediate reaction of most salespeople is to think of ways round this obstacle. I have seen salesmen driven to desperate actions by the sheer frustration of finding all normal methods of communication blocked: 'confidential' telegrams, disguised voices, 'nobbling' homeward buyers, and so on. One can only admire the determination and ingenuity of such efforts, but often they become necessary through lack of subtlety and common sense from the outset.

The attitude of the salesman towards secretaries generally, is particularly important in this context. Secretaries are not the chattels of their masters; they are normal, intelligent people performing an essential business function. Many female secretaries are in the job because they have decided on a business career rather than a domestic one, and as such are very independent ladies who respond badly to male chauvinism. Any hint of patronization, arrogance, connivance or flattery, therefore, is bound to introduce psychological barriers. If the salesman starts out by attempting to work with the prospect's secretary rather than getting past her, he will ultimately have fewer problems.

The first stage is to discover the secretary's full name, while remembering to use only her surname in the first instance, as the salesman needs to show respect in order to gain it, and the Christian name mode with a stranger is never advantageous. Having discovered who the secretary is, and how to address her, the next step is to get her assistance. The best way to do that is to ask for it. Obviously, the only help the salesman really needs at the outset is to be put through to Mr Prospect. If this results in resistance, then the salesman needs to offer more specific reasons why the secretary should help him meet her boss. Often, by simply stating his situation and the need for assistance, while showing an appreciation of the secretary's responsibilities, the salesman can achieve positive results.

'I am sure Mr Prospect is constantly approached by salesmen wishing to sell to your company, and he doesn't have time to see them all. I realize it is part of your job to help him select those salesmen whose products could bring most benefit to your company. The product I need to discuss with him is not only bringing significant benefits to some of your competitors, but is also closely allied to company policy, and only he can decide upon the validity of the advantages involved. When would you suggest is the best time of the week to contact him?'

It is very important to make the secretary realize that her importance is appreciated, while at the same time introducing a decision criteria which is outside her scope and thus demands the involvement of Mr Prospect. 'Company policy' and 'competition' are useful devices in this context.

Having said all of that, it is clearly better for the salesman not to get involved with the prospect's secretary other than at the courtesy level. Often the manner of the salesman's approach can get him straight through without any resistance. It is therefore important that his attitude is bold without being familiar, thus suggesting an existing relationship between the prospect and himself. This does not infer the use of Christian names!

Of course, the salesman cannot be sure that the prospect will be in the office when he calls. In this situation it is best that he rings off, after establishing the best time to call back, avoiding any further discussion with the secretary. In his eagerness to sell, he might just sell himself out of a reason for calling again!

Dealing with management

The managing director

Most salesmen, particularly in industrial and commercial selling, know that making initial sales contact at the managing director level has significant benefits, including, above all, a greatly improved chance of winning the order. Yet a significant proportion of salespeople, having acknowledged the wisdom of this approach, ignore it. Why are salesmen so reluctant to apply this piece of obvious common sense by avoiding the one person who has absolute authority to say 'yes'? Perhaps the reason is conscious or subconscious fear and inadequacy! I know that sounds a bit strong, but it's worth considering. I suppose you could say it is laziness, lack of intelligence, or the deliberate choice of an easier option that makes salesmen attempt to sell their products 'down the line'. But you will probably be wrong! The average citizen is conditioned to accept the inadequacy that is implied by his position within the social hierarchy. Against an historical backcloth of Kings and Queens and the autocratic power of Church and State, the average child is systematically exposed to the authority of parents, schools, church and police, and military and governmental bodies, augmented by the humiliation of high technology and the threat of a nuclear holocaust. In such circumstances it is quite understandable that the subconscious of 'the man in the street' is attuned to inadequacy and fear of authority, despite possible protestations of his conscious mind to the contrary. Consequently, the managing director who sits as king within the social order of commerce, is a manifestation of power and greater minds. Clearly, this is an illusion, but to overcome it still needs an enormous effort.

The first stage in overcoming a reluctance to approach managing directors is to try and understand who and what they really are. The fact is they are usually quite ordinary people. They feel just as vulnerable and aware of their mortality as anyone else, and their position of relative power comes as a daily surprise to them. They, more than anyone else, appreciate that they have less job security than they had at lower stages of their career. Managing directors lose their jobs, have marriage crises, and worry about their health, like anyone else. My very first sales manager always recommended the 'Emperor's new clothes' approach to young salesmen who were nervous about approaching and meeting very senior clients. 'The silly idiot is going around in the nude!', he used to say. 'He's sitting there behind his desk stark naked and only you have the perception to see it!' It always worked rather well if ever I became over-awed by rank. I wonder if any of those senior executives in the West Riding of Yorkshire ever knew what my source of confidence and enthusiasm really was! A managing director is just a guy doing a job. Sure, there are a few arrogant megalomaniacs around, but I venture to suggest you will come across more of these in middle management than at the top. Managing directors are usually very busy men, involved in meetings most days of their lives. For this reason one usually has to plan well ahead and approach the first appointment with a professionalism that is sensitive to his activity and responsibility. But, after all, that's not so different to getting to see most other people.

What do managing directors wish to hear?

As a general rule, managing directors are primarily interested in financial benefits, whereas middle management wants to know about performance and technical efficiency. In, for example, the sale of a palleting system to a warehousing and distribution company, the warehouse manager will have a real influence on the final decision. He will be extremely interested in the ability to increase the efficiency of space usage, ease of application, dimensions of pallets, load bearing capabilities, effect on existing fork lift equipment, etc. On the other hand, the managing director's interest in such aspects will be minimal so long as middle management is satisfied that the equipment will do the job. What he wants to hear about is savings, related to feature benefits which can bring about increased company growth and profitability.

> 'This system, which is already enjoying considerable success with many other companies in the same line of business as yourself, will not only bring about a significant increase in usable warehouse space and improve the efficiency of your operation, but will also enable you to provide a higher level of customer service. This means you should be able to both delay capital investment in further premises for the foreseeable future and increase revenues by virtue of greater storage capacity and more efficient service for customers who might otherwise go to your competitors. This could make a considerable contribution to the profitability of your company.'

Managing directors want to know about ways in which they can improve total company performance. This usually brings about a relative disinterest in aesthetics, mechanics, and the ambitions of divisional or departmental managers. Their concentration is on those factors which are closely related to the company's, and therefore their own, survival.

The hazards of the middle management contact

If you were to ask any salesman how he would feel about subcontracting his selling responsibility to a biased third party, he is unlikely to greet the proposition with much enthusiasm. Yet, that is what selling at the middle management level usually means. The salesman puts his sales argument to whichever individual lack of endeavour, insufficient foresight, or accident has thrust upon him, in the hope that this person will argue with the decision-maker on his behalf as strongly and with the same interests in mind as the salesman himself. A vain hope indeed!

If there is anyone who ought to understand managing directors, it's a managing director. If such a man was to return to direct selling you can be assured that any initial approach, other than straight to the top, would not even be considered. His reason, apart from the obvious logic of the decision-making process, would be that managing directors are usually much more objective and decisive people to negotiate with. After all, these are some of the essential qualities which got them their positions.

In general terms, the point of initial sales contact automatically becomes the 'hierarchical ceiling' beneath which the salesman's subsequent negotiations will take place. He can easily move down the scale, but not up. This situation is not brought about by the reluctance of people higher up the organization to become involved. It is rather the inability of many people in middle management to react objectively to the process of allowing the salesman to address their peers in order to obtain a decision, primarily because of the personal inadequacy that such an action implies. For such people, an admittance that they do not have the necessary authority to make a decision is an affront to their pride. Thus they attempt to give the impression that their influence upon the decision-making process is so profound that it amounts to the same as having ultimate authority, or conversely, that they have the power to prevent any contender from entering the consideration process. This is very difficult territory indeed! As I suggested earlier on, there is always a greater chance of running into the friendly neighbourhood megalomaniac at middle management level than at the top. Unfortunately, particularly in larger organizations, such a person may well have a truly strong influence on the final decision, or in some cases, may actually have the final word.

An approach to the managing director, rather than creating political barriers, typically offers opportunities for getting around the reluctant middle manager problem. It may well be that in the case of a particular salesman's product decisions can be made below board level. On the other hand, it could be that the managing director in question would not contemplate the possibility of making a final decision without the involvement of all the managers who will be directly or indirectly affected by the product concerned. This, however, in no way detracts from the wisdom of making the initial contact with the chief executive, as he is the best source of information concerning the people who have a real, as opposed to assumed, influence on the final decision. To approach middle or senior managment with the opening statement 'Your managing director has asked me to discuss this matter with you' is substantially stronger than most overtures otherwise available to the new business salesman.

Finally, once the salesman has opened the managing director's door, he should endeavour to keep it open. He will not only need to address that source of influence again before the sales negotiation is over, but also needs to bear in mind that his competitors will be doing the same. To lose contact with the managing director, once established, is to run the risk of giving competition exclusivity of access to the ear of the actual decision-maker.

Sales enquiries

Sales enquiries are generally initiated by (a) your company being a market leader, or (b) by virtue of specific marketing activity. There are some companies whose market status is such that most end-users considering a new purchase will automatically include them, even if they have no intention of ultimately purchasing that supplier's product. *Rank Xerox* in photocopiers, *IBM* in computers, *ICI* in chemicals, are typical examples. But even for large and successful companies such as these, self-generated enquiries represent only a small proportion of new business sales. Most sales enquiries are generated by advertising, exhibitions, press announcements, and other forms of product promotion. These are not only essential, expensive and time-consuming processes, but are completely worthless if they do not result in new business. It is remarkable, therefore, that many salespeople whose companies have invested so much money and effort into creating these potential business opportunities, throw it all away by abusing the final product of their endeavour with delay and mishandling.

The effect of failing to respond quickly to sales enquiries should be obvious. If a potential buyer enquires, he usually wants to start the buying process immediately, not next year or even next week. Therefore, delay can only result in giving the initiative to competition or cause the potential customer to lose interest. There is only one way to deal with a sales enquiry—urgently. And there is only one person who can do the job—the salesman! That must seem like rather an obvious statement, but the fact is many salespeople are so indifferent to sales enquiries that they respond in a manner most likely to minimize the chances of success.

The most important consideration in handling sales enquiries, other than promptness, is prospect qualification. Any large scale promotional activity is sure to result in a significant proportion of inapproriate prospects. Sorting out students from managing directors is a job for a salesman, not a secretary, an office manager, or the marketing department. There is no merit at all in sending out advertising literature *en masse*, perhaps with a covering letter, to all enquiries, in the hope that the truly valid prospects will identify themselves. Life isn't like that! A tremendous amount of time and money can be spent on typing, administration, postage, sales litera- ture, etc., in order to give equal priority to waste paper hoarders and active buyers. How much easier and effective it is if the salesman makes a tele- phone call to the enquirer and simply asks why the enquiry was made in the first place. Valid prospects can be handled straight away, long term 'suspects' can be processed as a secondary priority, and the time waster can be appropriately dealt with. There's nothing more frustrating than making a delayed response to a prospect only to find they have just placed the order elsewhere. 'I'm sorry. I thought you weren't interested!' What else can they say?

Prospect qualification

It's always depressing to lose a sale. Even the acceptance that 'you can't win them all' is cold comfort on the day when the outcome of months of concerted effort is total rejection. Losing orders is not only a source of anguish for the salesman, it is also a monumental waste of time and money for both he and his employer. Of course, there is one excellent method of reducing the number of lost sales and that is only to get involved in those sales situations where you are absolutely convinced you are going to win. Believe me, that statement is not as flippant as it might first appear! Pros- pect qualification is as important an element of the selling cycle as the close itself.

There is a great degree of personal ego within the selling process and this is often a barrier to objectivity. How often one sees a salesman with the bit firmly between his teeth grimly battling on with a lost cause when it is apparent to everyone except himself that there is no possible hope of suc- cess. It is a simple fact of selling that the motives of apparently potential buyers are often devious no matter how sincere they may appear. It is also a fact that many buyers do not have the courage to say 'no' to an insistent salesman who is determined to propose his product, even though they know full well that it is inappropriate. This leads to two distinct areas of prospect qualification:

Validity of business opportunity.
Validity of proposition.

Whether your prospective client was generated by personal approach or by a formal request for tender, there are many reasons why he would want to tag you along although there is no real hope of success. Here are some typical examples:

1. The buyer wants a comparative quote just in case the supplier he has already chosen is over charging.

2. The buyer has already made his decision, but wants to give his colleagues and superiors the impression that his recommendations are the result of a detailed analysis of a cross section of potential suppliers, as well as demonstrating his democratic attitude towards all vendors.

3. The buyer is committed to a particular design philosophy but out of curiosity would like to consider the implications of a different approach.

4. The buyer knows that his company could never afford the type of sophisticated system he has asked you to propose, but through academic curiosity or delusions of grandeur he encourages you to continue with your fool's errand.

I am sure there is a host of other contrived and innocent motivations for persuading some buyers to mislead salespeople. With this possibility in mind, the salesman should do everything possible to avoid involvement in such abortive activity by qualifying the actual need.

There are many ways of verifying the intent of the buyer. For instance:

1. Ask the buyer to pay for any initial feasibility study on the understanding that the charge will be refunded in full should your company be given the contract. This is not a completely reliable device, but the sensitive salesman can often tell from the buyer's reaction just how serious he really is.

2. Ask the buyer in a courteous and well-considered manner whether your type of solution is too expensive, too complex, too powerful, too early, too big, too political, etc.

There are very few buyers who will say 'no' when the truth is 'yes'. Having said all that, there must be at least ten lost causes created by salespeople themselves, for every one inflicted on them by unscrupulous buyers. By and large, people do not like to say 'no' when someone offers to do something for them, particularly when no charge is involved. Prospective clients are no exception to this rule. They don't like to say things like, 'You would be wasting your time', or even 'Clear off!' It makes them appear to be intolerant and prejudiced. So when the eager and blinkered salesman comes rushing in, more often than not the buyer will let them get on with it. It is his way of playing fair.

So what should the salesman do? Once again, he should have his own checklist of fundamental questions to ask both the client and himself before getting deeply involved in the selling process. Here are some possible considerations:

1. Do the inherent company or national politics of this situation make my product unacceptable?

2. Does this company really have a need for my product?

3. Does my company have the product/skills to provide a valid and cost effective solution to the problem?

4. Does the prospect have sufficient funds available to afford the type of solution we are likely to propose?

5. Has a fundamental decision already been made in the context of either design philosophy or product type which will invalidate our particular approach?

6. Can we meet the delivery date?

7. Can we afford this business, i.e., will it be profitable?

I am sure you can think of many more. However, it is important to apply such disciplines as a fundamental part of a day-to-day selling activity, rather than merely acknowledging their inherent wisdom. For me, the ultimate prospect qualification is simply to view the product through the eyes of the potential buyer and ask myself, 'Would I buy it if I were him?' Alternatively, 'Could I buy it if I were him?'

Spotting tomorrow's successes and failures

It is as important to be aware of the source of tomorrow's new business prospects as that of today's. It is, therefore, essential that the salesman has an awareness of the significant areas of decline and growth within the companies and markets throughout his territory. Of course, it is tempting to 'do a Mr Micawber' and wait for sales prospects to turn up. It's easy to sit around the office moaning about the company's lack of promotional activity or the need for a direct mailing campaign. However, the salesman can do a lot for himself when it comes to spotting tomorrow's probable winners and losers in the business world. This is an important and rewarding activity because it helps the salesman to identify new prospects which might be less obvious to his competitors. It can also help him to take early action to protect his company's interests when bankruptcy might be on the horizon for his existing clients.

Spotting potential winners and losers in the business world is a complex process which even 'City experts' are unable to perform with absolute consistency. However, there are some tell-tale signs which can be a pointer to future performance.

The well-informed, territorial salesman is a conscientious reader of the national and, particularly, local business press. This way he gets to know about many of the companies who are enjoying success and suffering failure. By identifying companies whose apparent growth and success is the product of strong and aware management, the salesman can often locate new prospects which would never appear in the usual trade directories and thus be less likely to involve intense competitive activity.

It is a good practice to keep a prospect file of local companies, based on press cuttings declaring sales achievements, market prospects, financial reports, etc., which can be an efficient pointer to present and future business potential and an indicator of significant growth and decline. In both circumstances, the implications can be significant, with much to be gained or lost, as pre-warning can enable the salesman to exploit either situation to his advantage. The well-informed salesman is one who knows where new business opportunites are most likely to occur. Unfortunately, he cannot rely on an out-dated edition of *Kompass* to tell him all he needs to know in order to be in the right place at the right time.

Spotting declining companies is a very difficult process and there are two approaches that can be used. One is my own particular 'early warning system', especially relevant to existing clients. Obtaining the right input is difficult but it can say more about a company's future than it knows itself. Simply, attempt to discover what proportion of the company's revenue actually comes from new customers and new product developments. If the proportion is in single figures, or less than the current rate of inflation, the company is potentially stagnant surviving only on its revenue 'flywheel' and thus increasingly at risk to competition. The other, and more positive approach, is to take out a formal credit rating and obtain a copy of the most recent annual report. There are several sources for gaining this type of information, ranging from Companies House to *Dunn and Bradstreet*. The salesman should pay particular attention to details such as:

Turnover and rate of growth.
Value of order book.
Stock levels.
Total of outstanding debt.
Total of outstanding credit.
Days credit given by creditors.
Days credit taken by debtors.
Tax liabilities.
Outstanding borrowings.

If the salesman can also discover the proportion of capacity used and investment in new products, so much the better. The combination of all this information can give a pretty accurate appreciation of the company's future prospects.

Having said all of that, the salesman should make no hasty judgements.

If he thinks he has a client about to go bankrupt or a prospective first-time user needing an earth satellite, he really ought to discuss it with his manager first.

4.

Territory management

'Genius does what it must, and Talent does what it can.'
Edward Lytton 1831–91

One of the casualties of currency decimalisation was the shilling. Today, we have instead the five pee or 5p. This reminds me of two most important selling considerations. One provides the answer to the question 'What is marketing?', and the other is the key to territory management. Marketing is said to be about having the right Product in the right Place at the right Price with the right Promotion and generating the right Profit. The 'shilling' of territory management is somewhat more succinct: Poor Planning Promotes Pathetic Performance!

If selling is to be truly professional it must always be based on a plan. There has to be a systematic approach to maximizing the use of time, evaluating territory and prospect potential, maintaining records, etc. There is no exception. Every aspect of the selling process demands organizational commitment, imagination, and absolute attention to detail. Yet, important as such responsibility might be, it is not effective if it achieves anything less than the highest possible call rate. For only in this way can the maximum number of prospects be generated and thus the optimum level of business obtained. Territory planning is unarguably essential, but there is no substitute for hard work. Plan well and work hard and the law of averages will always work in your favour.

Every salesman should be a farmer

It is rather a sweeping statement to say that farmers are either good or bad. But one tends to notice those farms which are clearly prosperous, well managed, efficient, and using up-to-date and well-maintained equipment, and, at the other extreme, those farms which are clearly disorganized and ramshackle, with equipment left rusting in the fields and which barely manage to scrape a living.

However, let us forget the incompetents and failures and concentrate on the good farmer, his responsibilities, the job he has to do, the way he goes about his tasks, and the circumstances in which he operates. In most cases

44

the successful farmer has a predominance of fertile ground which can be relied upon, given the right climate conditions, to be very fruitful provided he tends it with care. This is where most of his endeavour is concentrated. He may also have less fertile land only suitable for a limited range of produce or only fit for grazing. He accepts the fact that no matter how much investment of time and money he makes, the potential yield will always be minimal. He therefore gives it a much lesser proportion of his time. He may also have completely new land, either recently purchased or reclaimed, that apparently has significant potential; but tomorrow, not today. He therefore works on it whenever he has the opportunity, or perhaps devotes some time to a 'crash programme' of land enrichment with a firm time scale in his mind of how he is going to treat it, what he is going to grow on it, and when he intends to start his first planting. In most instances he will also have some barren 'scrub land', which he accepts as worthless and seldom visits. He certainly has no intention of wasting his time trying to grow crops on stony ground. In other words, he has a total picture of his land, equipment, and livestock, and knows where best to invest his time. There is little room for sentiment.

Every day he spends some of his time walking or driving around his land, just to see how everything is getting along. He knows he can't leave the farm to look after itself. A sick animal identified in good time may be saved by early treatment, whereas neglect would probably involve the cost of replacement. On the other hand, he may wish to see the effects of his new irrigation or fertilization methods. As he wanders along, he considers ways in which he can overcome the problems and exploit the opportunities he has identified within his boundaries of responsibility.

Making an early start and working until the day's jobs are completed in their logical sequence is the farmer's unavoidable routine. The cows are milked at the same time of day, morning and evening, because that is what they are accustomed to. Any deviation will result in a significantly reduced yield.

If the weather makes a planned job impossible then he doesn't sit around moaning, he fixes his broken baler or does some other job he's been saving for a rainy day.

The efficient farmer rotates his crops and so retains the vitality of the soil. He not only maintains variety, but also keeps abreast of market demands and economic fluctuations. He must have the knowledge and courage to turn his back on well-proven produce, if need be, and grow new crops that may be more profitable. To switch from dairy to beef cattle is a large step to take in both practical and economic terms, but if EEC legislation, market prices, or technological development offer better opportunities, they must be grasped. Many farmers have gone into liquidation by firmly refusing to acknowlege the advent of change.

Keeping accurate and up-to-date details of all activities is an essential

45

part of successful farming. Which crop was planted when? What did the crops cost? What is the current price and market trend? What strain of seed did we plant before? What is the effect on cashflow? What is the tonnage per acre? Without reliable knowledge of what might be, what is and what went before, the farmer's chances of failure are extremely high.

All this means, in other words, that the farmer is a good 'housekeeper'. He constantly keeps a firm eye on his land, the seasons, the crops, and the weather so that he is sure of the best time to harvest. There is a right time for everything; to oppose the logic of the seasons is simply to court disaster. Now that's not so different from territory management, is it?

Time management

It is said that time is money. But time is the medium within which we apply our skills and talents, assets that have greater value, and therefore require greater care and consideration in their use, than something so indiscriminately distributed as material possession. Yet even the allocation of human attributes has no fairness or logic. It appears that time is the only thing that is evenly endowed upon us all; and I suppose one could even argue about the justice of that!

One of the most significant differences between low and high achieving salespeople is their individual management of time. Time wasting is a temptation in any job which allows complete freedom of action; and few jobs offer more opportunities for contrived or unconscious deception than selling, at least in the short term. The absence of continual supervision leaves the salesman free to organize his own time. That is why self-discipline is so important in selling; no other job provides greater scope for dereliction of duty. If you want to play golf instead of making sales calls and try to justify your actions to the world and yourself by pronouncing on the value of business contacts on the fairway, that's entirely up to you. If you find yourself unable to resist extended lunches and coffee breaks when there is business waiting to be closed, that's your decision. If you feel it is more important to sit in the office and get your files looking really slick instead of spending the time prospecting, do what you must. Yet never lose sight of the fact that one day you will need to declare the profitability of your activities. There is no point in fussing around with an immaculate recording system if the same information can be retained by less sophisticated and time consuming means. It is not that top salespeople wouldn't like, or couldn't create, a neatly typed clerical masterpiece, it is just that they are always too busy selling! The real achievers in selling always have a very positive set of priorities. They continually sort their tasks into those that must be done immediately, soon, eventually, or not at all.

Client categorization is an excellent means of ensuring that selling time is used effectively. Clients and prospects may be rated 'A', 'B' or 'C' according to their potential, and the frequency of calling and application of time allocated accordingly. For instance, 'A' clients may be those with a qualified business potential in excess of £50 000 per annum, 'B' clients over £5000 and 'C' clients below. It may be decided that 'A' clients should be seen at least once every month, 'B' clients every three months (in other words, every third trip) and 'C' clients every six months. The duration of individual calls may also be planned in accordance with potential, if that is feasible.

Knowing *how* to apply one's energies is no more important than knowing *when* to do so. There are times of the day that offer greater potential than others for maximizing the effect of your endeavours. For example, it is important to have no preconceived ideas about the times of day when clients are likely to be unavailable. If competitors assume that certain times of day and days of the week are unsuitable, surely that represents an opportunity. As far as planning and administration is concerned, there can be no better time of day than the early morning for really getting things done. At that time of day the mind is fresh and the world is not cluttered with the inconsiderate pressures of visitors and telephone calls. Once the habit of an early start is established and the discipline of tackling the big problems first becomes second nature, the salesman is two steps ahead of the game. With a refreshed and alert mind and the blessing of uninterrupted thought, major difficulties can suddenly become minor problems, and armed with the success of early achievement the salesman can greet the day with confidence and enthusiasm.

Monday mornings and other excuses

We used to have a regular routine. Every Monday morning each salesman was expected to complete his claims for business expenses, up-date the prospect hot-list, and complete any outstanding call reports from the previous week. The arrangement mostly worked quite well, but there was one character who regularly missed the midday deadline. However, he was the company's most successful salesman, which earned him a little extra flexibility so the situation never became a problem. One day I asked why only he was regularly absent from the office on Monday mornings, bearing in mind the administrative arrangements and the time of the week. To my surprise he told me it was one of his best times for meeting clients and prospects.

To all intents and purposes he was an average fellow, with none of the articulate charisma that the uninformed normally associate with salespeople. However, he had a prospect portfolio at least twice as big as any other salesman and a much greater call rate. In fact his ability to make more calls than his fellows, thus generating more prospects, was due almost entirely to his refusal to accept any of the common myths concerning the time parameters which are supposed to govern the scheduling of appointments.

Many salesmen believe that selling cannot generally be conducted on

Monday mornings, Friday afternoons, and on any day before 10.00 am or after 4.30 pm and between midday and 2.30 pm; the notable exception being the occasional lunchtime appointment, which can often be related more to self indulgence than selling. The very fact that the belief in these apparently unavailable hours is so widespread makes them particularly fruitful to the more objective salesman. It also begs the question as to whether the lack of direct sales activity at the beginning and end of the week is more a reflection of inadequate salesmen than reluctant buyers.

The most important call is the first call of the day, for it tends to dictate the pattern of subsequent sales activity. A familiar and extremely negative approach to planning sales calls is to assume that everyone has masses of post to process before anything else can be done. Another negative assumption, particularly in major cities, is that most people do not reach their offices until after 9.30 am. The answer, simply, is make the first appointment each day for 8.30 am. You will soon discover, which people are usually around at that time. You will be surprised how many senior executives normally arrive at work before 8.30 am or are willing to arrive a little earlier to see you. Most companies do not finish distributing their mail until well after 9.30 am, which gives plenty of time for discussion before the postal ritual. Appointments after 4.30 pm are often more difficult to arrange than early morning calls. Nevertheless, many senior executives are prepared to stay a little late in their office if they believe it may benefit their company, particularly with someone who is also prepared to give up some of his own time. As far as lunchtime is concerned, the determined and well-organized salesman can work right through the lunchtime period if need be. This ability is purely a function of keeping effective client records. There are two fairly consistent features of lunch periods; they normally last for one hour and usually start any time between midday and 1.30 pm, i.e. many people have returned from lunch before others have left for theirs. The question is who lunches when, and that is where detailed client records are essential.

Most salespeople could significantly increase their existing call rate by using their selling time more effectively, resulting in increased rewards for both salesman and company alike. There are many disciplines and techniques which can contribute towards more profitable sales activity, but none can bring more significant results than simply getting to the first call by 9.00 am at the latest every day, knowing which clients lunch when, and disregarding any generalizations about proper and improper times to call.

Organization and documentation

Call planning

A call planning system has several significant benefits, not least of which is the facility for comparing what was achieved with what was orginally intended. It also allows the salesman to awake each morning free from the significant demotivation of being virtually unemployed. Yet these are not the only benefits of operating an effective call planning system.

A salesman who is out of touch with the people supporting him is likely to be out of touch with sales success. Any secretary will tell you how difficult it can be to contact salespeople whenever urgent situations arise. Yet it is absolutely essential that rapid communication with the salesman is achievable at all times. Many salespeople operate like undercover agents, surreptitiously creeping from one clandestine meeting to another and breaking cover only to collect their expenses and receive further briefing.

It is undeniable that where there is mystery concerning the activity of any salesman, there is also a considerable likelihood of inefficiency. People seldom hide those parts of their nature which might increase their esteem among their fellows. So, when a salesman cannot be found it could mean that he is disorganized, dishonest, lazy, inefficient, certainly not management material, and possibly looking for a new job. However, the most likely failing is the lack of an effective call planning system.

A call planning system is simply a device which helps the salesman to construct a logical sequence of future sales calls taking into account such factors as geography, call frequency, and client category as well as any special situations and priorities. It is a system that tells the salesman and his supporting colleagues Who? When? Why? at a single glance and as such is an essential device in terms of both efficiency and discipline. A single form is all that is required to create efficient means of communications. The essential elements are obvious:

Time/Day.
Company.
Name of contact.
Telephone number.
Purpose of call.
Appointment or cold call?
Overnight address and telephone number.

By being sent a copy of the completed document prior to the salesman's departure all supporting people are in a position to provide the right kind of assistance and generally do their jobs properly.

As far as the making of appointments is concerned, it is important that a call planning system is accompanied by efficient, geographically-orientated client records in order to facilitate both sensible routing and the possibility of unscheduled calls on existing and prospective clients in the same locality. It is also preferable that the call plan be generated as much in advance as possible. Most people manage to keep their diaries full at least a week ahead, so a two week lead time tends to create less 'busy signals' and often avoids the pressure of 'squeezed in' appointments. Another good discipline is to arrange the first and last appointments for each day before those in the middle. It gives much greater flexibility for fitting in other appointments and is usually worth at least a couple of extra calls a week.

The organization of calls

Salespeople generally spend about a third of their time travelling. That's an incredible waste of selling time! It is therefore likely that they could gain more benefit from concentrating on the more effective use of travelling time (i.e., selling time) than on those disciplines principally designed to improve the techniques of selling.

It is clear that the number of calls can be significantly increased by the more effective use of travelling time resulting from conscientious planning and organization on the part of each individual. The most essential tool is a map of the salesman's territory with his home base and location of each client and prospect clearly marked. A colour coding system to distinguish between clients, prospects, industries, products, special situations, etc., is particularly useful. Artificial territory zones can then be created which encompass each logical geographic grouping of these existing areas. These coloured zones should be regarded as primary territory and the remainder as 'sheep' country where activity is relatively passive. After all, the salesman is not obliged to cover a large geographic territory merely because it has been allocated to him. If a special, perhaps industry-orientated, campaign or a self-generated prospect creates a need for departing from the primary selling zones, then it should be regarded as a possible extension of an existing zone and approached with that zone in mind. If the prospect turns out to be worthless, then the journey includes the opportunity of calling on existing clients and prospects on the way back, thus avoiding a completely wasted journey.

A simple, but effective, discipline is to ensure that the first call of the day or trip is the one furthest away. All subsequent calls should then be planned in order of decreasing distance from home. This approach has several benefits for the salesman, particularly related to increasing the number of selling calls. However, the biggest advantage is simply that of making the longest journey while he is fresh and the shortest when he is tired. Sometimes a circular calling route or 'round trip' is more applicable than a 'straight line' journey. In these circumstances the furthest client from home might be best visited halfway through the day. If this is the case, the nearest call to home should still be last. A few minutes should also be spent studying a road map before setting out, deciding upon the shortest total journey which will embrace all the planned visits. There are usually several alternative routes and good planning could easily mean an extra selling call.

Client records

Client records are essential, not only for keeping a consistent record of all the activity that went before, but also to assist planning ahead. Where there is a multitude of client and prospect contact it is easy to forget what happened when, who promised what, and the action that was actually taken. Any sales manager will tell you that the best salespeople keep the most efficient, rather than the most comprehensive, client records.

Perhaps because of a congenital hatred of paperwork, most salespeople are badly organized when it comes to the maintenance of detailed records of their sales activity. A cursory view of the salespeople around you may reveal a variety of eccentric methods for retaining information: backs of envelopes, last year's diary, tatty index cards, a cardboard box in the car boot, and the like. Amazingly, many such people are out on the road selling products intended to increase the efficiency and productivity of the client! Remember the parable of the mote and the beam?

Client records have more uses than just a reminder and planning system for the salesman. They are essential in circumstances where someone new has to take over the situation. This could involve a relief salesman during periods of sickness or holidays, the result of a whole or partial reorganization of territories, or even the permanent departure of the salesman to another employer. Whatever the reason, the salesman who inherits someone else's territory will have enormous problems without a record of what went before.

Imagine an urgent telephone call from an irate client taken by the secretary of the salesman sunning himself in the Mediterranean:

'We have just received a communications modem which doesn't appear to have the transmission characteristics we were expecting. We have an urgent situation here! Can you send someone round to sort out the problem please?'

The secretary gets the correct name of the company, but not the name of the caller. She then reports the situation to the sales manager. No problem, the salesman's client records quickly reveal the company's address and telephone number, the name of the chief engineer, a note of the order taken on the last visit, and the department head who required a high speed modem. It is then a matter of checking with the dispatch department to see what has been sent. Then, having asked for the appropriate department head by name, the sales manager is quickly able to deal with the problem. Without established records the situation could be quite different. The dispatch documentation might reveal some information, but:

1.   Who actually ordered the product?

2.   What was promised?

3.   In what circumstances was it ordered? (Was it understood to be a trial or what?)

4. Were the dispatch details correct? The address, version of product, etc.

5. What are the names of the people involved and their responsibilities?

6. Was any support promised? If so, what?

7. For what purpose is the product being used?

8. Was a detailed proposal ever submitted that might provide some useful background?

9. Were any alternatives discussed?

10. Did the salesman actually take the order, or was it someone else?

The existence of up-to-date client records could answer many, if not all, of these questions and help someone with no prior knowledge of the situation to give the salesman the kind of support he would wish for in his absence. Without them a minor problem could easily be aggravated into a crisis.

Client records need to be up to date, accurate, flexible, accessible, and legible. Many salespeople use basic record cards containing name, address, telephone and contact details, merely noting the date of each call. This is fine for some products, and if information for each call, such as what happened, what was achieved, object of next visit, and anticipated date, can also be briefly contained, so much the better. However, the higher the product value and thus the longer the selling cycle, the greater the need for detail. In such circumstances something more comprehensive is called for, and the kind of client records I prefer are file folders kept in alphabetical order by client. Inside the front cover is all the basic details on the client, including turnover, number of employees, names and positions of all persons in buying positions, best times to call, type of industry and markets, potential and existing products in use and competition, together with a simple one-line-per-call record of each call made, on whom, about what, and when. All detailed call reports, proposals, correspondence, press cuttings, client's own product and corporate literature, and any special notes are then kept in the file. Once this kind of system has been set up it is relatively simple to maintain, for most entries consist of a few written words together with any relevant material that may transpire. It has virtually unlimited capacity, for all the salesman has to do when preparing a call is consult the file to find all out he needs to know. For anyone 'picking up the threads' there is all the detail of action and background to provide real continuity.

The whole process of maintaining effective client records is a question of both personal discipline and self survival. It may be a struggle and a bore when you first start out, but very soon it will become so much second nature that you will wonder how on earth you managed to survive without them. Come the next recession, maybe you won't!

The in-call report

One of the worst things a salesman can do is rely on his memory; and I guess that also applies to most other people in business. If a salesman assumes or accepts that he has a bad memory and caters for such inadequacy accordingly, he is half way to remembering everything.

The call report is probably the area where the salesman tends to leave most events and actions to memory, yet this is the aspect of his activity where it is essential that no observation or promise of action to be taken is forgotten. How many salesmen do you know who write out most of their call reports once a week, and only then because their managers collect them on a weekly basis? This is a grossly inefficient situation with nothing to recommend it. Firstly, it makes a significant task out of what should be a simple exercise. Secondly, it relies on the vagaries of the human memory which as a recording device tends to concentrate on 'highs' and 'lows' with an overlay of random amnesia. Thirdly, it potentially delays the initiation of actions to be taken by up to a week. Fourthly, call reports can be overlooked altogether, creating a picture of sales activity which is less than actual performance.

The best place to write out a call report is during the call. A client will never object to a salesman's request to take notes during a meeting. After all, such an action is a confirmation of the salesman's desire to do a thorough job and a call report produced during the sales call is likely to represent a true record of everything that transpired.

A call report created directly after the call, may be sitting in the car, even using a cassette recorder, is certainly preferable to the once a week fiasco, but is less reliable than the direct response of the in-call report. Documentation produced in this way is immediately available for action; perhaps a copy to back up a telephone call to the technical department to act upon a complaint or to the sales manager to act upon a useful piece of information about competitive activity. This approach is the only truly efficient way of sales recording when you really think about it, for the function of call reports is substantially more than providing an historical record.

Checklist and questionnaires

Many kinds of industrial and commercial selling involve the production of a sales proposal or quotation which in turn requires a detailed survey to collect all the relevant information so that the best available solution can be offered to the prospective client. While the information one collects in every such exercise is virtually unique, by far the greater proportion of questions the salesman needs to ask recur from client to client. Yet, despite this repetition, salespeople very often approach the survey situation on a one-off, 'play it by ear' basis. This means that the chances of getting all the information needed is a direct result of experience, memory, and a considerable amount of time. The use of standard checklists within the sales survey is an excellent method, not only of increasing the efficiency of collecting essential information, but also for aiding the lesser-experienced salesman within an unfamiliar application or industry.

Let's take, for example, the sale of a manual accounting system for a sales ledger application. Most of the questions that need to be asked are obvious to someone who has sold a sales ledger system before:

1. How many sales ledger accounts do you have?

2. How many new accounts have you opened over the past year?

3. How many ledger postings do you expect on a daily and month-by-month basis over the next year?

4. What is your accounting discipline? (Balance brought forward, balance brought forward by month, open item.)

5. How many days average credit is being taken by debtors at the present time?

6. What about integration with invoicing and stock control?

All straightforward questions for the configuration of any sales ledger system. Of course there is also a need to cover non-standard input under the heading of 'Any Other Requirements', but 80 to 90 per cent of the questions will be the same, whichever company is being addressed. So why not have a data collection form for each application or type of product, containing all the standard questions? The related benefits are considerable:

Greater accuracy.
Fewer omissions.
Less time consuming.
Assists relatively inexperienced personnel.
Formal confirmation of client's needs.
Greater investigatory discipline.

The areas of possibility are not limited to relatively simple areas such as accounting and business management. The specification of all kinds of equipment, materials, and services usually involves a considerable amount of repetition. This is not an original idea; I know of many companies who have been using sales survey checklists for years. If you are in the business of specifying products and don't already use this kind of sales aid, I suggest you start to devise your own as soon as possible. I can assure you that it won't be long before you are wondering how you ever managed to generate a proposal without one. It also makes an excellent document for the prospect to sign, just in case there is any subsequent argument about the task that was undertaken.

5.

Communications

'He has flashes of silence that make his conversation perfectly delightful.'
Rev. Sydney Smith 1771–1845

The basis of communications

Communications is the topic that business people typically discuss after a management disaster which came about because they failed to keep all interested parties informed. Communications is a familiar component of retrospective wisdom: it is anathema to the autocrat, pointless to the arrogant and puzzling to the insular.

The ability to communicate effectively is the hallmark of any truly successful person, whether their day-to-day activity is in business, politics, religion, or purely social survival. For some people the ability to communicate is instinctive, a genetic accident, a natural flair as rare as common sense: for others it is a hard-earned skill resulting from years of training, studying, real-world experience, and patient application.

Communications is largely about remembering nature's ratio of two ears to one mouth. It is about listening rather than simply hearing; having constant consideration for every party with even the slightest interest in, or influence upon, a given situation and keeping them informed at the right level. By right level, I don't mean a constant flood of information or indeed the gesture of an occasional out-of-date memorandum.

A past colleague of mine once neatly summed-up the inadequate communications of the company where we worked together as 'mushroom management': 'Feed 'em plenty of bullshit and keep 'em in the dark!' In this case he was highlighting, not only a failure to communicate with client and employees, but also the way in which some people and companies limit their communications to promoting either their own interests or distributing misleading company propaganda.

It has been said before that communications is a two-way street. I agree with the general intentions of that analogy, but not its detailed application. Simultaneous communications, when both people talk and neither listens, can often be more misleading than total silence. I believe that the responsibility for effective communications lies with the transmitter. Okay, I know I

56

have already emphasized the need for listening, but someone within the communicative process must take prime responsibility for ensuring that the total process is complete, i.e., message sent, message received, and message understood.

Message received and understood

One of the most significant areas of communications failure is where both parties believe it is the responsibility of the other to complete the process of communicating. It must be the transmitter who has the ultimate obligation to ensure that any communication is completely understood by the receiver, because, apart from any other reason, the recipient cannot request a re-transmission or interpretation of the message if he is unaware that it was ever transmitted. Make no mistake, nobody at all is too dense to understand. It is the responsibility of the initiator of the communication to transmit at whatever level, speed and volume, and in whatever language that will best be understood by the recipient.

The use of technical jargon personifies the arrogance and insularity of the non-communicator. It is as if such people deliberately seek a means of ensuring misunderstanding and confusion. What makes matters worse is the tolerance and apathy of recipients whose pride will not allow them to confess their inability to understand, assuming the confusion is a reflection of their own ignorance rather than the foolishness and insensitivity of the transmitter. Technical jargon and scientific gobbledegook might do wonders for a salesman's ego, but it is unquestionably the salesman who speaks the buyer's language who will get the business.

The principal objective of person-to-person communications is to transmit ideas, feelings, impressions, emotions, messages, etc., with a minimum of distortion. This is seldom achieved in the absolute sense as very often something gets lost along the way. Sometimes the recipient hears something in a message that the transmitter never intended. Often the message is never received at all. These failures in communication happen because of a wide variety of forces which contrive to dilute, pollute, or misdirect the intended message.

In selling particularly, although this subject is just as applicable to any type of person-to-person interaction, a significant objective of communications is to achieve a predetermined and favourable response. This is a principal skill of selling; the ability of the salesman to present a communication in a way which will be acceptable to the recipient and create a path to mutual understanding. This demands sufficient sensitivity and objectivity on the part of the originator of a communication to assess the human characteristics of the recipient and the external forces which might affect his reaction, so that the correct route can be chosen to achieve the desired response. This route to the common ground of mutual understanding often requires the negotiation of a large number of emotional and psychological barriers.

The following schematic chart gives some idea of the processes involved and the potential obstacles to effective communications. As I have already said, no one is too dense to understand, and successful communication is the responsibility of the initiator. He must do whatever is necessary to establish understanding right from the start.

Obstacles to communication

Speaking in the same tongue as the recipient does not always ensure understanding. There can be barriers created by the semantics of the spoken word, the nuances, the context, the emphasis, the mannerisms, the expression, the colloquialisms, those elements of language which can innocently, or sometimes deliberately, corrupt the meaning intended by the transmitter. How often we hear the expression, 'A complete misunderstanding'. You can blame the person sending the message every time!

There are many other obstacles too, not the least of which is the credibility barrier which is generally created by having insufficient knowledge of the environment in which one finds oneself: not knowing the size or nature of a company, its products, marketplace, etc; having insufficient knowledge of one's own products; not knowing the rank, role, or status of the recipient. The recipient will very often ask himself the question, 'Why should I communicate with this person, he doesn't understand me, my business, my problems, or his own products?'

Then there are the personality barriers, perhaps the most difficult of all. What is the nature of the person with whom one is attempting to communicate? The manner one might employ for establishing the right level of rapport with an extrovert car salesman would certainly be different from the approach one might use with an introverted academic. It takes a lot of application and experience to have a meaningful amount of success in that respect. Nonetheless, 'knowing your man' is an essential part of effective communications.

Ethnic and social demarcations also hold many pitfalls for the unwary. In fact, there is such a large number of potential disparities between the transmitter of a communication and the recipient—educational background, political affiliations, cultural background, artistic taste, etc.—that everybody falls foul of them at some time. One can only be aware of the possible pitfalls and be most sensitive to the personality of individuals in the communicating process. It is too much to hope that one will never destroy the communications process by the occasional *faux pas* or, indeed, by dropping the most resounding clanger every so often.

The charade barrier is very common in selling, and a very difficult one to overcome. It is a habit of most people to hide their real feelings and attitudes behind a façade of interest and agreement because it is easier that way. A typical situation is one where the buyer pretends to be interested, but his mind is elsewhere because he has clearly decided to buy from

The logic of person to person communications

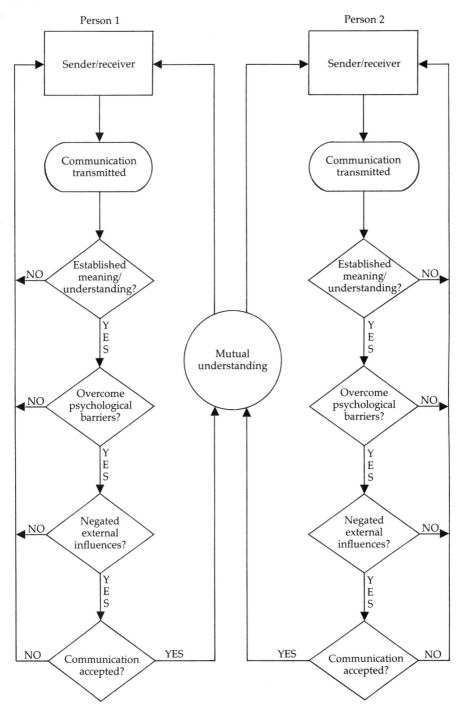

somebody else, but because he's a nice guy he doesn't want to hurt the salesman's feelings. This, besides being dishonest, can waste a lot of time for the unwary salesman. Communications should never be a downhill, one-way street. If the recipient agrees with everything, and apparently wants to make contact, the only way to discover the truth is to ask him searching questions about why he agrees, what alternatives he envisages, and would he be prepared to commit himself. This usually reveals the true situation.

Then there are external force barriers to contend with. The effects of company edicts, politics, union pressures, image, social attitudes, etc., can produce communication barriers which are extremely difficult for the transmitter to overcome. It is one thing persuading a buyer that a product is good, but it's something else to get him to actually buy it contrary to company policy. A comprehensive knowledge of a company, its operational peculiarities, and the personalities involved, is essential if the salesman is to have any real chance of overcoming such obstacles.

Two ears and one mouth
Another stumbling block for effective communication is the listening barrier, which affects the transmitter and receiver alike. Hearing is one thing, listening is another. The only way one can know if a communication has been received and fully understood is to receive feedback from the recipient. The only way a salesman can understand the needs of the buyer is to listen. For many salesmen the time which should be spent listening is used for thinking about what should be said next. This is typified by the salesman who suddenly interrupts the buyer in order to make a sales point which has suddenly occurred to him. The buyer could be saying anything—from, 'I just gave the order to the previous salesman' to 'where do I sign?' Either way the message will be lost to the non-listening communicator.

'There are none so deaf as those who will not hear.' This old adage sums up the kind of person who will not accept a communication which is contrary to his ideals and beliefs. This 'dyed in the wool' mentality is anathema to the creative salesman. There are so many people one meets in life who believe they know exactly 'where it's at'. They have a comfortable pigeon-hole existence of well ordered conformist routine which makes them totally unresponsive to new ideas. Such people can be identified by their use of expressions like 'we've tried that before', 'that doesn't apply to us', 'we're satisfied with our present supplier', 'there's no point in changing', 'we've managed very well up to now', and so on. Bull-at-a-gate tactics seldom work with these people. One has to dismantle their argument step by gentle step.

This may seem unnecessarily complicated, when all one apparently does is say something and somebody hears it and reacts accordingly. However, all one has to do is look around at the mess the world is in to begin to understand the complexity of communications as they relate to common understanding. The reasons why people fail to communicate with each other are as wide and various as the complexities of the human psyche. Awareness of this reality is half the communications battle. The other is a mixture of patience and sensitivity, and simply working at an understanding of what motivates the individual person.

The veil of mystique

Many industries and occupations are shrouded by a veil of mystique. The general effect of this is to make those who are outside feel inadequate and those inside smug, secure, and superior. I must confess that the inside of a wristwatch always gives me a feeling of profound inadequacy. It is clear that there is an enormous gulf between total ignorance and a little knowledge. To disregard or exploit this information gap causes much fear and distrust outside a particular industry or occupation. For example, how secure do you feel in the fields of computers, drugs, biological engineering, nuclear power, and laser technology, in comparison with the technicalities of your own product? I venture to suggest that for most people within those industries, the complexities and implications of *your* product will be equally bewildering to them.

The ethics and responsibilities of product promotion within the public domain is a separate subject and one which I do not intend to discuss. However, technical salesmen in particular have an absolute responsibility for presenting to all directly and indirectly interested parties the truth and practicalities of their industry and its products. They must at all times deal in realities rather than 'black-box panaceas' and technological fantasies. In this way their comments and attitudes in both the business and social domain will contribute to greater public understanding, rather than uninformed distrust. If you think this does not apply to you, just consider yourself for a moment. You must surely have experienced a small surge of pleasure at some time when an acquaintance or a first-time user asked you to explain a technical aspect of your product, and you did so in a considerate, even paternalistic manner, enjoying every moment of it. It doesn't take much to go one stage further into the whole ego trip of blinding the unsuspecting victim with science and technology, quickly reducing him to a bewildered heap with a total mental blockage on the whole topic. This desire for personal aggrandizement lives, unfortunately, in most of us.

It is so important for technical salesmen, in particular, to limit their dialogue with users and social contacts to basic facts that are sure to be understood, for there is always a chance that today's gobbledegook could give birth to tomorrow's Luddite.

There is more than one way of making a point

We are all subject to the vagaries of interpersonal communications. We are all emotional beings despite the exteriors we present to the world. As if in a post-box, we look out through a slit; insecure and secretive, needing to be liked, wanting to be right.

When people communicate to us by voice or by letter we unconsciously carry out our own interpretation of it, which varies considerably according to our emotional state at the time. The same words can please or offend, depending on our state of mind. It is so easy to 'get the wrong end of the stick' because of a gesture, a look, the intonation, or the semantics of language. If this is the potential attitude of the recipient, then there is obviously some value in considering the possible effect of a communication before it is transmitted. There is always more than one way of making any statement, and always an unoffensive way to make a point.

Fuelling the fire of annoyance

I recall an instance late in 1981 when I was involved in a telephone conversation that fully demonstrated how business can be lost simply as a result of assumption, patronization, and lack of sensitivity. I have an oil-fired central heating system and, oil being the price it is, I shop around every time I buy a consignment. There is so much competition among suppliers (in my locality at least) that oil prices are not only in a continual state of flux, but with a bit of haggling, can be reduced quite significantly. On this occasion I went through the *Yellow Pages* to find the best currently available local price. Having already telephoned a number of companies, I spoke to this particular supplier:

'What is your best price for 2300 litres of thirty-five seconds oil?'

'What is the capacity of your tank?' said the voice at the other end.

I was a little surprised.

'Oh, 500 gallons, or whatever that is in litres.'

'You mean 600 gallons.'

'No 500.'

'It can't be, there's no such size.'

I was beginning to have some doubts about my memory. After all, the tank was installed over ten years before. Then again, I was reasonably convinced that I was right and anyway I didn't see what it had to do with my opening question.

62

'I guess I must have an unusual one then, because I'm fairly sure its capacity is 500 gallons.'

'Well, you may have that impression sir (he was becoming a little patronizing) but they don't make them in that size. You will find that yours is 600 right enough.'

By this time he had achieved maximum penetration of my left nostril!

'All right', I said, motivated only by the tolerance that many years in selling inevitably bestows, 'assuming my tank has a capacity of 600 gallons, what is your price for 2300 litres?'

'Fifteen pence a litre', he said.

It was the best price I had been quoted by far.

'And when could you deliver?'

'Within the next 48 hours', he responded enthusiastically. 'Can I take your order?'

'Certainly not', I replied. 'Most of your competitors are offering same day delivery and yours is the worst price I've been quoted.'

I put down the telephone and felt a bit foolish afterwards; lying and cutting off my nose to spite my face, but it was a sincere reaction at the time. Besides which—I enjoyed it!

From the salesman's point of view it is essential to anticipate the effect of every communication, particularly when using the telephone. There are many situations where it is important for him not to say exactly what he thinks because to do so would be destructive. Very often the best strategy is to make a point against himself when he feels like making one against his client. The responses to 'I don't understand' could be many:

'I'll go through it again!'

'It's quite simple really.'

'You can't have been listening.'

'What! All of it?'

When the salesman turns it against himself and says something like:

'I'm sorry, I didn't put it as clearly as I should',

he makes a real contribution towards developing a healthy environment for negotiation. Take another example:

'Our problem is unique.'

'No it isn't.'

'That's what they all say!'

'What makes you think that?'

'We could always "bend" our solution for you.'

To contradict is destructive, and unnecessary. It is far better for the salesman to agree, then qualify the statement:

'I imagine it is rather complex, but we have solved similar problems for several companies in the same industry as yourselves.'

One often seens the inconsiderate use of language at work in communications between management and subordinates:

'You have failed!'

is so much more destructive than:

'You have not enjoyed the success we know you are capable of!'

One demotivates, the other challenges.

Demonstrations

Demonstrations are seldom a roaring success. They usually fall into two categories, satisfactory or disastrous. A satisfactory demonstration is one where the salesman is able to prove to the client that all the claims he has made about the equipment are valid. As with the sales proposal, there are no surprises, merely confirmation of product features already discussed. It is a situation which enables the potential buyer to move from the unknown to the familiar, in product terms. Unfortunately, most demonstrations fail to meet these simple objectives, and all for the same reason—lack of forethought and planning.

By far the most important aspect of a demonstration is deciding upon those features which are relevant to the client's needs and concentrating upon them. A demonstration which exposes equally every aspect of a machine's performance, is not an effective selling exercise, as irrelevant features serve only to confuse. What is the point of displaying even the most impressive function of the equipment if the potential user has no need for

64

it? It is therefore essential that the salesman decides which facilities are of interest to the client, well before the event, and concentrates upon those.

The organization of a demonstration needs a lot of planning and consideration.

Firstly, the overall administration. Where will the demonstration be held; at an existing client's premises, or one's own? When is the machine available? Is the client available on that day? Who will be attending on the prospect's behalf? Who will be needed on the salesman's side? Will refreshments be required? Does the client need to be met or collected? What relevant literature will be required—equipment, software, proposal?

Then the product itself. It must be the one on which the prospect is about to make a buying decision, the one he is expecting to see; not a bigger one, or a smaller one, or one with different features. This must be established well in advance. The demonstration should be rehearsed well before the event and also immediately prior to the live run, in order to cater for any last-minute hitches. If the salesman needs the assistance of technical staff, they should be involved right from the start.

The demonstration itself should be structured, stepping from one relevant feature to another, with a natural pause wherever appropriate to agree the related benefit. The salesman must be in control of the demonstration throughout, whether it is he or a technician who is actually 'pushing the buttons'. This is best achieved by a philosophy of: 'Tell them what you're going to show them, show them, then tell them what you've shown them.' However, this control should not be too rigid or formal. If the demonstration takes place in a present user's premises, it is essential that the prospective and existing customers have the opportunity of talking alone. After all, a satisfied user is a company's best salesman.

Under no circumstances should the salesman abuse the product either physically or emotionally. To kick the motor, or doubt the intellectual capability of the engineer, only serves to degrade the product and reduce the chance of a sale. The salesman's respect for the product must be made apparent. He doesn't need to go to the extreme of caressing it, but his actions and attitude must demonstrate that as far as he is concerned it is the best equipment in the world.

One final thing—the salesman must never forget to say 'Thank you', both verbally and subsequently in writing, to all the parties involved. The prospect for attending, the existing client for the use of his equipment and hospitality, and his colleagues for their assistance. There is always a next time!

Presentations and visual aids

There is a well-established saying which tells us 'a picture is worth a thousand words'. It is clear that people generally remember, in greater detail and for longer periods, things they have seen only rather than heard

65

only. For instance, people typically remember faces and forget names. Clearly, information which is received by way of both sight and sound must have a compounding benefit, as one has the effect of stimulating the other. Compare, for instance, the accuracy of routing instructions for driving to an isolated spot received over the telephone with a drawing or map received through the post. The visual description is almost certain to be more meaningful. Yet compare both with the interactive process of having the route explained by someone with the aid of a map. The latter process must always put over the necessary information more accurately and memorably. This is undoubtedly true of the selling process, as the benefits of using visual aids to emphasize and clarify the sales message are considerable.

Sales literature usually comes under the heading of visual aids, but to be effective it has to be specifically designed to augment the sales story and it has to be used properly. Many company brochures, leaflets, catalogues, etc., tend to take the form of technical specifications and related company and product information which is normally of greatest value after the sales call rather than during it.

If pictures are to emphasize or clarify, they must be compatible with statements the salesman wishes to make.

'This is what the product looks like.'

'This is the kind of information the system produces.'

'This graph shows the relationship between output and consumption.'

'This is how one of our existing clients uses the product.'

Flip charts
Flip charts are a useful form of visual aid, particularly when it comes to emphasizing key words and statements or displaying the relationships between figures. One should not limit their potential to those metallic easels, present at all sales meetings, which often need an IQ in excess of 150 to erect them, yet collapse immediately prior to the climax of the presentation. The use of desk-top flip charts of about A3 size, make much more sense when dealing with very small numbers of people. However, it is always essential to present the information in an entirely professional manner, as nothing reduces the impact more than a scruffy presentation. You don't have to be an artist; if you can't produce neat lettering yourself, find someone who can. For a really important presentation, why not employ the services of a commercial artist? You will be surprised how much top-class professional artwork can enhance the image of your company and product. One useful tip for remembering important points during a presentation: write them in pencil in the appropriate place, clear enough to be seen by the presenter, but not the audience.

'Flogging books' and film shows

I have always maintained and employed a 'flogging book' as a permanent source of visual aid to assist in the selling process. The purpose is to collect items to which one can quickly refer in order to emphasize a sales point: written extracts and pictures from the press and company brochures, tables of information, sample documents, pictures of products and accessories, pictures of reference clients, price lists, sample advertisements, etc. I am convinced that no salesman should be without one—but it must always be kept up to date.

The use of movie films and photographic slides can also be very effective in exploiting the impact of sight and sound. One primary advantage is the ability to temporarily demand the total attention of the client:

'Switch off the light and take the 'phone off the hook, we're going to have a picture show!'

However, like any other selling aid, done well they are a boon, done badly, they can be a disaster. Here are some basic rules:

1. Check that all the equipment has been received and works well before the event.

2. Make sure the film you received is the one you requested.

3. Make sure the cables are long enough to reach from the source of electricity to the point of presentation, and that the plugs fit!

4. Thoroughly practice the presentation in its entirety as close to the event as possible.

5. Count the number of people in the room before you switch off lights. You wouldn't want to lose any would you?

Sales sensitivity

Contrary to popular belief, super salesmen are not brash, hard-nosed individuals. The salesmen who consistently enjoy sales success are basically creative and therefore sensitive individuals. In the selling context, sensitivity means the use of the senses to gather the maximum amount of information required in order to secure the business. This essentially involves sight and sound.

By using the eyes, one can gain a significant amount of detail concerning the buyer's emotional state. Keep looking at his hands and his eyes; you can bet you're in bad shape if your subject is constantly tapping his desk. He is likely to be bored, upset, late for a meeting, trying to get a word in edgeways. You may even be in the wrong office! If he doesn't look you in the eye he could have no authority or funds, already placed the order with someone else, be lying through his teeth, or simply hates the new tie you were given for your birthday.

By and large, salesmen talk too much. In any negotiating situation—be it a normal sales call, a demonstration, or a presentation—the customer should contribute at least two-thirds of the dialogue. The only effective method of sustaining this balance is to keep asking relevant and well-conceived questions. Listening is bloody difficult! The 'don't give me the order yet, I haven't finished what I'm saying' syndrome is extremely common.

Due primarily to a lack of pre-call planning, many salesmen find themselves constantly thinking about what they are going to say next, rather than listening to what the buyer is saying now. Many selling opportunities are lost in this way. Having conditioned oneself to the constant discipline of listening, one then has the problem of creating a dialogue within which the buyer provides information that can be used as a basis for closing. This comes from the use of 'open' questions rather than 'closed' statements to which the response can only be 'yes' or 'no'. For example, 'Are you happy with your present system?' The answer of 'yes' or 'no' does not significantly advance your knowledge of the total situation. Whereas, 'How could your current system be improved?' will reveal not only the present level of satisfaction, but could also give you a number of areas to which the benefits of your own product can be related. Information such as, 'We have serious problems during peak loads', or 'We find spares difficult to locate', or 'Our existing equipment keeps breaking down', can form the whole basis of your ultimate sales success.

It is quite easy to inflict this discipline on yourself by ensuring that every question you ask starts as follows:

Why . . .?

How . . .?

When . . .?

Where . . .?

Who . . .?

What . . .?

Which . . .?

The response cannot be 'yes' or 'no'; it must result instead in the contribution of information by the prospective buyer.

There is a particular time when the 'closed' question is appropriate and that is when you ask for the order—and you will, won't you?

What makes people tick?

Very often the order can be lost due to the buyer apparently acting in such an irrational manner as to confound the salesman. 'Why on earth did he do that? I don't understand it.' Every angle was considered, all the possibilities explored, the alternatives analysed in a logical manner, yet the buyer chose not only some other product, but one which was clearly not the best for the job. Had the job of selection been his, the salesman would certainly not have made the same choice, even to the exclusion of his own product—so who can blame him for losing the order?

This kind of situation is more common than one might think, but rather than being an irrational act on the part of the buyer, it is often an error of judgement by the salesman. When you think about it, such unexpected behaviour occasionally confronts us all, sometimes in a business environment, but often within a social setting. You create a strategy or make an approach based on what you consider to be the likely reaction, and suddenly you are shocked and disappointed to discover that your ideas are rejected in preference to an alternative which is so clearly inappropriate, inferior, too expensive, or even stupid. Yet the fact remains, you have been rejected, the decision has gone against you, and it's difficult (but not impossible) to get it reversed.

So, why do people sometimes act in what appears to be an inconsistent and illogical way? The answer is that they usually don't, at least not from their own point of view. One of the big mistakes we all make in life is to expect other people to work to the same pattern of social behaviour and selection criteria as ourselves. This seldom happens. What we may consider to be a minor and transient phenomenon can have a profound and permanent impact upon others. On the other hand, our own momentous and unsolvable problems may be seen by others as trivial matters with an obvious and simple solution. To a great extent this must be a combination of our individual chemistry, parental influence, environment and social conditioning, education, influence of the media, personal experience, and the shadow of the Church flung from the Middle Ages. We all appear to have an infinite capacity to produce a unique reaction to an endless number of variable situations. In other words, it is very difficult to judge how any person will react in a given situation, despite the apparent logistics involved. There is, of course, no precise way of solving this psychological problem, all one can do is try to avoid falling into the trap of expecting people to do the same as oneself in the circumstances. The nearest one can get is to work hard at getting to know the real person behind the façade; what motivates them, what do they like, fear, want, expect, know, etc.

Don't send a memo

There is a kind of communication that an old friend of mine calls the 'write and tear up' letter. It is a document written in the heat of the moment, an impulsive reaction to a situation that one considers unreasonable in some way. The source of antagonism could be anything—the apparently unreasonable behaviour of a peer or subordinate, a client who appears to have acted unfairly, the experience of using a service or product which falls below expectation, or even the receipt of an inflammatory letter from someone else. Perhaps within the conflict of wanting to say something *immediately*, yet doubting the possibility of stating one's case in an articulate and logical manner in one's current emotional state, the creation of a letter may seem to be the only available means of a satisfactory response. In fact, it probably is the best thing to do. The trick is not to send it; at least not until you've had time to 'sleep' on it. It's surprising how inadequate and over-stated such letters can appear in the cold light of the following day. Yet at the same time the more pertinent points can be extracted, and with a clearer mind one is better equipped to respond effectively to the problem, that is if there still appears to be one. Then you tear up the original!

There is another kind of letter which is far more common and far more destructive than the impulsive reaction letter: the 'face to face cop-out' memorandum. I'm sure you've seen lots of them before:

'With immediate effect all salesmen must complete the enclosed sales activity form declaring calls made, reasons for calls scheduled but not made, products sold, and any change of client category, as well as stating likely requirements of such clients by product for the coming 12-month period.'

Or perhaps:

'Dear Mr Salesman, during the past three weeks there has been a marked decline in your call rate, yet a considerable increase in your business expenses. I trust you will put this matter right with immediate effect.'

Or even:

'Dear Mr Sales Manager, I am appalled at the quality and general presentation of the new sales brochure which is an insult to the intelligence of our clients and the sales force. Surely we could have employed a specialist to do the job rather than someone who obviously knows nothing about our business!'

The possibilities are endless, yet somewhere within the selling world hundreds of such destructive articles are cast adrift on a sea of discontent every week of the year.

It is no good hiding behind a memo, particularly if you are a manager. If you ask your subordinates to perform additional or unusual tasks, they need to have reasons why. They need to know if the demand is justified in terms of apparent benefit without creating an inbalance or disadvantage for someone else, particularly themselves. Asking people face to face instead of telling them by memo has both the advantage of providing acceptable justifications and the possibility of improving the effectiveness of the original plan through discussion with, and contributions from, all the parties involved. It is easy to be lulled into the complacency of thinking that writing a memo is a precise and time-saving method of communication. In some ways it is, but not when trying to persuade people to make additional effort or change their working methods.

Instructional memos should be like sales proposals, they should confirm actions already agreed by face-to-face discussion. The telephone is seldom an exception to this rule.

So, if you want the sales force to handle a new sales reporting document, wait until the next sales meeting and tell them why the company needs the information and how the individual salesman could immediately or ultimately benefit. If you think one of your salesman is 'swanning around', make an excuse (if you need one) for meeting him some place and let him know about the impression he is giving. And salesmen, if you feel critical about the company, its management, or a particular operation, let it rest until you have the opportunity of a relaxed moment with your boss and first ask him his opinion about the matter. Once you know where you stand you can modify your reaction accordingly so as to make your opinion known without unnecessary antagonism. After all, that sales literature you absolutely hate is possibly your manager's own creation, the fruits of a monumental creative effort over several weekends, and furthermore, his family thinks it's terrific!

6.

Initiating the sale

'Grace is given of God, but knowledge is bought in the market.'
Arthur Hugh Clough 1819–61

Preparing the sales call

One of the essential ingredients of sales success is the ability to achieve professional credibility. In other words, the establishment of absolute confidence on the part of the potential buyer in the competence and reliability of a particular company and its salesman. To a great degree this is a function of fluency in one's own products, the client's needs and the related sales benefits.

Back in the 'sixties, when I was a trainee salesman with *IBM*, I was involved in a role playing exercise in which I was the salesman making a call on a prospective buyer for a computerized accounting system. I had known for a couple of days that I was going to be involved but, for a number of reasons, I didn't get round to much preparation before the event. However, armed with all the arrogance of applied ignorance, and the confidence of knowing I was fairly quick on my feet, I launched myself into the call. The buyer (the sales trainer) told me about his problem, putting particular emphasis on his interest in sales invoicing. As quick as a flash I waded in with a barrage of information on the power of our system and the speed at which his documentation could be produced. I really had the bit between my teeth when my peripheral vision noticed considerable hilarity among the audience. You see, I was the only one who had not been given details of the actual situation that the sales call was intended to reveal. It turned out that the imaginary company manufactured battleships at the rate of three a year and dispatched the same number of invoices annually to the appropriate government departments. Apart from the fact that they clearly had no need in that instance for anything more than a reasonably sharp quill pen, I had made myself look quite silly, simply because I had failed to prepare the call and ask the right questions. I had destroyed my personal credibility by being uninformed.

My reason for telling this story against myself is to highlight the importance of pre-call analysis and planning, which consists of four main consid-

72

erations: personal organization, sales objectives, client information and product knowledge. These disciplines are fundamental to selling of every kind, whether the product is carbon paper or nuclear power stations.

1. Personal organization

Do my actions and appearance give the impression of someone who is well organized and reliable? This question is particularly relevant when it comes to pre-call preparation:

1. Has the appointment been confirmed?

2. Have I agreed an approximate finishing as well as starting time for the meeting?

3. Is this company actually on my sales territory?

4. Which is the best way to travel there and how long will it take?

5. Have all the travel arrangements been made?

6. Is my car clean and free from problems, with sufficient fuel for the journey?

7. What is my plan for the structure of the call?

8. How will I open the interview?

9. Am I well prepared for the subject to be discussed?

10. Am I well stocked with basic sales literature?

11. Will I need any special sales aids?

12. Have I been asked to bring anything with me?

13. What objections are likely to be raised and what will be the logical rebuttals?

14. What unexpected events could possibly occur?

15. Do I need any assistance from my sales manager?

16. Does my appearance give a business-like impression?

2. Sales objectives

Every sales call must have a reason for taking place other than the obvious intention of selling something. The pre-call consideration is always the same: what is the reason for this meeting and what objectives do I intend to achieve? This will certainly lead to a number of other questions that are unique to the individual situation, in terms of the problems and opportunities that exist and the stage the negotiations have reached. On the other hand, the deliberations could be of a more general nature:

1. Is the person I am meeting the real decision-maker? If not, what will be my strategy for rectifying the situation?

2. What sales documentation/literature should I leave behind after the meeting in order to stimulate continuing interest?

Forget 'courtesy calls'—they are not within the repertoire of the professional salesman.

An essential ingredient of selling is the ability to identify a specific need or desire and then apply to it the most appropriate solution within one's product portfolio. This inevitably demands a clear understanding of the potential buyer's situation and the capabilities of one's own company. This calls for a lot of information for both sides of the equation.

3. Client information

Have I carried out sufficient research into this company's size, product, and market-place, in order to have a real appreciation of the likely business opportunities which may arise? In other words:

1. What is the correct name of the company and the person I am visiting?

2. Is this company part of a larger organization?

3. Do we already deal with any other related company?

4. What is their financial situation?

5. How many employees do they have?

6. What is the true nature of their business?

7. What are the likely areas of requirements?

8. Am I calling on the actual decision-maker, and what do I know about him?

9. Has my company been in contact with this prospect before? If so, what proposals were made in respect of what requirements?

10. Can any of my colleagues supply me with information on this prospect?

11. Do they already use products similar to the ones I am selling? If so, who supplies them?

12. What is the market situation within the prospect's particular industry?

4. Product knowledge

Do I really have a complete understanding of my own product portfolio, particularly in those areas most likely to be applicable to the prospect?

1. What questions will I need to ask in order to both appreciate the nature of any requirement and propose the means of satisfying it?

2. Which of our products is this company most likely to require?

3. What are the likely benefits to the prospect?

4. Do we have any existing clients in the same business and which of our products do they use?

5. Am I authorized to use them as referees?

6. Do I have complete details of specification, price, and delivery?

There is no limit to the questions that might be asked in each of the above four areas of consideration and it is up to the individual salesman to decide what is appropriate to his situation. Only when this total process has been completed, can the salesman be completely ready to proceed with the sales call itself.

The structure of the sales call

Continuing sales success cannot be achieved by constantly playing it off the cuff. The most capable senior salespeople, with the kind of knowledge that should make them the best qualified of all for handling their selling in an impromptu manner, are in fact the ones who are most heavily committed to planning in every aspect of their selling activity. Experience has taught them that sales achievement is a direct function of personal organization and planned selling.

While most aspects of planning are discussed in Chapter 4, I would like to deal with the sales call in particular in order to highlight the importance of planning as a precise day-to-day discipline rather than merely a general housekeeping strategy. Many salespeople, especially those who are working within a relatively static marketplace and who call regularly on the same clients and supply a virtually unchanging product, can convince themselves that selling to a pre-determined pattern is a complete waste of time. They become 'order takers'. Yet, experience shows that no matter what the product or marketplace, whether boiled sweets or bulldozers are involved, any salesman wishing to rise above the level of mediocrity must totally understand and accept the need to work within a planned structure conditioned by product capability and the individual buyer's needs.

The sales call can be divided into six stages.

1. Attention

Having completed the appropriate pre-call preparation, the first objective of the sales call must be to establish an approach which will gain the undivided attention of the individual buyer. This is best achieved with an opening statement that gives the salesman's reason for being there, and why it is in the buyer's interest to listen carefully and become involved: 'Tell them what you're going to tell them!'

2. Qualify

It is important to establish as early in the sales call as possible whether the contact is a valid prospect for the sales proposition. Is there a real need for the product? Can the prospect afford it? Are you speaking to the right person? Does he have the authority to place an order? Effective pre-call preparation will answer many of these questions, but not all of them. A considerable amount of precious selling time can be wasted by failing to ask these fundamental questions right from the start. It is not uncommon for buyers, often for reasons of misguided courtesy, to allow the salesman to go right through the whole sales presentation before letting it be known that there is not the slightest possibility of doing business together.

3. Credibility

As discussed in Chapter 9, it is easy for the salesman to be convinced that the sale is made, once the buyer acknowledges both his need and a desire to possess the kind of solution presented to him. Unfortunately, what can often happen is the achievement of acceptance without commitment. The buyer agrees with the proposition, but feels there is less risk and perhaps greater gain to be had by pursuing the same deal with some other, perhaps better known, supplier. This often happens when the salesman fails to establish the professional credibility of his company, his product, and himself. Telling the 'company story' and referring to relevant existing clients can greatly assist in this area, whereas the professional credibility of the individual salesman is a direct reflection of personal organization and knowledge.

4. Interest

The next stage is to do whatever is necessary to establish real interest in the proposition being put forward. This cannot be achieved by a rambling, unprepared presentation lacking in visual aids. Furthermore, the buyer is unlikely to show much interest if he has no real need of the product. Only effective pre-call planning and prospect analysis can ensure applicability.

5. Desire

Gaining the buyer's interest does not necessarily imply a desire on his part to actually possess the product concerned. This can only be achieved by emphasizing those feature/benefits which are likely to appeal to the buyer concerned. This knowledge comes from effective pre-call research and really listening to what the prospect has to say during the meeting.

6. Close

The best time to ask for the order is usually towards the end of the structured sales call, but not necessarily. As discussed in Chapter 9, the ideal opportunity to 'close' the sale could occur at any stage of the negotiation. Whatever the circumstances, the most important sales objective within a particular call is the buyer's acceptance of a specific proposition from the salesman. This could take the form of a final or interim close, or just an agreement on further action to be taken.

In summary, the sales call should take the form of a pre-determined structure, with planned objectives within which the salesman can control both predictable and unforeseen factors. This can only be achieved with a strategy that contains complete understanding of the capability of one's own products and the likely requirements of the potential buyer.

So much for that brief look at the framework of the sales call. The next consideration is how it should be put into effect. There is only one way: start at the beginning, keep the dialogue on the predetermined path, and listen intently.

Opening the interview

The opening of a sales call is one of the most critical stages, whether it involves a new prospect or an established user.

Firstly there is the immediate impression. A loud tie, a crumpled collar, untidy hair, a trendy suit, can create as much of an emotional obstacle as arriving an hour late.

Having overcome the subjective hurdle of personal appearance, the salesman is then immediately into another critical stage of the selling process: the opening gambit. What is the best way to open the conversation? The possibilities are endless! 'Good morning Mr Prospect. Sorry to be late, I got held up on the motorway. The traffic was terrible. It was just as bad last night, it took me two hours to get home from the match. Good game mind . . .' Or alternatively: 'Good morning Mr Prospect. My name is Peter Out of The Integrated Suspender Company. We were founded in 1841 by Fred Smith who unearthed some golden plates while playing golf with Abraham Lincoln. . . However, some minor technical problems caused the company to delay its initial product launch until last week!' These may seem exaggerations, but I can assure you that every day hundreds of salespeople start their sales calls with similar meaningless banter. Let's face it, the prospect fully appreciates the purpose of the visit and is not expecting a missionary or social worker. He is expecting to meet someone who will try and sell him something. The salesman should at least be courteous enough to confirm the buyer's assumptions.

So what is the best way of opening a sales conversation other than the customary salutations and confirmation of credentials? The answer can be found in effective sales preparation, related to the prospect's business situation. The sales call cannot get onto the right footing until the reason for being there is firmly established.

'I understand that your principal area of business activity is related to the mass production of electrical components. I imagine this demands a lot of skill, particularly related to the management of stock and production. We have been able to assist many companies within your industry to achieve considerable savings by the use of our production control techniques. What methods do you currently employ to maximize efficiency in these areas?'

Or perhaps:

'I understand you have recently won a contract for the construction of ten miles of motorway. My company supplies earthmoving equipment to most of the major civil engineering contractors in the UK. What are your present arrangements for such equipment and your likely requirements and plans for the new project?'

The buyer will usually be too busy to indulge in timewasters and will really appreciate salespeople who get quickly to the point. There is no more effective way of winning the buyer's attention and respect than simply getting on with the business at hand in a well-informed manner. After all, if there is anyone with more to benefit from the effective use of time than the buyer, it is the salesman.

There are of course, many possible variations of initial approach, according to the nature of the product, the prospect, the salesman, and the sales situation. Let us look at some of the possibilities:

The introductory opening:
'Good morning Mr Prospect. My name is Stan Dardoyle of the "International Petroleum Company". We are specialists in the provision of lubricating oils for high-precision engineering.'

The product opening:
'Good morning Mr Prospect. My name is Mandy Lifebote of the "Marine Products Company". I would like you to examine this new stainless steel hawser coupling.'

The question opening:
'What is the current rate of down-time on your filtration equipment?'

The benefit opening:
'This electronic ignition system could reduce your petrol consumption by as much as 15 per cent.'

The interest opening:
'Have you seen this type of liquid crystal display before?'

78

The shock opening:
'If you suffered a major fire today, how would you finance the cost of rebuilding?'

The survey opening:
'We have been able to bring about considerable savings for many companies such as your own. I would like to have the opportunity of surveying your present methods in order to see where our services would be most applicable in your particular case.'

The reference opening:
'We supply this product to one of your major clients and they suggested you might also care to benefit from its use.'

It may well be that the chosen opening consists of a combination of such statements and questions. Whatever the case, the 'opening gambit' must fit the circumstances and be based on thorough pre-call analysis.

The sales presentation

The achievement of company, product, and personal credibility, plus the creation of interest in, and desire for, the product, is generally achieved within the sales presentation. However, its principal objective is to open the door to the demonstration, specification, and proposition of the product.

The sales presentation is a preconceived plan that enables the salesman to control the course of the sales interview, and, in so doing, achieve the objective of the call. The principal factors are:

1. *Pre-call preparation*   Analysis of the prospect's situation, as well as the relevance of one's own products.

2. *Deciding on the objectives*   A clear definition of the purpose of the call in terms of specific aims.

3. *Establishing the format of the call*   Using the structured sales call as a means of delivering the message and applying the chosen selling strategy.

However, planning alone does not guarantee a successful sales call. The manner of delivery is just as important. There is no doubt in my mind that the most important element of the sales call is the enthusiasm of the salesman for his product and his company. There is nothing quite so contagious as enthusiasm, or destructive as the lack of it.

There are also a number of disciplines that need to be observed at all times. Here are just a few:

79

1. Never overstate or exaggerate, use only the facts you know to be true.

2. Avoid the use of superlatives when making claims on behalf of your product and your company.

3. Do not denigrate your company, your product, your colleagues, or your competitors.

4. Be sure everything is clearly stated without ambiguity of any kind.

5. Continually check for understanding.

6. Refer to previous experience with satisfied clients.

7. Be courteous, attentive, respectful, and tolerant, at all times.

8. Do not argue; at most suggest there may be some grounds for disagreement and leave it at that.

9. If you get side-tracked, memorize the point of digression from the call-structure and quickly work the conversation back.

10. Remember that people who interrupt are not listening—and that includes yourself!

Despite all of these considerations, of course, there are no guarantees that every sales-call will go the way you planned.

Avoid the condensed presentation
A common situation is where the salesperson arrives promptly, only to be told that urgent and unforeseen circumstances have called the buyer to an urgent meeting, leaving him with only a few mintues before rushing off. Now that is both unfortunate and unreasonable! So, there you are, with an early appointment, planned call, and agreed exit time, all wound up and ready to go, and the carpet is pulled from under your feet. The immediate temptation is rapidly to give a brief synopsis of all the points you wish to cover, or alternatively attempt to discuss in detail one aspect of your presentation and discard the rest. Never be drawn into either of these traps! The buyer has effectively already left you! He is almost certainly mentally preparing for his urgent meeting, and your dialogue serves only as a distraction from his immediate problem, and is therefore a source of aggravation. His presence is a courtesy, no more, and one cannot possibly sell anything in such an environment. More to the point, a summarized sales call will probably destroy the justification of any unexpurgated repeat performance at a later date.

There is only one satisfactory method of handling such a situation. Take the pressure off the man by telling him you understand his problem and feel it would be better for both of you if your discussion was rescheduled. Consequently you do not wish to take up even the small amount of his

80

precious time he has courteously allocated to you. Simply, make another appointment for the earliest convenient date for both of you. He will not only be grateful for your consideration, but will also remember your good manners and professionalism on your subsequent meeting.

So much for the framework and disciplines of the sales call, but this is only a process through which the sales benefits, some more attractive than others, are expressed.

Sales benefits and advantages

The sales close cannot be applied until a reason for buying has been established. This clearly demands the buyer's acknowledgement that he has something to gain from the proposed transaction. Most types of selling involve the use of 'feature benefits', i.e., those particular aspects of a product or service from which the buyer is able to derive a meaningful gain. These represent the basis of the sale rather than the product itself. The identification of relevant benefits is not merely a function of the product, it is more a question of compatibility with a known need or desire of the buyer. In other words, no matter how enthusiastic a salesperson feels about a particular product or its application, an apparent benefit is not a benefit until the buyer accepts it as such.

During the course of the sales negotiation, one will usually hear the words 'benefit' and 'advantage' used as if both words mean the same thing. However, in the context of selling, I prefer to think of these words as having a significant semantic difference. This has an important disciplinary effect on selecting the right feature on which to base the sales close. Let me give you a definition in order to make this a little more clear. A sales *benefit* is a gain which can be achieved by the purchase of a given type of product or service. A sales *advantage* is a sales benefit which can be obtained from one supplier only. For example:

The benefits of buying central-heating oil from 'Home Fuels' and 'Express Oils' are that they are substantial and reputable companies, they can supply the required quality of fuel, their prices are competitive and they can deliver within 24 hours Monday to Saturday. However, 'Express Oils' have the sales advantages of providing a 'topping-up' service at the bulk-delivery price, local maintenance and a 24-hour answering service, because these facilities are not available from 'Home Fuels'.

In other words, *benefits* are those aspects of a sales proposition which are needed or desired by the buyer and must be firmly established by the salesman in order to equal, and therefore cancel out, similar claims by competitors. This is sometimes referred to as 'me too' selling. Sales *advantages* are those benefits which are unique to the salesman's own product and are the primary justification for asking for the order. It is what I call the 'American

81

discipline'. Concentrate your selling efforts on the USA (Unique Selling Advantages)!

Creating a matrix of significant benefits available from competitors can be a very rewarding exercise for the salesman. This provides an objective view of both the benefits and unique advantages of one's own products in relation to the competition. The salesman then has a clear picture of the advantages that need to be emphasized and the competitive claims that have to be countered within the sales presentation. However, the salesman cannot always depend on having clear and positive advantages over other suppliers. Often the competitive edge may be no more than a variety of benefits, which, despite being matched on individual terms by a number of competitors, have the largest accumulation in one's own product. In some circumstances the salesman may have no apparent advantage other than having convinced the buyer of his personal integrity and reliability. And make no mistake, any salesperson who has a positive lead over competition in such emotional considerations, has very powerful advantages indeed.

However, in many sales situations the greatest advantage of all is from having taken the trouble to analyse the benefits and advantages related to the potential buyer, the competition, and oneself, and having acted accordingly when competitive salespeople may not have; and that is more often than you would believe.

The qualification of sales benefits

Of course, the basic assumption implied in the application of sales benefits and advantages is that one actually understands what they are. Unfortunately, a great many salespeople would not recognize one if it hit them between the eyes. On so many occasions salespeople forward reasons for buying that are virtually meaningless due to weak presentation. For example:

The 'Superflop' computer terminal offers a variety of very attractive advantages:

1. Total flexibility of use.

2. Local processing capability.

3. Ninety days delivery.

4. Data can be transmitted at 9600 characters per second.

Now all of that sounds completely reasonable doesn't it? Whereas in reality this kind of statement, irrespective of product type, is likely to be meaningless to most potential buyers. One can never assume that the buyer under-

82

stands the implications of a stated sales benefit as clearly as oneself, so it is essential that the salesperson always qualifies any sales benefit by way of two very significant considerations:

1. Is it relevant?
2. If so, what does it mean to the potential buyer in real terms?

This leads us to two very important sales disciplines related to the identification of meaningful sales benefits.

1. The *'So what?'* test.
2. The *'Which means that . . .'* interpreter.

In the first case the process is very easy. All one has to do is put oneself in the buyer's position, state all the apparent benefits one at a time and simply ask the question 'So what?' after each one. It is surprising how few apparently powerful advantages are able to satisfy the demands of this unassuming phrase. Let us examine our sample advantages in this context:

1. Total flexibility of use.
Such a nebulous statement could embrace a multitude of desirable facilities. *'So what?'* Maybe the potential buyer doesn't want flexibility, what he wants is a simple unsophisticated device, the more inflexible the better.

2. Local processing capability.
'So what?' Perhaps he wants to avoid local processing, that's why he's considering the purchase of a terminal linked to someone else's computer rather than installing one of his own.

3. Ninety days delivery.
'So what?' This is of no value if the prospect needs six months to prepare for its installation.

So much for identifying relevant sales benefits, but that still does not establish reasons for buying. A bald statement of feature benefits very often means little to the potential buyer, he needs to know how these benefits apply to him. This brings us to the 'Which means that . . .' interpreter. This is a device for creating a bridge between the superficial sales benefit and a statement that provides a definite reason for buying. Back to our example:

4. Data can be transmitted at 9600 characters per second.
Such a statement would appear to have some difficulties with the *'So what?'* test. However, when augmented by the 'Which means that . . .'

interpreter we offer something the potential buyer understands and may find attractive. '. . . the peak-loads of printing which occur every Friday can be handled within the working day, whereas slower devices demand overtime working, which is inconvenient and increases operational costs.'

It will be seen that the effect of the 'Which means that . . .' interpreter is to cause the sales benefit to move from the general into the specific.

In summary, if an apparent sales benefit is to qualify as a reason for buying it must be viewed through the eyes of the potential buyer, and be:

1. Presented in terms of its effect rather than merely its nature.

2. Described in a manner that is clearly understood.

3. Accepted by the prospect as being applicable to his particular situation.

7.

Disciplines of the sales negotiation

'Remember, that time is money.'

Benjamin Franklin 1706–90

The content and objectives of the sales call differ considerably, not only from product to product and industry to industry, but also in accordance with the length of the selling cycle. (The typical period of time between first contact with the potential buyer and the eventual placement of the order.) As a general rule, the more expensive the product the longer the selling cycle. Therefore, with products such as fast-moving consumer goods, one normally expects the sale to be completed during the first call on the prospect, which implies that such things as surveys, feasibility studies, formal proposals, etc., are not part of the normal scenario. However, capital equipment, for instance, can involve numerous calls and a selling cycle that could run into years. A considerable amount of product evaluation, formal presentations, extensive documentation and multi-tier selling situations extending from the shopfloor to the boardroom, could also be involved. In such circumstances the purpose of a call could be merely to achieve a single step of progress towards a long-term goal.

In this varied selling environment one cannot expect each call to follow a consistent pattern, no matter how much pre-planning is applied. This is dictated, not only by variations in product type, but also by the circumstances which may prevail at the time. It is essential, therefore, that salespeople maintain flexibility within the confines of the structured call, yet never lose sight of their objectives.

This chapter considers some of the situations that are likely to exist once the salesman has progressed from the initial stages of introduction and presentation to the heart of the sales negotiation. It is important to remember what was said in Chapter 1, 'Why do people buy?' Knowing what and why the prospect is likely to buy must constantly be a primary consideration.

Selling solutions

I know it's a little dishonest, but when I go to an exhibition I sometimes pose as a potential buyer. I wander on to a stand and hang around on the off-chance that someone might be interested in selling me something, but particularly in the hope of discovering some new sales technique, or for the mere satisfaction of seeing a good salesman at work. I am usually disappointed. I know it is easy to criticize people who work on exhibition stands; it is an exhausting business, and, inevitably, it will sometimes show. Nevertheless, I find it extremely difficult to tolerate those salesmen who appear to be incapable of relating their product to the problems of the potential client.

I remember once attending a computer exhibition and was appalled by the number of times I became involved in variations of the following conversation:

'Can I help you, sir?'

Having resisted the temptation of a straight 'No thank you':

'Yes, I'd like some information please. I'm interested in the possibility of installing a computer.'

'Then you've come to the right place, sir. I'd like to tell you about the "Microcheap 99". The basic model comes with a 32K processor, full qwerty keyboard, twin double-density one megabyte floppies, a 100 cps matrix printer and a green on black 24 × 80 VDU. The system includes. . .'

I don't suppose that means a lot to anyone outside the computer industry, and to someone contemplating their first excursion into the mysteries of electronic data processing, it could be enough to put them off for ever. The product happened to be a computer, but it could have been anything from a fighter bomber to a fire extinguisher.

Throughout my tour of the exhibition hall, not one single salesman asked me about the nature of my problem, and for what purpose I was considering the use of computers. After the exhibition I was speaking with a very experienced salesman I knew. He told me how a prospective client had visited his stand, and when asked what business he was in, said he was from the wholesale grocery trade. The salesman asked if the prospect had a stock control problem, and explained how computers could be used to overcome problems of inventory control. The man was delighted!

'I've been looking at computer equipment at this exhibition all day,' he said, 'and you are the first person who appears to have any understanding of what my business problems might be!'

All the salesman had to say was, 'Do you have a stock control problem?'

Potential buyers of equipment and services really want to discuss solutions to problems. Their interest in tools is minimal, for technical specification alone does not guarantee the experience to understand the requirement or the ability to satisfy a buyer's need.

I told the salesman about my own experiences at the exhibition, and his reaction summed up the situation very succinctly. 'These guys can't seem to get it into their heads, what they are selling is a hole in the wall, not an electric drill.'

This true story highlights some of the most important aspects of selling: two-way communications, listening and evaluating. What does the prospective buyer really mean, want, need, understand? What conditions, forces, emotions will influence his reasons for buying? What is his real problem as opposed to the one he has described or the one he believes he has? The only route to the ultimate satisfaction of the buyer's need is through careful and continual consideration of every element of the environment in which the sales negotiation takes place.

Situation evaluation

If any of my children ever ask me what they should do to succeed in the world, the first thing I will suggest is that they avoid the frustration of expecting other people to have the same ethical and moral standards as they set for themselves, and secondly, to evaluate each situation in which they find themselves from every conceivable view point, rather than just their own. I am sure this will give them a perpetual advantage, no matter what their chosen vocation, but particularly if they should take up a career in selling.

Situation evaluation is a discipline applicable to all relationships, be they in a business or social context. The process is simple in conception, but potentially complex in application. It is more than just seeing the other person's point of view; it is the analysis of every influence affecting the achievement of an ultimate goal. The objective could be anything from getting an order to agreeing a bank loan.

Many salesmen take the blinkered approach of seeing the selling objective purely from their own point of view—'I'm selling a good product at a reasonable price, so there can be no intelligent reason for not buying.' Smarter salesmen also view the matter through the eyes of the potential buyer and attempt to evaluate and anticipate his practical, emotional, and political motivations and modify their approach accordingly. Unfortunately, it is seldom as simple as that, as there are usually other forces outside the control of the seller and the buyer which can have a profound effect on the ultimate decision.

Let us take an apparently simple situation. A salesman is re-negotiating a contract with the technical director of an existing client company involved in Government contract work. The technical director has total authority to handle all negotiations. Therefore, the salesman can reasonably assume he has made the right level of contact. Now, let us look at possible peripheral situations and external influences which are either ignored by, or unknown to, one or both of the participants in the negotiation.

1. A major division of the company wishes to use an alternative type of product, but their demands are being ignored by the technical director. Consequently, they are exerting considerable pressure on the managing director for authority to use an alternative source of supply.

2. The technical director has handed in his resignation and is joining one of the salesman's principal competitors.

3. The Government department which provides most of their business is insisting on the use of another supplier whose products, unlike the salesman's, are approved at ministry level.

4. The most significant of the clients' Government contracts is coming up for renewal and they are not sure of retaining the business.

5. The technical director is greatly influenced by the opinions of both his deputy and his secretary.

6. The managing director has been 'wined and dined' by a significant competitor, despite the fact that he turned down a similar invitation from the salesman's company.

7. The salesman's company is about to sell out to one of its major rivals and plans to run down the current product range.

An unusual array of possibilities perhaps, but even one such unanticipated influence can result in the failure to sell. Whatever the circumstances, every aspect of the sales situation must be analysed on a 'What if?' basis, in terms of all potential influences bearing upon negotiations, particularly as far as all involved persons are concerned, even though it may not be possible to counter all the situations revealed. Any sympathy which sales management might have for business lost through 'head office interference' or 'unforeseen events' is, in my opinion, often misplaced. It simply indicates that the salesman has exercised insufficient control over the situation due to inadequate analysis of the total sales scenario.

Evaluating the competition

There is another crucial aspect of the sales situation that also demands close analysis—the competition! It is essential to have a complete understanding of which competitive suppliers will be proposing what in order to have a clear picture of the relative strength of one's own product features.

It is too easy to make assumptions and to underestimate the strength of other suppliers through lack of perception, arrogance, or even laziness. Total enthusiasm for both product and company is absolutely essential if the salesman is to enjoy continuing success. Nevertheless, this should not be allowed to develop into a kind of tunnel vision that focuses only on the glory of his own company's offerings.

One often sees advertisements or hears claims that suggest a particular product is vastly superior to the offerings of competitors, who, one is led to believe, are still in the Middle Ages. Such statements are, at best, brash and naïve. This kind of optimistic euphoria can be misleading to the potential buyer as well as to the salesman, who is actually out peddling the product. Salespeople are particularly susceptible to their own propaganda.

It would be marvellous to have a commodity for which there was a real need, yet no competition, but this is seldom the case. If there are other products available for broadly the same purpose, then there is competition. And to assume that all competitive products are inferior is an arrogance that will ensure more failure than success. While it is rather a sweeping statement, it is reasonable to say that there would be no such thing as competitive products if they did not have some appeal to certain buyers. This being the case, the salesman must regard all competitive products as equal to his own, for indeed they are in some circumstances.

What does the buyer really want from the product he is considering for purchase? Here are a few possibilities that come to mind:

1. Ability to solve a given problem or perform a particular task without overkill or underkill.

2. Availability of a special feature to satisfy an unusual need.

3. Positive resale potential with an attractive profit margin.

4. Quick delivery.

5. Low cost.

6. Company or personal status.

7. Political advantage.

Only a fool would believe his product to be unquestionably superior to those of every other vendor in all of these few considerations. So, it is essential that the salesman has a complete awareness of his own product and company as well as the needs of the prospective buyer and the relative capabilities of competitors.

There is a quick method for providing objective analysis of any sales situation which, despite its simplicity, appears to be much neglected. It is called the Competitive Evaluation Matrix and consists of two stages.

Firstly, a comparison between the principal needs of the potential buyer and the ability of competitive suppliers to wholly or partially satisfy them. This means you have to discover not only who your competitors actually are, but also have a comprehensive knowledge of their products. Secondly, a comparison between the feature benefits of one's own products and those likely or known to be proposed by competitors. The first case is an analysis of *need* and the relative ability of suppliers to satisfy it. The second is an analysis of the *means* by which these suppliers will attempt to satisfy that need.

In the case of a competitive situation involving a mini-computer-based system, the prospective buyer's axis of the matrix may include requirements such as:

1. Packaged programs for all commercial accounting, payroll and stock control applications.

2. Program packages for forecasting and financial planning.

3. Electronic mailing capability.

4. Up to 30 on-line interactive terminals.

5. Maximum of 1 second response time.

6. 6 remote interactive terminals via switched network.

7. Ability to operate in remote batch mode.

8. Up to two megabytes addressable on-line storage.

9. Maximum of 4 months for delivery.

Along the opposing axis are the names of competitive suppliers and within each element of the matrix their relative capability is declared. Some will be able to completely satisfy the needs of the prospect, while others will have a partial or total inability to provide what is required. In this way the salesman has a more objective view of his competition, while still mindful of the reality that the best product doesn't necessarily win the order.

In the second phase, one side of the matrix consists of the salesman's product and the principal competition, and the other contains the product features that are likely to be proposed and their relative performance one against the other, perhaps even using a scoring system and certainly noting specific factors of particular strength or weakness.

1. 'Yes, the "XYZ Computer Company" can propose a financial planning system, but it will be bought in and they have never previously installed one.'

2. 'Yes, the "ABC Computer Company" can handle 30 on-line interactive

terminals, but cannot guarantee a maximum of one second response when all are operating simultaneously.'

Once the second phase is completed, the salesman has a clear picture of the client's needs and the strength of the competition. More importantly, though, he can see the strengths and weaknesses of his own sales argument and act accordingly.

Feasibility studies

So much for the necessity of analysing the sales situation. This, in many cases, cannot be achieved without first establishing the potential buyer's need. In most kinds of selling related to non-consumable products, the sale is preceded by a survey or feasibility study resulting in a formal document showing the specification of the proposed solution—services and/or equipment, details of price, delivery, etc.

Feasibility studies (sometimes called sales surveys) are a well established part of industrial and commercial selling. Yet sales are continually lost because the specification obtained by the salesman was inadequate or incorrect. Following some common sense guidelines can help prevent this.

1. Qualify the problem to be studied
The salesman must ensure that the right problem is being investigated; which is not always as straightforward as it might first appear. It is easy to accidently omit essential facts yet include irrelevant ones or even misunderstand the client's requirements to the extent of proposing a solution to the wrong problem! It is therefore most important that once the salesman believes he has a complete grasp of the apparent needs, he confirms this with the client. If competition is involved there is no harm in confirming that their activity is also confined to the same area of investigation.

2. Get all the facts
There are many ways in which essential facts can be forgotten, or never asked for in the first place. Nothing should be left to memory: nothing assumed. The use of survey questionnaires, based on previous experience, is an excellent device for ensuring that all the basic questions relating to a given application or specific piece of equipment are posed. This enables the salesman to concentrate on any special or unusual requirements.

3. Go and look at the problem
The salesman should not limit his input of information to those facts provided by the client's appointed representative. He must go to where the problem resides and look for himself.

4. Be sure to speak to everyone involved
Very often the people with the least authority have the most responsibility.

It is essential, therefore, to speak to every person who is involved with the existing problem and likely to be affected by whatever solution is chosen. This applies from the shopfloor to the boardroom. This kind of complete dialogue can help the salesman identify those exceptions that can so often swing the balance between success and failure. There is also the added benefit of introducing the system or product to the real end users, on whom success will ultimately depend.

5. Be open minded
It is very easy for a product to be turned into a 'solution in search of a problem' because of preconceived ideas concerning its potential. One should always listen carefully to everyone and make no assumptions during the feasibility study, particularly at the operational level. Many original ideas can come from people with substantial working experience of a given application area.

6. Keep the solution within reason
It is essential to know the prospective buyer's budget before starting a feasibility study, as there is little point continuing if budgetary limitations make the solution impractical from the start. On the other hand, a 'blank cheque' does not reduce the salesman's responsibility to propose a product or service that is good value for money.

7. Get approval for any extras
There are often opportunities to expand the solution beyond the area of investigation or cost initially envisaged, but don't ever make the mistake of pursuing such possibilities without prior approval from the decision-maker.

8. Keep going back to the decision-maker
It's always a good thing to keep the decision-maker's door open. A regular progress report can be of considerable advantage to the salesman preparing a large-scale, long-term study.

9. Qualify the facts
A feasibility study often involves volumes from which equipment, supplies, or services are subsequently planned. They could apply to workload, materials, information, process, power, etc. Considerable semantic risk is involved in the use of such words as *estimated, potential, anticipated, possible, probable,* etc., in relation to *volumes,* as a design or specification can only be based on facts. Whether such information from the buyer is real or estimated is not relevant; but, in order to avoid any misunderstandings, the salesman must contact the decision-maker stating his understanding of the volumes concerned, before proceeding with the final specification of the

proposed solution. Getting the buyer to sign the completed survey questionnaire is by far the best form of approval.

10. Thank everyone involved
Never forget to thank everyone who has assisted in the completion of a feasibility study, including your own sales support people. With a bit of luck you will be returning, having won the order, and it's good to work with people who know their contribution is appreciated.

11. Get the client to pay for the survey
The sales prospect to avoid is the one who doesn't really want to buy anything, but is interested in mounting an investigation into the nature of his problem and the range of possible solutions, thereby getting some free consultancy. If the salesman suspects he is involved in this kind of affair he should propose a consultancy fee subtractable from any subsequent order. It is often a useful sales strategy to make a charge for all in-depth feasibility studies. This tends to make the client take the outcome more seriously, and at the decision stage recoverable study costs can be a very strong influence upon the buyer's choice.

The feasibility study is a crucial stage of many sales situations. It is difficult enough to win the order, so why increase the odds by making the wrong proposition?

The sales proposal
Once the process of investigation is complete, decisions have to be made concerning the type of solution that is to be put forward. In the case of capital goods, particularly, this normally takes the form of a document detailing every aspect of the product being proposed, together with the way in which it will be operated, the purpose and implications of its use, price, delivery, etc. It is a compilation of all the factors which condition the decision to buy, and is commonly known as the sales proposal. It is merely a confirmation of agreed prices and product specification, benefits and advantages already established, and images already created. It re-states why the prospective buyer should buy from the proposer and contains no surprises for either party. Above all, it is not an alternative to the sales close.

Many salesmen make the mistake of going through the selling cycle without considering the sales proposal until the last moment. Many benefits can be gained from an individual file for every qualified prospect, containing information useful for the proposal stage: names of relevant personalities, special client needs, competitive information, press cuttings, advantages and benefits (particularly those identified by the client), details of current costs, etc.

The size of a sales proposal is neither a measure of the supplier's professional credibility nor the buyer's status. The aspects of a proposal which make the most significant impression are concise, comprehensive, and non-ambiguous content, easy location of information, and the quality of overall presentation. Added to this there is the benefit of a synopsis of the total proposal, to enable the client to grasp quickly the total implications. This is particularly relevant if the document is necessarily technically complex or multi-faceted. An effective solution is to start with a brief 'management summary', giving a précis of the main sections of the whole document, highlighting the most significant areas by using the same section headings. In cases where a decision is made in committee, the technicians tend to read only the technical page in depth, accountants the financial page, and so on, so a management summary allows people to get an overall appreciation of your proposition without having to read the whole document in detail.

Nothing but the truth
The sales proposal must contain only the whole truth. I am not suggesting that sales people normally tell lies, but they can easily indulge in wishful thinking: claims for products yet to be proven in the field, stating company experience as a reason for buying when it does not exist locally, delivery promises based on anticipated cancellations or a possible increase in production, etc. A proposal once accepted is a commitment. The seemingly trivial additional facility, or the especially early delivery date could subsequently involve unnecessary expense or embarrassment which could convert the whole deal into a loss-making project. 'Reference sells' have also to be handled very carefully. They must be relevant and their use authorized.

Once the proposal is complete, everyone who is involved with the supply of the proposed products must be able to check what they have been committed to. Very often they will have ideas for improving the proposition. Most of all, the salesman must ensure that his direct superior reads the proposal and is aware of the obligations that are being entered into on the company's behalf.

Finally, there are two essential disciplines concerning sales proposals:

1. Always deliver it personally. There is nothing more likely to suggest disinterest than sending a sales proposal through the post.

2. Do not go to all the trouble of preparing a detailed sales proposal if the order can be achieved just as easily without it. Sometimes a brief letter can be just as effective.

Don't sell futures

The 'whole truth' of the sales proposal leads to an aspect of the sales negotiation which is worthy of particular mention; the temptation of becoming involved in pre-release products.

Salespeople are employed to sell their company's current product range. They are not employed to sell products that are yet to be formally announced or those they assume could be made available with a little persuasion. Despite this obvious responsibility, salespeople regularly become involved in sales negotiations for products that are not actually available.

A good example of this unfortunate practice was once described to me by a salesman, who, during new business prospecting, unearthed a potential user where negotiations were already in progress. However, his company could not currently match the prospective client's requirements, but he had been told about a forthcoming new product that was just what this organization really needed. So, he gave an outline description of the new equipment to the prospect, putting particular emphasis on its superior cost/performance, and arranged a special preview. The prospect held back on his other negotiations and the salesman dropped all other sales activity in order to concentrate on getting the show together. On the day before the event, the salesman was shocked to hear that the demonstration would have to be cancelled! Not through a temporary fault, strike, or illness, but because the parent company had decided not to release the product. As simple as that! There was nothing to be done. The waste of the client's time, as well as the salesman's, could not be recovered; but, even more disastrous, the salesman's personal credibility and that of his company had been undermined.

This story highlights the risks involved in rushing into sales negotiations with products which are in one way or another unready for use, rather than bowing out gracefully. Competing with a prototype against an established product, no matter how much better the new one might be, usually results in a lot of sales effort for little return, and, in many cases, a total loss of professional credibility. The salesman should always bear in mind that qualifying the sale applies just as much to his own company's capability as the buyer's requirement.

Reference selling

Third-party references can be a powerful selling device within the dynamic situation of the sales call and the formality of the sales proposal. Most salespeople have a number of clients who are completely satisfied with the products or services they have received. Their colleagues will also have similar clients, so that their company as a whole will have a broad selection of contented users involving a variety of industries, locations, and company types. These existing accounts can be a very valuable aid for persuading prospective users to buy.

The main qualification of a valid third-party reference is its relevance. There is no point in mentioning a prestigious account like *Rolls-Royce* when your prospect is in the chemical fertilizer business—unless he has a sideline in aero engines! If reference selling is to be truly effective, it is best organized at the company level. A record of satisfied clients by application, industry, company size, equipment type, location, and person to contact, can be generated and held by a responsible senior executive, such as the marketing manager, so that truly relevant references can be supplied on application.

Of equal importance to the relevance of a reference sell is the client's willingness to be a referee. Some companies simply do not want to be bothered, and their wishes must be respected. In addition, it is important that contact by off-territory salespeople does not interfere with the salesman who has responsibility for the client concerned. Therefore, reference clients must always be checked, through the salesman concerned, for their current willingness to participate, their present level of satisfaction, and their availability in terms of the intended visit.

Keep a low profile!

There are three ways of pursuing business references—telephone, letter and, most importantly, by personal visit. While the salesman should always participate in such visits, it must be remembered that the lower his profile, the greater the credibility of the reference sell. The salesman is merely the courier in such an event and must leave the prospect and the client to their own particular truths. After all, the existing user is generally going to compliment, otherwise he would not have been selected as a referee. Also, existing users are normally eager to re-affirm the wisdom of their original choice.

The hospitality of referees must never be abused. Always arrive promptly and make the visit brief, and let the client know his assistance is appreciated. A letter of thanks soon after the visit is both courteous and good business sense.

The inclusion of a list of reference clients in the formal proposal is a fairly common practice, but this is worthless unless the names involved are those of companies already visited or discussed in detail, and therefore familiar to the client. Very often prospective clients will not make contact with a referee. In such circumstances the reference sell can still be useful if a buyer is procrastinating because he feels that the transaction contains an element of risk. The best way to provide reassurance is to put him in touch with someone who has already handled the same situation. Once he knows his dilemma is not unique he will feel much happier about committing himself:

'I can understand your difficulty in making a final decision on our proposition Mr Prospect. I know Mr Positive of "Allied Farming" had just the same uncertainties before he ordered our "Superfeed 123" for a similar application. Why don't I get him on the telephone for you, so that you can either have a word with him now or perhaps arrange to call on him later today? I am sure he would be delighted to help.'

More often than not the buyer will either take up the offer and get the necessary reassurance, or simply take the salesman's word for it and give him the order.

Attacking the competition

One of the basic rules of selling is that one should never 'knock the competition'. Undoubtedly, this is an excellent sales discipline but one which is subject to misinterpretation. Clearly, slandering one's rivals is, not only discourteous, but also implies elements of fear, envy, dishonour, etc., which will not gain you the admiration of the potential buyer. It can only destroy your own credibility. On the other hand, it is an essential responsibility of all salespeople to gain fluency in the specification and capability of competitive products, so that they have real understanding of the strengths and weaknesses of their opponents' products compared to their own.

To declare truthful and undeniable product related facts within the selling procedure is by no means defamation of a competitor's character or professional credibility. Salespeople should not allow the 'don't knock the competition' syndrome to inhibit them from highlighting their advantages over the competition's products in an accurate, ethical manner. This demands absolute discretion and sensitivity for there is sometimes a very thin line between constructive and destructive truth. Any reasonable code of behaviour will forbid abuse of the reputation or character of a competitor, whether the attack be full-frontal or innuendo. Comments such as the following are completely unacceptable, whether they are true or false:

'You can't rely on the "XYZ" company.'

'The "XYZ" company doesn't understand the business.'

'The "XYZ" company made a complete mess of the job.'

'I hear the "XYZ" company is going down the tube.'

'The "XYZ" product is a load of rubbish.'

They are purely an attempt to enhance one's own status by discrediting others, and it usually has the opposite effect. Even stating the shortcomings of the competitive products needs to be handled in a very sensitive manner. Merely to state that 'The self start mechanism of the "XYZ" generator is unreliable', is to appear jaundiced. More to the point, the comment can be completely self-destructive if the potential buyer subsequently reveals he has no requirement for the feature in question.

Highlighting the weaknesses of competitors
One of the best methods the salesman can use to highlight the inade-

quacies of competitive products is firstly to establish the product features required by the potential buyer. This list can then be augmented by unique feature/benefits of his own product that the buyer accepts as being desirable.

It is then a simple process to use this information for creating a matrix of feature performance in respect of the principal competitors, thus indicating their relative shortcomings without direct affront. One often sees this form of comparison in press and advertising related to motor cars and similar products—'Who else provides you with a digital ashtray at no extra charge?'

There is nothing wrong with establishing that the potential buyer will derive significant benefits from a particular product feature while, at the same time, highlighting the fact that competitors in general, or one in particular, cannot supply a similar feature or match its performance.

'While the speed of the "ABC" photocopier is similar to ours, the average cost per copy is a penny more and it does not have an auto-stacking feature.'

This kind of mention of the competition is not only acceptable but, in most circumstances, is also essential. The salesman can never rely on the prospective buyer having a complete dossier of information on all potential suppliers. In many cases the statement of facts that some sales 'purists' might construe as 'knocking the competition' will be seen by the buyer as a welcome source of data for his decision-making process.

Another method of highlighting weaknesses in competitive products is to establish the benefits of a unique feature of one's own product to the point where it becomes a positive want that is unavailable elsewhere. This kind of opportunity does not occur very often but needs to be exploited when it does.

'We are as yet the only company to replace the traditional electromechanical servo with a microprocessor. This will provide you with increased reliability and reduced costs which were hitherto unavailable. Competitive products without this new facility would effectively deprive you of such savings.'

If that is 'knocking the competition'—keep at it!

8.

Overcoming sales resistance

'If you want to win a man to your cause, you must first convince him you are his friend.'

Abraham Lincoln 1809–65

The nature of sales objections

When a buyer raises an objection or asks an awkward question, it does not mean that the sales negotiation is going badly. Quite the opposite. It usually indicates real interest in the sales proposition and a wish to stimulate rational and evaluative discussion on its validity, i.e., the buyer needs to be totally convinced.

It is unfortunate that the term 'sales objection' has somehow crept into the selling vocabulary without being identified as the negative expression it really is, responsible for much self-inflicted, irrational anxiety for many salesmen. There is seldom such a thing as a sales objection! *The Oxford English Dictionary* describes an objection as 'An expression, or feeling, of disapproval, disagreement, or dislike'. This kind of extreme reaction occurs so infrequently within the normal selling situation that it is unworthy of consideration. However, the buyer can be expected to demand information, ask questions, or even decline an offer, very often in a vigorous or even abrupt manner. But that is not so unlike any other person-to-person interaction. A sales objection, so called, is not an attempt to belittle the salesman or destroy the credibility of his sales argument.

It should not be seen as a personal affront or a rejection of the sales proposition; quite the contrary. It should be welcomed as a clear indication of the buyer's interest and involvement. If you think a sales objection is worrying, consider the implications of the prospective buyer who says nothing! The sales objection should always be seen for what it really is—a plea for more information.

Even the objection 'Not today, thank you!' is really another way of saying 'You have not provided sufficient information to convince me that it is to my advantage for us to do business.' Therefore, sales objections should be welcomed rather than feared, for they indicate the involvement of the prospect and the route to the heart of the selling procedure.

It is also worth considering the apparently frivolous, but very real, point, that the buyer who has already decided to buy often wishes to make the salesman work for the order rather than 'handing it over on a plate'.

The importance of being flexible

Because there is an infinite variety of buyers, salesmen, products, and situations, the range of possible sales objections is endless. However, it is possible to divide them into broad categories of type. Similarly, the ways in which such resistance might be overcome can be broadly categorized. However, just as important as this is seeing the ideal moment to respond in order to achieve optimum effect. Should it be immediate, thus getting the problem out of the way and allowing the buyer to relax, or should it be delayed because the natural progression or demonstration will answer the question more meaningfully later on? There is no infallible answer to that question, other than to highlight the absolute need for salespeople to be totally flexible in their approach and reactions at all times.

Apathy and inertia

Possibly the most common type of sales resistance the salesman has to overcome is indifference or an unwillingness to change the status quo. Apart from a host of quite plausible explanations the buyer may offer, there are often other, more profound, but unstated, reasons. Change can imply many things for the buyer:

'What will be the personal effect on me if the currently acceptable situation is worsened by change?' (*risk*)

'If the current situation is acceptable, why should I involve myself in additional and otherwise unnecessary effort?' (*personal effort*)

'Does change imply that the choice I made previously was not the best one?' (*personal credibility*)

These are real fears that have to be allayed, usually by convincing the buyer that there is no risk yet much personal gain, as existing users have already proven the product and are now enjoying the benefits (i.e., 'reference selling'). As for the credibility of his previous purchase, the buyer needs to be assured that it was the best decision he could have made at the time, due, perhaps, to lack of awareness of the product now being proposed, or because there was no alternative product available at the time, or whatever.

The power of the personal defence mechansim should never be underrated and the inertia of complacency and habit must never be ignored. Such circumstances demand positive stimulation—'If you want the fruits of sales success, first you have to shake the tree!' That does not imply a need for shock tactics, but rather emphasizes the importance of having

100

something to say which from the start wakens the buyer to new ideas. The means of achieving this effect depends on the circumstances, but it must say, 'Here is how you and your company can benefit by changing your current practice!' There are no magic phrases in this, or any other aspect of selling, which guarantee the desired effect. But, knowing the likely areas of interest through effective pre-call preparation, there are many appealing, or even provocative, direct statements that can stimulate the interest of the buyer. This must, of course, be delivered with conviction and enthusiasm:

'This service/product will. . .

. . . increase your profits.'

. . . improve your efficiency.'

. . . enhance your stature.'

. . . lower your costs.'

. . . give you advantage over your competitors.'

No buyer worth his salt can afford to ignore the opportunities offered by such statements. After all, that is the purpose for which he is employed. Nevertheless, it is up to the salesman to establish that the process of change is a justifiable and acceptable course.

Emotional considerations

One thing most of us have in common is the process of buying. The fact that this usually occurs in the retail marketplace does not make the emotional aspect of our individual decision-making process radically different from that of a professional buyer. If the item of clothing does not fit or if we don't wish to change from our accustomed brand of detergent, we say so; if we are not sure which pair of shoes is most suitable, we procrastinate and if we have never bought stereophonic equipment before, we question and deliberate. So, when a businessman is presented with a sales proposition by a professional salesman, he is most unlikely to accept it without question or reservation. His reactions are much the same as our own would be in similar circumstances and he needs to be handled with the same intelligence, courtesy and sensitivity as we would wish for ourselves.

Despite these rather basic observations, many salesmen make the mistake of increasing sales resistance by their persistent attitude. How often have you gone into a retail shop or been visited by a door-to-door salesman and found yourself being pressurized into buying something you don't want? There is nothing more likely to put off the typical prospective purchaser than being browbeaten with arrogance and insensitivity. Selling is not a gladiatorial occupation but a process of gentle persuasion.

101

There is no point in attempting to overcome sales resistance by increasing sales pressure—it can only have the opposite effect. Trying harder should not be confused with selling harder, as one seldom benefits from confrontation, particularly in selling. Outmanoeuvre perhaps, but never overpower; don't fight sales resistance—neutralize it. Once established in the buyer's mind as an antagonist rather than a friend, the salesman is doomed to failure. There is always tomorrow, and the minimum requirement of any sales call is to leave in complete confidence that one is welcome to go back and try again.

Possibly the most critical point of the sales call is the way in which it begins. A declaration of intentions right from the start can do much to ensure cooperation and avoid confrontation: an enthusiastic, friendly, and positive opening statement of what the salesman wishes to say and wants to learn, related to his company's product and the client's needs, followed by real proof of his understanding of the buyer's industry and knowledge of his own products. This will quickly establish the kind of personal credibility that leads to good rapport, and which, by its very nature, neutralizes many of the transient, emotional reflexes of the sales negotiation. Like all human relationships, 'starting out on the right foot' is essential for 'staying the course'.

Sources and kinds of sales resistance

Sales objections are either valid or invalid. Many are entirely appropriate as they reflect uncertainties about the product or service, perhaps a need for more information or even misunderstanding. Others are merely a subterfuge to delay a decision or hide the real reasons for not wishing to buy. The separation of these two categories is a difficult, but necessary, task, for without this knowledge, such sales resistance is unlikely to be overcome.

Valid sales objections
Valid sales objections should always be welcomed, for they are a statement of truth which implies interest in the sales proposition. These can be divided into two further categories—positive and negative. Positive statements mean, 'I am interested but I need more information' or, 'Yours could be the right product but you haven't completely convinced me.' In other words, positive steps towards close of the sale. Valid sales objections which are negative are really saying 'I understand your proposition but I truly have no need or justification for your product or service' or, 'I have no funds to pay for your product or service whether I need it or not.'

Invalid sales objections
Unfortunately, it is easy to confuse valid/negative sales objections with those which are intended to mislead, i.e., invalid objections. Statements like 'We don't need any' and 'We can't afford it' are very often excuses or

deliberate attempts to negate the sales proposition. Sometimes invalid objections are raised for reasons of personal insecurity, because of an inability to understand the product being offered. However, it should always be remembered that in selling nobody is 'Too dumb to understand', the onus is always upon the salesman to ensure that the appropriate information has been conveyed and understood.

In this kind of situation the buyer is likely to generate sales objections which are intended as a diversion from personal inadequacy, as few people have the humility and strength of character to admit they don't understand. Some invalid objections are merely an attempt to avoid any possible conflict from directly saying 'No!', others may simply stem from a reluctance to hurt the salesmen's feelings.

Nevertheless, all objections should be treated as valid, no matter what interpretation may be put upon them. Any buyer is bound to react negatively to an objection that is ignored or treated lightly. To even imply that a sales objection is invalid will, more often than not, lead to antagonism which can only result in a sterile selling situation.

While there are many types of sales objection, there is no truly definitive method of anticipating when they will occur and the form they will take. However, being forewarned is forearmed, and much benefit can be derived from categorizing recurrent sales objections by type and meaning to form the basis of a personal checklist that can be augmented by new situations as they occur during the selling round.

Basic types of sales objection

Need for information

This is not really sales resistance at all; it is more likely to be a reflection of the buyer's inability to proceed due to a lack of pertinent facts.

He is really saying, 'I am undecided' or, 'I am having to say "no" because I have not received sufficient information to do otherwise.' In effect, most of the following types of sales resistance are merely subdivisions of this request for further information, sometimes stated, often implied, that can occur at any time during the sales negotiations. It is worth remembering that most buyers adhere to that old adage: 'When in doubt, don't!'

Subterfuge

This is more of a buying tactic than a sales objection, whether it comes in the form of complex chicanery or simple excuses.

When a buyer uses these means it can be interpreted in many ways, none of which are endearing. They are usually manifestations of weakness, incompetence, deviousness, insincerity, bad manners, questionable ethics, etc., but, sometimes, a result of naïvety and ignorance. Such tactics can usually be seen for what they are. Subterfuge can take any form, from weak excuses to blatant lies. Like all professional abuse, it is best ignored or side-stepped.

Prejudice
Preconceived ideas that are used as barriers against the logic of the sales 'argument'.

Prejudice is not only a recurrent and frustrating aspect of selling, but also one which is a true test of character for the professional salesman. Many buyers have preconceived ideas about products and companies, due to unsatisfactory personal experience in an indirect context, or a variety of completely unacceptable factors, from hearsay to bribery.

Whatever the reason, prejudice is usually emotive and illogical, and must be handled with extreme sensitivity.

Lack of enthusiasm
This is more of an attitude than a precise objection, but it is equally as negative.

It is a non-specific attitude which often occurs at the beginning of a sales interview. However, it can be sustained throughout if the salesman is making insufficient impact to gain the attention and interest of the buyer. As such it should be regarded as a self-inflicted sales resistance.

Insularity
Subjective sales resistance which feeds upon the effect of the sales proposition itself rather than the product.

'It's not my style' and 'It does not apply in our case' are common statements of this introspective attitude. It is not necessarily a criticism of the product or the sales proposition but it does reflect a lack of flexibility on the buyer's part, or even a failure to face up to his prime responsibility, i.e., constantly seeking the best value for his company's investment. Again, sensitive selling is the order of the day.

Inadequacy
Sales resistance that reflects demotivation due to a lack of ability to comprehend or make a personal commitment.

Making a decision, even for an experienced buyer, creates a certain amount of insecurity. After all, his basic hope and intention is to make the right decision every time, even if he knows this to be an impossible task. Many factors can promote a lack of confidence or even apathy and none more readily than an inability to understand. An essential part of the salesman's role is to inspire confidence in the product, the company, and himself. This cannot be achieved unless complete understanding has been established at every stage of the sales negotiation, not just in terms of product specification, but also method of use, terms of business, etc.

Status quo

Resistance to any aspect of the sales negotiation which requires a change in current practice and makes otherwise avoidable demands upon the buyer.

There can be many reasons for not wishing to 'rock the boat' other than apathy and inadequacy already mentioned. Many buyers deliberately attempt to avoid change because it demands extra effort from them, and extra work that they believe could be put to better use elsewhere.

Change can also bring with it costs that are not actually part of the sales proposition itself. A change of computer type may involve rewriting all existing programs; a change of truck manufacturer may mean abandoning existing stocks of spare parts and having to retrain mechanics. Political forces (see 'Politics') can also be a reason for maintaining the status quo.

Product resistance

Sales resistance directly related to criticism of the product, or incompatibility between the 'problem' and the 'solution'.

This should be treated as objective argument, even though in many cases the root cause may ultimately turn out to be entirely subjective. More often than not, it takes the form of objection to price, performance, delivery, service, presentation, guarantee, suitability, etc.

Credibility

A stated or implied declaration of no confidence in the salesman, his company, or his product.

Unless 'professional credibility' in every respect is established right from the start, there is little chance of sales success. It must, therefore, be the salesman's prime objective, using whatever means are at his disposal, to ensure there are no doubts in the buyer's mind concerning the integrity of any aspect of the sales proposition.

Affront

When the buyer takes exception to a statement made by the salesman.

As I keep emphasizing, sensitivity is a vitally important aspect of selling. This, by and large, consists of an ability to interpret and anticipate the reactions of the buyer to statements and actions made or to be put into effect. Looking, listening, and thinking are the critical elements of this process. One is less likely to offend if one has considered the possible reaction to what is about to be said, i.e., 'Do not engage mouth before switching on brain!'

Misunderstanding

A reaction based on an illogical interpretation of clearly-stated information or a reasonable assumption based on badly presented facts.

This must be accepted by the salesman as profound personal failure.

105

While effective communication must be of equal benefit to both buyer and seller, it is the salesman who must bear total responsibility for achieving complete understanding on the part of the client.

Self-aggrandizement
Sales resistance contrived by the buyer in order to demonstrate his status or knowledge.

Fortunately, this is not a very common occurrence, but it can be rather disconcerting when it does happen. It is usually meaningless banter that usually has to be endured for as long as it takes to side-step the conversation.

Politics
Sales resistance which relates to the buyer's company hierarchy and its machinations rather than the product or its supplier.

This nebulous sales resistance is probably the most difficult of all to overcome. It can manifest itself at a variety of levels; international, corporate, inter-company, divisional, departmental, or personal. 'If it was up to me, I would go ahead, but it's against company policy', is a fairly typical statement of political sales resistance, that is relatively easy to respond to. The really difficult political problems are those which come from absolutely illogical decisions or direct refusals without any valid explanation. In such circumstances, the salesman must identify, not only the seat of political influence, but also the route to it, in order to have any chance of survival.

Silence
Unstated, or implied, sales resistance.

Just because the buyer has not thrown the salesman into the street or reacted in some other demonstrable fashion, does not mean he accepts what he is being told. This is a common occurrence among sales people, particularly those new to the profession, who, for reasons perhaps of nervousness or enthusiasm, are swept along by their own rhetoric without considering the likely reaction of the recipient. While some buyers may be so introspective, inadequate, or insecure that they blanket their negative feelings in silence, it is usually more a matter of being swamped with statements rather than questions, or being asked questions where a movement of the head is sufficient response.

Stalling
Playing for time rather than making a conclusive statement or decision.

'I need time to think it over', is the classic reaction of a buyer who cannot put forward plausible reasons for not buying. This usually means one of two things: he is not absolutely convinced about the benefits of the possible transaction; he has the prospect of a better deal elsewhere but wishes to hang on to this one just in case the other doesn't work out.

106

'Last ditch stand'

A final and often contrived sales 'objection' which frequently occurs immediately before the commitment to buy.

To some degree, deciding to buy is rather like jumping into the deep end of a swimming pool, without the benefit of testing the temperature or knowing the depth. No matter how confident you might be and no matter how attractive the proposition, you don't really know whether or not you've done the right thing until you've bought it and tried it. So, that final, irrevocable moment of decision inevitably leads to momentary insecurity. Decision is always followed by mental relief, even if there is still uncertainty as to whether or not the decision made was actually the best one. The typical buyer is no different from the average citizen. That brief spell of insecurity that follows the moment of decision and precedes final commitment is often manifest in a sales objection that is really a need for assurance and should be seen for the buying signal it really is.

This is by no means an exclusive list, but it does cover most categories of sales resistance. This, inevitably, leads to the more demanding question of what one should do about them, so I will be returning to those same objections later. In the meantime, let us consider the broad disciplines and implications of applying the appropriate selling response.

General responses to sales objections

The first rule of overcoming sales objections is never to contradict and seldom dispute. Clearly, the level of understanding and friendship between buyer and seller has some bearing on this statement, but even the strongest relationship can be severely affected by the simple statement 'You are wrong.' The aim must, therefore, be to remove the objection without causing offence. This is not simply a matter of identifying a predictable statement and responding with a standard phrase. There is an absolute need for sensitivity and awareness in terms of how and when a sales rebuttal is applied.

It is so easy to compound a selling problem by making a response which gives an impression of arrogance, patronization or even hostility. As in any kind of rigorous discussion, the best method of achieving acceptance of your argument is to dilute the apparent strength of your counter in order to lower the defences of your 'opponent', and thus achieve greater effect. Later on we will discuss specific techniques for overcoming certain kinds of sales objections, but, as a general rule, it is worth remembering that any rebuttal, tempered by a pre-statement that exonerates the buyer from any blame for being at odds with the seller, not only strengthens the rebuttal but also the relationship. 'I'm sorry, I didn't explain that as clearly as I ought', is so much more acceptable than, 'You obviously haven't understood, so I'll explain again.' Similarly, there are pre-statements, varying in degree of emphasis, that serve the purpose of taking the sting out of the rebuttal yet enhancing its effect.

'I'm sorry if I mislead you.'

'That's a good point.'

'If I were in your position, I'd probably take the same view.'

'Most of my existing clients had the same initial reaction as yourself.'

Such statements are then followed by the actual rebuttal, usually linked by use of the word 'but' or 'however', as in:

'I know you have a lot of experience in this area. . .

. . .but this is a completely new development with unique features/ benefits that could significantly increase your profitability. Take this one for example. . .'

The importance of good timing

Ideally, a sales objection should be met with the appropriate rebuttal as soon as it is raised, for once cancelled out, it is unlikely to interfere with subsequent negotiations. If the objection is ignored or deferred, it is likely to become overemphasized in the buyer's mind and distract him from following issues that may be more important. There are, however, some situations where delaying tactics are both justifiable and unavoidable.

Sometimes the buyer will ask for price details before he really knows about the product or its feature/benefits. Such demands must always be resisted for premature revelation of costs can destroy the sales proposition by virtue of the psychological burden that may be created. This is a difficult situation to deal with for the mental barrier that ensues is likely to be unstated.

'I don't know what you are offering, but I'm sure I can't afford it!'

In other cases, sales resistance occurs that can be dealt with more effectively later in the sales story, perhaps by way of demonstration, or simply because it comes over more effectively or automatically at a later stage in the presentation without destroying its natural flow. If this is so, then the buyer not only needs to be informed accordingly:

'I'm glad you raised that point: I shall be covering it in detail in a moment',

but also reassured that his query has not been forgotten, should the interval between question and answer be extended. On occasions, objections

108

may be raised which are irrelevant, out of context or deliberately misleading. The salesman cannot afford to be lured into these diversions. It is, therefore, essential that the buyer is made aware of the need to stick to the framework of the presentation for purposes of clarity and continuity, whilst at the same time declaring a willingness to cover any outstanding questions once the sales story is completed. Whatever the absolute reality may be, the slightest suggestion that any sales objection is trivial is as good a way as any of finding oneself back out on the street.

The very best time to overcome any sales objection is before it is actually raised, i.e., by anticipation. This has many benefits. Sales objections that are introduced and overcome by the salesman have much less emotional significance than those introduced by the buyer. Similarly, answers to anticipated questions have the effect of defusing them. It also enhances the credibility of the salesman by making it clear that there is no attempt to hide anything. There is no risk of contradiction if the objection is self-introduced, as this reduces the risk of conflict. Most objections to a given product are recurrent, and therefore the salesman is unlikely to have trouble in identifying and introducing them when he chooses rather than when the buyer does. This clearly demands they occur early in the sales presentation, and in accordance with the nature and circumstances of each particular selling situation. It goes without saying that this essential selling skill demands intelligent pre-call preparation, based on a comprehensive understanding of the product, the industry, the application, and the client.

There are, however, some objections that cannot be rebutted at all; those which are accurate and justifiable statements concerning the product. Salespeople must only deal in truth. To deny faults and claim feature/benefits that do not exist is a sure means of permanently destroying a client relationship, and thus all chances of ever achieving sales success from that source.

Essential disciplines

While the principal purpose of this sub-section is to identify the kinds of sales resistance that are likely to occur and the means of overcoming them, it is also important to highlight the related selling disciplines that must be obeyed in order to avoid the exaggeration of sales objections or the introduction of avoidable problems.

Be respectful

Always show respect for the views of the buyer. Often you may disagree, sometimes you may know for an absolute fact that he is wrong. What you are very unlikely to discover is the basis of his reasoning or source of information. Perhaps he has been misinformed or is burdened with the unenviable task of taking an illogical political stance? Respect is a reflective process; the more you give, the more is received in return. But what is

109

respect if not the establishment of personal credibility, and how likely is sales success without it? In other words, the respect you gain for yourself is a direct function of the amount you show to others.

Listen

Merely to hear is not enough. Very often, what has been said is of less relevance than why it has been said. Complete understanding of the buyer's statements and questions and the generation of effective responses can only be achieved through undivided attention.

Very often the salesman will suddenly interrupt the buyer with either an anticipated answer to the buyer's unfinished question, or even with a statement that is completely out of context. In such circumstances, one can only conclude that the salesman believes his own dialogue to be more important than that of the buyer! From the buyer's point of view, people who interrupt are not listening, and people who are not listening don't deserve to get the business. And they usually don't!

Think

Don't leap in with a sales rebuttal. Always pause for thought, no matter how briefly, so that you are sure your response is valid, i.e., don't jump to the wrong conclusion. This will also indicate to the buyer that his statement is important and has been given due consideration. Once again, we get back to the reflective quality of respect. The buyer is likely to give as much consideration to the salesman's reply as is given to his question.

Don't argue

By all means, reason, rationalize, persuade, and explain, but never argue or tell the buyer he is wrong. 'Full frontal' argument is seldom to the saleman's advantage, for it inevitably becomes a win or lose confrontation which puts the buyer/seller relationship at extreme risk. This does not mean that opinions should never be expressed or that open discussion is prevented. It is simply a matter of avoiding the emotional conflict and criticism implied by contradiction.

Keep objections in perspective

It is very easy to let sales objections get out of proportion by over-reacting to them or dwelling upon the subject. The salesman's response to every question must be balanced and concise and, once relevance and acceptability are established, the topic must immediately be dropped from the discussion.

Qualify

It is important to look beyond the face value of a sales objection. Is the objection valid, is it subterfuge, why is it being raised, what is the real

110

objection? Buyers often create a lot of 'flak', simply because they are not convinced by their own argument, or find it necessary to cover up an unstated objection that they believe to be untenable or embarrassing. Those who lack the honesty and humility to say 'I cannot afford it', are more likely to say something like 'It doesn't suit me' or 'I have no need of it.'

Keep calm
Never react strongly to provocation. No matter how annoyed or irritated you may feel about the buyer's question or response, always react in a relaxed and rational manner. This is the only way to recover or maintain the perspective of a sales negotiation and avoid the risk of creating a negative environment, thus damaging the credibility of the sales rebuttal.

Don't patronize
Many salesmen fall into the trap of exploiting the enormous gap between a little knowledge and total ignorance. Particularly in the area of new technology products, there is a great temptation to take the 'ego trip' of telling the first-time buyer everything in baffling detail. There is nothing more likely to destroy personal credibility than the implied arrogance of becoming a self-appointed expert.

Check for understanding
Do not assume that your response to a sales objection is automatically understood or accepted. There is only one way to find out—ask!

Be an ally
The raising and answering of sales objections should not be seen as some kind of tennis match with the desk as the net. The successful sales negotiation is one where both parties win, having achieved mutually beneficial objectives. By reinforcing the buyer's case wherever possible, and agreeing with his arguments when they are clearly justifiable and not at odds with his own product and company, the salesman can do much to create a bond of common understanding.

Be prepared
Never go into a sales situation without at least attempting to anticipate the possible sales objections and the appropriate rebuttals.

Make a note of it
New situations and types of sales resistance occur all the time. The salesman can be forgiven for not having the right answer first time, but not when it recurs. It makes a lot of sense to note down any sales objection that is experienced for the first time, so that an appropriate rebuttal can be

created by way of simple evaluation, personal experience, or advice from fellow sales people.

Know your product

Without real understanding of the total scope of a product, it is not possible to fully exploit all the sales opportunities that may occur or may be created. Many products offer the possibility of creative or 'conceptual' selling, due to their many potential variations of specification, and the multitude of applications for which they may be put to use. Only by gaining knowledge of every facet of a product, and by studying all the ways in which it has been applied to date, can the salesman be fully equipped to exploit its maximum potential. And, by doing so, he may gain the considerable personal satisfaction of making a sale as a result of his own expertise and ingenuity.

Know your customer

More often than not, sales success depends on identifying the real problem. This can often differ radically from the one that the potential user thinks he has. In order to discover this, the salesman must be conversant with the nature of the buyer himself and the nature of his industry, the mechanism of his company, the scope of its applications, its fundamental needs, and its resources (manpower, expertise, finances, etc.).

Always be ready to ask for the order

The opportunity to wholly or partially close the sale may occur at any time, but particularly after successfully overcoming a significant sales objection. Always be prepared to ask for the order when the opportunity arises, the next chance may not be so easy!

Dealing with sales objections

Overcoming sales objections and closing the sale have in common the absence of any particular technique or formula that is best for a given situation. There is no magic phrase that can be thrust into the discussion at the appropriate moment in order to disintegrate the buyer's resistance. Flexibility is paramount. While it is feasible, and indeed desirable, to anticipate sales objections, it is extremely difficult to judge when they will occur and the form they will take. Some types of sales resistance, particularly those of emotional and political origin, are completely unpredictable. It is, therefore, essential that salespeople develop total fluency in all the basic techniques of handling any type of sales objection, whenever it may arise. The process of converting conversational 'problems' into 'opportunities' demands considerable versatility in approach and delivery. The fact that a certain technique was effective in overcoming a particular sales objection on a previous occasion, does not mean it will work again in a similar situation elsewhere.

Sales sensitivity is, as ever, a significant factor in taking the right action; maybe this technique, maybe that, maybe a combination of techniques. Fluency in handling sales objections can only come about as a result of considerable study and practice, certainly in the classroom but particularly in a 'real life' selling environment.

Another essential component in successfully overcoming sales resistance is the maintenance of a positive attitude, not only towards sales resistance, but also to individal selling situations. I have already stressed that a sales objection is normally a declaration of interest, rather than outright rejection or personal affront. Likewise, prospective clients must be viewed in terms of their potential for success, rather than possibilities of failure. A typical example is the prospective buyer who declares a lack of interest in a new proposition through loyalty to his existing supplier. Is the way barred? Is it best to walk away? Not a bit of it. This is, in reality, a very attractive situation, for a client with such loyalty, once secured, can be expected to show similar allegiance to a new supplier. So, off you go into your presentation of the benefits to be gained from a second or alternative source! The difference between success and failure is often the difference between positive and negative thinking.

So much for the generalities. Let us now look at some of the well-established techniques for handling specific kinds of sales resistance. You may already know some, or even all of them, but by different names.

Direct denial

Direct denial is seldom the appropriate reaction to a sales objection because it is a form of confrontation that can quickly get out of hand. No one reacts kindly to being contradicted and, when the source of such irritation is a person who is trying to sell something, to take offence is a very good excuse for saying 'No!' For this reason, many buyers deliberately contrive to make unreasonable statements in order to throw the salesman off balance and create a negative selling atmosphere. Yet there are occasions when this kind of response is unavoidable and the risk of putting the buyer and seller on 'opposite sides of the fence' has to be taken.

Clearly, the content of a direct denial is important. No matter how one says 'You are wrong!', the effect upon the recipient must be the same. Nevertheless, using this method depends as much on delivery as it does on the choice of phrase. Let us consider two kinds of 'direct denials', in response to an inflammatory remark from the buyer:

'Your system will not work!'

This is hardly a statement the salesman can ignore:

'Oh yes it will!'

This kind of emphatic response is likely to cause tension that will quickly destroy all chances of ever achieving sales success. It is uncompromising and antagonistic, and, however delivered, will very likely result in early termination of the sales negotiation.

'This system is already working very successfully within several organizations similar to your own. I can assure you it will work just as efficiently for you as it has for them.'

This is still contradiction; the buyer is still being told he is wrong. But the statement is reinforced with a reference, so that it becomes implied fact, rather than opinion. It also has the effect of redirecting the denial, and therefore part of the blame, to a third party. Even so, the manner of delivery is still very crucial.

Innuendo, gestures, semantics, and physical expression have a considerable influence on the meaning of words. It is, therefore, essential that a 'direct denial' is delivered with good humour or serious interest and concern for the buyer's circumstances. The smile, for instance, is a most disarming device, which can be used to great effect, even though it may sometimes be a considerable strain to do so.

The real difficulty of the 'direct denial' technique is that it is a thoroughly automatic response to an attack on your product, your company or yourself. While this might be seen as an admirable characteristic, it can be so spontaneous as to lack the necessary finesse demanded by a sensitive situation. In the final analysis, the only valid test of a direct denial is whether or not it meets the objective of a given stage of the sales negotiation, i.e., provides the buyer with the information he requires, overcomes his fears, strengthens the buyer/seller relationship, and prepares the way for the close of the sale. A direct denial, however seldom provides this kind of opportunity.

Indirect denial

As you might expect, the 'indirect denial' is a very close relative of the 'direct denial', above, and usually refers to specific instances where experience is different from that cited or anticipated by the buyer. It is not a contradiction backed up with facts, it is the explanation of third-party experience that is contrary to the buyer's fears and leaves him to draw his own conclusions. To repeat the previous example:

'Your system will not work!'

'I can understand your reaction. That's how Mr Smith of "Staybrite Castings" first responded to the proposition, but the system we installed there last year has brought about many benefits and continues to operate most effectively.'

This approach does more than redirect the source of contradiction from the salesman to a third party. It also removes the onus of possibly being wrong from the buyer's shoulders. In other words, Mr Smith of 'Staybrite Castings' was wrong, so being misinformed is not an ignominious position!

However, citing third parties is not without its hazards. Some buyers may take exception to the assumption that what is right for another company is automatically right for them. In some circumstances, the buyer may see himself as an expert on the matter in hand and may not take kindly to suggestions that he is not infallible. There is also a danger that the introduction of a competitor as a third-party reference may create an obstacle to the early development of a good buyer/seller relationship.

Turnaround

The 'turnaround' or 'boomerang' method aims to convert a sales objection into a reason for buying. The salesman simply takes the positive stance of regarding the sales objection as a vehicle for strengthening the working relationship between the buyer and himself in pursuit of the best possible answer for both parties. It is a device which starts out with an expression of agreement, followed by a resolution to help the buyer solve the problem he has highlighted.

> 'Your system has many attractive features, but it is far too expensive to justify any possible savings.'

> 'I'm glad you've raised the question of savings. Let's see how the system could be applied to your particular circumstances and estimate the relative cost/benefits.'

There are several well known introductions to the 'turnaround' method:

> 'That's a good point.'

> 'That's why I'm here.'

> 'I'm glad you reminded me.'

> 'I'm pleased you brought that up.'

They are all designed to introduce the 'turnaround' and, in so doing, achieve several objectives:

1. Reduce the apparent significance of the sales objection.

2. Convert the situation from a negative to a positive stance.

3. Reinforce the 'partnership' of the buyer/seller relationship.

4. Remove a sales barrier.

5. Progress the sales negotiation further towards the close.

Paraphrasing

The 'paraphrasing' technique is, in effect, a repeat of the buyer's question in reassembled form, followed by a statement that is intended to carry the sales negotiation further towards the close by accomplishing a variety of objectives:

1. Lessening the impact of the question or putting any exaggerated statement into perspective.

2. Showing you intend to answer the question but first wishing to check that it has been correctly understood.

3. Making it clear that you are not intimidated by the question.

4. Satisfying the buyer that his question is being taken seriously, and that his point of view is appreciated.

5. Generating a 'breathing space' while deciding upon the best response.

6. Converting the sales objection into an answerable request for information.

For example, the buyer may be concerned about the implication of a total product change:

'The relatively small savings you are proposing hardly justify our putting ourselves at risk by replacing what has always been a thoroughly reliable system.'

'I recognize that your present system is extremely reliable, as it should be, and, as is our own. I also understand the implied risk of any kind of change, particularly from something which is familiar to something which is completely new. Clearly, you need to be satisfied on reliability and the ease of changeover and would like to see it demonstrated.'

Paraphrasing is not simply the process of repeating the buyer's question. It is an acceptably modified restatement that enables the sales negotiation to progress. In the example, above, paraphrasing is used to advance the dialogue towards the buyer's acceptance of a formal demonstration of the system.

Agree and counter

This kind of rebuttal is perhaps the one most commonly used by salesmen and is often known as the 'yes . . . but. . .' technique. In fact, its use in selling is so popular that most experienced buyers will instantly identify it for what it is—that is, they will completely disregard the 'yes' element and react to the 'but', as if it were an outright contradiction. Experienced salesmen will, therefore, cloak their use of this method by the use of less predictable dialogue.

The 'agree and counter' comes in a variety of forms. Let us consider five variations:

1. Agree and counter with additional benefits   This technique is a two-step counter, consisting of an initial concession to the buyer's objection, followed immediately by previously unstated features and benefits that have the effect of offsetting or overcoming the objection concerned. It is a turn of phrase attuned to strengthen the bond of mutual agreement to carry the buyer over the difference between what he has said and what the salesman wishes to say.

> 'We've used continuous linen towels for years now, and have found them satisfactory. And many people in our line of business appear to think the same.'

Agree   'I can appreciate your reluctance to change from a product that has served you well for so long and certainly their use is widespread. . .

But   . . . However, there is an increasing trend towards paper towels due to their hygienic superiority and lower cost per individual user.'

To have simply said:

> 'Linen towels are less hygienic and more expensive than their paper equivalent'

would have presented the same information, but would be much more likely to cause tension. If opposing claims are not diluted with agreement, they will usually be interpreted as blatant contradiction.

2. Agree and cancel opposing benefits   Sometimes the buyer identifies a valid shortcoming in the features or performance of the product relative to his particular needs, or an aspect of a competitive product that is superior. If the objection is valid, there is no alternative but to accept it gracefully. But this should be countered immediately with other relevant benefits that at least compensate for the disadvantage that has been highlighted:

> 'Your delivery period is much longer than that of your competitors.'

Agree   'Our declared delivery period is a firm commitment and as such

117

does represent a longer timescale than that stated by most of our competitors. . .

But   . . .Nevertheless, the superior cost/performance of our equipment will quickly offset any short-term gains made by products that are available more quickly. That assumes, of course, that your preparation for installation will not be put under unnecessary pressure by delivery at an earlier date. I most certainly regret that our lead time is extended but that is entirely due to ever increasing demands for our products.'

A word of warning! Sometimes the buyer will raise a genuine reason why your product cannot satisfy his requirements, while others can. Once this claim has been substantiated, the salesman should quickly curtail the sales negotiation, but without showing indecent haste. It serves nobody's interest to deliver an unsuitable product. On the other hand, there may well be alternative business within the same organization, either now or in the future. So, acknowledge defeat gracefully—it's an excellent way of maintaining professional credibility for both company and salesman alike.

3. Agree and translate into justification for buying   Very often the objection raised by the buyer is the very reason why he should be saying 'yes' rather than 'no'. It is, as I mentioned earlier, the difference between a negative and a positive viewpoint. This is a matter of interpretation that the salesman can use to great effect, but only if he does so with real understanding and sensitivity:

> 'Your survey of our needs and the report you produced is very interesting. I am sure you could help us to make significant savings. However, the current economic climate has severely affected our financial situation, resulting in a need to curtail all unnecessary capital investment for the time being.'

Agree   'Yes, it is clear that our system could reduce your costs as well as improving quality control and I can appreciate that the economic situation is affecting you in much the same way as it is troubling many of our existing users. . .

(You may notice that the 'Agree' element of the rebuttal can sometimes be modified to augment the strength of the 'bridge' between the agreement and the counter. That is, the addition of '. . .as well as improving quality control. . .' and '. . .the same way as it is troubling our existing users.' The former introduces an undeclared benefit in addition to one that has already been established; the latter implies that economic recession is not preventing other companies from putting similar proposals into effect.)

118

But . . .On the other hand, have you considered that any decision, other than to go ahead immediately with the implementation of our system, will, indirectly, cost your company significantly more than taking no action at all? The savings that you are able to make would start today if our system was installed. Any delay will mean the irrecoverable loss of both the financial savings and increased efficiency that our proposals will bring about, and could well represent a greater amount than the cost of investment.'

There are substantial risks, as well as advantages, involved in this technique, for, no matter how it is delivered, it could be seen to imply that the buyer has insufficient perception to appreciate the opposing logic of his own statement.

4. Agree, give reasons for buying, trial close   This takes the 'Agree . . . But. . .' approach a stage further, and takes in 'closing' which is an integral element of this and the following types of sales rebuttal. 'Closing' is dealt with in detail in Chapter 9, but for present purposes it is important to remember that the right time for closing the sale is often immediately following the successful rebuttal of a sales objection:

'I already have substantial stocks of your product.'

Agree   'I'm sure your confidence in maintaining substantial stocks of our product is justified by regular public demand. . .

But   . . .This is not a normal situation. We are about to stage our most comprehensive advertising campaign ever, employing television, the press, and high street posters, backed by special offer coupons distributed door-to-door, added to which we have this special one-time reduction in buying price to favoured distributors such as yourself. All of this means a greater volume of sales and high unit profit. This may temporarily involve a higher than usual level of stock, but this will be offset by increased sales. . .

Trial   . . .higher turnover, greater unit profit. Surely this is an opportun-
close   ity that could make a significant contribution to the increased profitability of your company?'

It will be seen that this 'three-tiered' rebuttal includes a request for confirmation that the benefits stated in the reply to the buyer's objection are reasonable. A positive response automatically brings the negotiation one stage nearer to the final close!

5. Agree, counter, conditional close   It is difficult to decide whether this is predominantly a rebuttal or a closing technique. It certainly includes an

119

element of both. This device is best used towards the end of the sales negotiation, where the buyer is perhaps making a 'last ditch stand' with one
remaining objection. It is devised to exploit the initiative of countering the
last remaining sales objection.

'Your equipment is obviously very good, but it's too expensive.'

Agree 'It certainly isn't cheap, but on the other hand, it isn't the most
expensive. One thing that never changes is the truth that we get
what we pay for. . .

But . . .If I can prove, via some of our existing users, that this system
can not only save you money but has a cost/performance at least
equal to that of our competitors, will you go ahead with our pro-
osals?'

Assuming a positive response to the 'But . . .' element, the counter may, as
in the example above, conclude in an agreement to visit established users
and witness a demonstration, or it may result in the production of information that disproves the client's objection. If this is performed satisfactorily, the buyer's acceptance of the proposition is automatically implied.
Notice the expression 'But . . . If . . .' as these are extremely powerful
words which, when used together, epitomize the conditional sales close.
This device is revisited in Chapter 9.

Let us summarize the benefits of using the 'agree and counter' method of
handling sales objections:

1. It infers respect for the buyer's point of view.

2. When a rebuttal is tempered by initial agreement, it dilutes the con-
    frontational implications of direct refutation.

3. Uncertainty concerning which of his claims are conceded and which
    refuted, has the effect of stimulating the buyer's interest.

4. It is an effective 'springboard' for introducing additional features/
    benefits.

5. It is an excellent device for leading up to a trial or conditional sales
    close.

Questioning

In some circumstances, a sales objection needs to be qualified, either
because the salesman does not understand it, because he feels it is unjus-
tified, or even a subterfuge. It could be said that salesmen tend to retreat to
questioning whenever they are in trouble. However, in this instance, I am

concerned with questioning being used as a positive device for progressing the sales negotiation and validating the substance of sales objections by putting the onus of proof upon the buyer.

Questioning is probably the least likely of all rebuttal techniques to instigate a confrontation, because it allows the buyer to make his own pronouncements while the salesman takes the apparently subordinate role of asking questions. However, questioning can, in some circumstances, create difficulties, or even embarrassment, for the buyer. Therefore, the salesman's manner of interrogation must be calm, quiet, and sincere.

The objective of this technique is to make the buyer reconsider his original objection, in the belief that such a review will either diminish its significance, or neutralize it altogether.

1. 'Your system does not cater for both Imperial and Metric values.'

   'That's true Mr Prospect. How essential is this facility to your needs?'

2. 'A product made of fibreglass is unlikely to be strong enough to meet our requirements.'

   'Do you think so? What are your precise requirements and what has your past experience of fibreglass revealed?'

3. 'Your equipment appears to be efficient but I'm not happy about its appearance.'

   'I must say, we do find that tastes differ radically from company to company, but how important is appearance in terms of the task to be undertaken?'

It's surprising how people in general respond positively to questioning by someone who is sincerely interested, particularly if it gives them the opportunity of expounding their theories or off-loading their problems. This can be an excellent method of revealing the 'hot-buttons' of buying motivation.

Blind eye

During the course of their work, salespeople are exposed to a great deal of 'flak'. In other words, some apparent sales objections are, in reality, meaningless banter, time-fillers or unconsidered comments unworthy of response. Unfortunately, many salesmen feel obliged to reply to any resistance which comes their way, and, in so doing, become involved in triviality, both time-consuming and distracting. Clearly, the salesman has positively to identify a truly irrelevant objection, as it is easy to give offence. Once convinced that a question is pointless, the salesman is best advised to proceed as if nothing had been said.

Examples of meaningless objections are numerous. Often they refer to irrelevant product features or the claims of competitors. Sometimes they can be a function of hearsay, speculation, hypothesis—the possibilities are endless.

Then there are familiar objections, like: 'We don't want any!', usually delivered before the salesman reveals the nature of his proposition. In my opinion this is a nonsense. How can a prospect not want any of something he knows nothing about? Best ignore it!

There are other pointless objections that do not justify direct response, but have an implied message that needs to be appreciated. Is the buyer really asking the salesman to leave, or is he concealing the reason for not buying? This is one of the many situations where sales sensitivity is of paramount importance; whether to take up issue or disregard it and carry on? There is little alternative but to trust one's instincts.

Inapplicability

This is a near neighbour of the previous item. The difference is that between irrelevant and inapplicable. Sometimes the buyer will raise a sales objection that he believes to be pertinent, when in reality the basis of his argument is incorrect:

'Your price is higher than that of other suppliers.'

'That may appear to be so, but our price includes delivery and installation as well as a complete supply of consumables, sufficient for approximately three months of normal usage. Our competitors treat these as extras. In total, our price is actually cheaper than that of most other suppliers of this kind of product.'

If the buyer is misinformed, he not only needs to be told, with suitable courtesy, but also wants to be told.

Postponement

Sometimes a sales objection is raised at an inopportune moment. To respond immediately may have the effect of destroying the continuity of the sales presentation. On the other hand, the question may automatically be answered at a later stage, perhaps by demonstration. Or perhaps the answer to the question will automatically occur later on. In such circumstances, it is reasonable, with the buyer's approval, to keep the answer in abeyance.

However, such deferment can lead to problems if allowed to go too far. Very often the buyer will worry about his question being overlooked, and will consequently become distracted from the ensuing dialogue as the importance of the outstanding question grows in his mind. This will reduce the impact of the presentation, and diminish the credibility of the feature/benefits. So, if the answer to a buyer's question is deferred, regularly assure him that it has not been forgotten. The cardinal sin, of course, is to leave without ever providing the deferred answer to a sales objection. The salesman may forget, but the buyer won't!

Comparison

Very often, the best way of overcoming a sales objection is to call upon examples that 'subcontract' the responsibility to a third party, while, at the same time, introducing an element of implied impartiality. On the other hand, the comparison could be made by citing a parallel example from the buyer's own experience:

> 'I recall Mr Williams of "Burton Textiles" raising the same question when we first put this proposition to him. There has never been a hint of such a problem since they installed it 18 months ago.'

> 'Of course, there will be installation problems, there always are. Look at the troubles you had when I installed your first computer, but look at the benefits you've gained from it since.'

Of course, you need to know your facts. Nothing destroys, personal credibility more than an incorrect 'reference sell', or inaccurate comparison.

Summary

No selling procedure is without sales objections; anything else is simply order taking. In every circumstance, objections should be seen for what they really are—demands for information that usually imply interest in the sales proposition. For this reason they should be welcomed and handled with enthusiasm. This cannot be done effectively without a real understanding of the various techniques and their objectives.

1. To answer both valid and invalid questions.

2. To allay any fears in the mind of the buyer.

3. To discover the real needs of the buyer.

4. To enhance the relationship between the salesman and the buyer.

5. To pave the way to the sales close.

One final thought. During the course of the selling round, salespeople are exposed to a wide variety of sales objections; some occur regularly, others infrequently. The latter are very difficult to counter. There is, therefore, much to be gained from compiling a list of sales objections, accompanied by rebuttals known to be effective. Such a list should not be limited to the experience of one salesman, but should represent the accumulated knowledge of his company's entire selling operation. It can be very helpful to have on hand the direct experience of fellow salespeople when exposed to a significant sales objection for the first time.

Here are some basic statements of sales resistance to start you off. Once you have established a basic rebuttal to these, you can make additions from your own experience and that of your colleagues.

1. 'We're not ready for your kind of equipment.'

2. 'We have too many other problems at present.'

3. 'It will cost too much.'

4. 'The unions will never agree.'

5. 'We've been through all this before.'

6. 'Our existing methods are adequate.'

7. 'We will have to change our present system.'

8. 'We don't have any real problems.'

9. 'We're not interested.'

10. 'We can use the facilities at head office.'

11. 'Your systems wouldn't work here.'

12. 'That doesn't apply to us.'

13. 'I'm far too busy to get involved.'

14. 'Our requirements are unique.'

15. 'Your system is not comprehensive enough.'

16. 'We wouldn't consider an imported product.'

17. 'Your main competitor is offering a discount.'

18. 'Your delivery is far too long.'

19. 'We are overstocked as it is.'

20. 'We just ordered a similar device from one of your competitors!'

Of course, some sales objections are easier to overcome than others. But bear in mind, when you meet an insurmountable objection, the importance of accepting defeat gracefully and so maintaining a good basis for business opportunities that may occur in the future.

9.

Closing the sale

'When in doubt, win the trick.'

Edmond Hoyle 1672–1769

Basic principles

It has been said that closing the sale is as easy as A B C—Always **Be** Closing! But, what is 'the close'? It is that point in the selling process when the prospect decides whether or not to buy; the stage at which success or failure to win the order is determined and the link between proposition and commitment made.

Some causes of failure

Many salespeople, particularly new recruits, appear to think that closing the sale is just a matter of knowing a special phrase or secret handshake. Unfortunately, it isn't that simple, as there is no special trick for ensuring success. Many salespeople, having handled the various stages of the selling process with distinction, have been known to crumble at the last moment when confronted by the need to ask for the order because the buyer has not offered it. This is possibly due to the intense psychological conflict between the need for success and the potential ignominy of failure. The fear of personal rejection implied by refusal is so profound that they are unable to expose themselves to the risk by asking for a favourable decision.

Generally speaking, salespeople who experience no significant problems in progressing positively through the stages of the selling process should be able to complete the close with equal ease. For such people, any problems they may have are almost sure to stem from lack of confidence, insufficient experience, or failure to continually and objectively evaluate their own performance. Make no mistake, a salesman who cannot close sales is not a salesman, he is, at best, an order taker. In other words, if you can't close, you can't sell.

There can be no greater handicap in selling than to suffer continuing uncertainty about one's ability to close the sale. It can become an emotional pressure that creates a negative feedback affecting selling efficiency at

125

every stage of the process. It is therefore a potential problem area, where any uncertainties need to be removed as soon as they are recognized.

For many of those who experience difficulties in closing, their real problem is a lack of perspective concerning the statistical odds of winning or losing, related to a given product within a given market exposed to whatever circumstances may prevail at a given time. The salesman is yet to be born who has never lost a sale. There is a substantial difference between striving to win on every occasion and actually doing so. The important thing is always to operate with success in mind; confidence and enthusiasm without blind optimism.

Without doubt, selling demands a certain amount of courage, but the need for this is not the exclusive province of the sales close. Cold canvassing, telephone prospecting, demonstrations, presentations, etc., all call for self-confidence which is but another shade of courage. But what kind of courage is this? It is nothing very illustrious, merely the strength of character to accept 'no' for an answer, without being overcome by humiliation and shattered confidence, and then spring back into selling, undaunted. It is the positive attitude of regarding 'no' as a challenge, rather than personal rejection. Any person without this capability should never be in selling.

Another problem, particularly common to new salespeople, is the inability to close the sale for reasons of self-imposed guilt. They either consciously or subconsciously regard selling as anything from begging to intrusion, coercion to deception. It is as if they believe that an order must be given without request; that to ask for it is a demeaning and unethical breach of professional code. They fail to see, or even consider, the reality of the benefits they are able to bring to the potential buyer, their ability to purvey knowledge where perhaps ignorance went before. It has to be said that any person who feels guilty about pursuing a selling profession should quickly find employment elsewhere.

There are some salespeople, and the ranks are not limited to those new to selling, who view many selling techniques, particularly closing, as forms of 'high pressure selling', as if to suggest that such activities are untenable on ethical grounds. In reality, what they really mean is that they are failing in some aspects of their job and are searching for an excuse. Asking for the order is not 'high pressure selling'. Bludgeoning some passive householder into buying an article he neither wants nor can afford might be so described, but finalizing a product presentation and highlighting the feature benefits with the statement, 'These are the reasons why you should buy, please can I have the order?', certainly cannot be.

Some salespeople fail to see the need to close the sale at all. They apparently assume that all they have to do is make a good presentation and the prospect will automatically give them the order. It is as if they feel entitled to the business so long as they put on a good show! To be fair, some prospects will actually do that—they may even go so far as to help the salesman out by asking if he is able to accept an order, but that does not happen very often. It has to be borne in mind that, in most situations, there are usually two opposing forces at work: competition and the natural inertia of the buyer. Most buyers need the final 'nudge' of the close to move them into a decisive frame of mind.

One common, yet rather silly, cause of failure to close the sale is over-immersion in the 'cut-and-thrust' of the selling process. Many salespeople become so bogged down in overcoming objections and pursuing sterile arguments, that it never actually occurs to them to ask for the order. This is often because they do not sell to any particular pattern, or operate within a selling structure that has the close as its natural aim. The close should not be seen as an isolated function, but as an integral element of the selling sequence, which the salesperson instinctively brings into effect at the appropriate opportunity.

Selling 'pressures'

One sometimes hears expressions like 'low pressure selling' and 'soft sell'. I do not wish to get into an argument on semantics or colloquial express-ions, but as far as I am concerned these terms are meaningless. All selling has periods of applied pressure. Asking direct questions, overcoming objections, and putting the record straight, all imply the application of some kind of pressure upon the prospect. But that is true of any debate that strives to gain common acceptance of new ideas or different approaches. The degree of selling pressure within any given situation is immeasurable, because there are no constant types of circumstances or personalities to measure against. Selling is about persuading. And per-suasion is about applying the appropriate emotional pressure in order to gain acceptance of a particular point of view. There can be no selling with-out pressure and this pressure may occur at any time. It is therefore reasonable to say that if we are to continue to use terms like 'high' and 'low' pressure, it might be better to categorize the former as 'selling' and the latter as 'non-selling'.

The closing situation

However intelligently a sales call is planned, and no matter how well con-ceived the structure of the sales presentation, selling is seldom as predict-able as we would like it to be. There is no definable single moment when the order is won or lost. The right time to close the sale is when the pros-pect is ready to buy. It's as simple as that! Neither is the opportunity for closing limited to one solitary chance, as there are usually several distinct occasions within the average sales negotiation when the chance to wholly or partially close the sale is presented to the salesman. It is up to the sales-man to grasp the opportunity when it arises. Such an opportunity may occur in the first few moments of the very first call, or it may take several calls and many months.

The psychology of the close

The close is probably the most important element of selling. However, I believe many salespeople have problems with closing because its importance has been emphasized so often that they see it in exaggerated isolation from the other integral components of the selling process. For them it has become a source of tension and anxiety which is entirely contrary to the best environment for the close. Thus, any selling pressure that may arise is not directly a function of the close itself, but a reflection of the tension and insecurity felt by the salesman. It can be this very anxiety that creates the kind of over-reaction, or even desperation, that negates what might otherwise have been a favourable decision.

As I have already said, prospects seldom ask to buy, mostly they rely on the salesman to make it easy for them. Let us be clear about one thing: making a decision to buy is not the same as agreeing to buy! Once a prospect has decided to buy he will very often hover on the brink of commitment, yet finds considerable relief in giving his consent and getting on with things. Any help the salesman can give to stimulate the process is usually welcomed.

'No'

Of course, potential buyers don't always say 'yes'; more often than not the answer is 'no'. Yet, there is seldom a situation in selling where the outcome is an irreversible refusal. Typically, 'no' really means something like, 'not on this occasion', not on the present basis' or 'not unless you can convince me that I have reached the wrong conclusion'. In other words 'no' should never be accepted at face value; at worst it should be regarded as 'no, but. . .'. Many salespeople who give up too soon are perhaps humiliated by the initial rejection, or only have sufficient courage for a single attempt at closing the sale. This could be for a variety of reasons, ranging from the implied intimidation of the buyer's status, to a basic misconception of what 'no' actually means in the buyer's terms. One of the best ways to success is not, generally, to accept 'no' for an answer. It is too easy to assume that 'no' means a potential buyer is completely written-off forever. The minimum objective of any sales negotiation must be to 'leave with the door open', having established complete professional credibility for one's company, product, and self, and the buyer's agreement to meet again within a given time-scale.

There is, however, a considerable difference between interpreting the real meaning of 'no' and refusing to give up until the buyer says 'yes'. An incessant barrage of dialogue, with the apparent intention of talking the buyer to the point of exhaustion, is not only bad selling but also a sterile

128

pursuit, as few buyers have time to waste and repetitive chatter is never appreciated. The fact is that once the sales 'argument' has been fully expressed the chances of talking the buyer out of the sale rather than into it become increasingly, higher.

Consider the buyer's problems

Those salespeople who have difficulty in asking for the order should also consider the opposing situation of the potential buyer. It is reasonable to suggest that the trauma of asking for the order is equalled, or exceeded, by the stress of deciding to buy. It is, therefore, quite understandable that the salesman will meet resistance from the buyer because of feelings of insecurity on the buyer's part that are just as profound as his own.

Just consider some of the buyer's problems: Will this product meet our requirements? Can we afford it? Does this product provide the best value for money? Will it be delivered in time to meet our urgent needs? Will this supplier still be in business next year? Has this company really got the resources to provide continuing maintenance and keep up to date with new developments? How will my position be affected if I get it wrong? etc. With such questions the buyer needs all the help he can get to commit himself.

Every buying decision has some negative areas which need to be overcome by an effective closing technique. In particular this demands the use of what seems to be a contradiction in terms: open-ended closing. Whether an interim or final closing technique is being employed there must always be room for continuing the sales dialogue, even if the buyer's response is negative to the point of outright refusal. Further negotiation must always be possible.

Timing

If there is one component of closing that is more important than any other it has to be timing—the choice of the right psychological moment to ask for the order. This does not imply a single opportunity for closing, as most sales situations offer a number of closing opportunities. The skill is in recognizing them for what they are whenever they occur. And that can often be much earlier than expected. Such opportunities must be 'grabbed with both hands', for the chances are that each one may be the last one, as: 'The order within reach today will be out of sight tomorrow.'

Consider the situation of the hesitant buyer: the salesman has made his pitch; the feature/benefits have been established; the order requested; but, the buyer is still uncertain. As far as he is concerned the proposition is in balance; there are reasons for and against it. Perhaps he procrastinates and gives superficial excuses, but he doesn't emphatically say 'no'. In such circumstances there may be a temptation to say something like 'I can see you are still uncertain and I don't want to rush you into anything. Why don't

129

you think it over and I'll come back and see you tomorrow.' Horror of horrors, don't ever do that! Hesitation prior to the point of decision is a perfectly normal response. (Aren't you the same when you are buying? If you are offered something you don't want, you say so immediately, whereas if you see something that is right you instinctively look to see if there's anything better available, even if you are reasonably convinced there is not. You carefully consider the alternatives, while the salesman may think you're dithering. So, why should it be any different when the roles are reversed?) No, don't ever agree to come back later. Will your sales argument be any stronger then? Of course not, so why should the fresh words you are serving today be more attractive tomorrow when they are stale? If the salesman falls in with the buyer's hesitation he is lost. In such circumstances the buyer is in need of assurance. This is the right psychological moment to secure the order! That is why top salespeople tend to take the pressure off in this kind of situation and move into a consultative role in order to create a relaxed environment within which the buyer can feel more confident. Browbeating at this stage is almost as bad as desertion.

Ultimately, the salesman succeeds by achieving the order; a moment of elation or relief. At this time there is a risk that the salesman will unduly relax. This must be avoided at all cost. There are three disciplines that have to be obeyed: react calmly to the decision; congratulate the buyer on his choice; leave quickly but without indecent haste. No buyer wishes to be a pioneer or do business with a loser. If the salesman's reaction is that of someone registering his first success, the buyer's confidence is sure to diminish. Over-excitement or profound relief can only give this impression. Having made a decision the buyer needs the assurance that he has done the right thing. Even though the salesman's loyalties are obvious, to commend the buyer on his choice is a most acceptable gesture that puts a seal of commitment on the agreement. Once this assurance is established there is usually nothing else requiring immediate attention, but there is considerable risk of further dialogue bringing uncertainties into the buyer's mind. Having made a decision, many buyers go through a process of self-recrimination and no salesman can afford to get involved in such a post mortem. It is therefore important to finalize the meeting soon after the order has been secured. This rule is not limited to low-value products where usually the only significant event after the close is delivery. Even high value and complex products or services are subject to the same discipline. Follow-up activity, such as arrangements for training, site preparation, maintenance, etc., are best dealt with on a separate occasion, for such discussions can always lead to second thoughts if dealt with on the day of decision. So, thank the man and go!

Summary
So much for the basic principles of the close. I may have given the impress-

ion that there is an awful lot to consider before putting it into effect. Well there is; but the principal factors can be condensed into eight areas of consideration.

1. The potential buyer must have absolute faith in the salesman, his company, and its product.

2. The potential buyer must fully comprehend the implications of the proposition.

3. The potential buyer must want to enjoy the benefits of the proposition.

4. The opportunity to close can occur at any stage of the negotiation.

5. There will be more than one opportunity to close.

6. Be prepared for a negative response, so that refusal does not terminate the negotiation.

7. Keep a calm exterior.

8. Having secured the order, leave as quickly as possible.

If the salesman is able to satisfy these conditions it is reasonable to say he has the situation under control.

Just one final thought on the psychology of the close. It seems to me that a lot of salespeople get disturbed about the close because they are constantly told by management and trainers alike that it is the climax, the very essence of selling. It is presented as the pinnacle of a pyramid of actions, disciplines and techniques that must be climbed in order to achieve success, rather than a natural step in a sequential process leading to a lasting relationship. Consequently, its relative importance has been exaggerated out of proportion. Maybe the skills of closing are taught the wrong way round. Perhaps, if we started by giving trainees a thorough understanding of the function of the sales close and worked backwards from there, it might be seen in its true perspective.

Disciplines and objectives

Jogging has become a very popular pastime for many people, primarily because it is an excellent way of keeping fit, but also because it is an activity independent of other people, can be pursued anywhere, and is very inexpensive. Some people have even graduated into running long distances, and ultimately into considering the marathon. To complete the marathon distance is the supreme objective of many of these joggers. But of those who attempt it, many fail to make the distance. It is a sad sight to see someone fail within sight of home; how pitiful to come so far and yet fail. It might be better never to have started out, for there are no prizes for failure, no real satisfaction in not completing the distance. What has happened in those last few minutes to cause the runner to stop? Foot blisters? Severe chafing? Dehydration? Pulled muscle? There could be all manner of reasons; but these are effects not the causes. The question is, could they have been avoided? Was the runner wearing the wrong shoes? Did he take precautions against chafing? Was he right to miss a drinking station? Did he increase his pace at the wrong time? In other words, he may have already been committed to failure long before he stopped, maybe even before he started out.

Working towards the close is very similar to running a marathon. If you are undisciplined, without a logical predetermined plan, and unsuitably equipped for each stage of the selling process, the chances of a success are very slim indeed. The salesman only has to do one thing wrong at any point and the potential buyer will switch into a negative frame of mind and merely wait for the right moment to say 'no' (which is usually at the moment when he suspects the salesman is about to ask for the order). Without doubt, it is very easy to underestimate the variety of disciplines that must be applied throughout every sales situation.

Obtain commitment
At every stage of the selling cycle the salesman should be striving to gain agreement and commitment from the potential buyer in terms of actions to be taken and benefits to be gained. As a further analogy, building up to a successful close is like constructing a house brick by brick in the correct sequence. If this is done effectively the buyer will assume he built it himself. It must therefore be so much in accordance with his desires that to say 'yes' will be a completely natural reaction:

'Yes, you can come and see me to discuss our milking methods.'

'Yes, you can visit one of our farms and look around the milking parlour.'

'Yes, we would be interested in reducing our consumption of animal feedstuffs and increasing our milk yield.'

'Yes, you can put in formal proposals for supplying one of your automated feeding systems.'

'Yes, installation by October would be acceptable.'

'Yes, we will give you the business.'

'Yes, you can have a formal commitment now.'

All commitments are not necessarily the direct response to a salesman's question. Many opportunities for commitment can come as a result of reversing a 'closed' question asked by the buyer. This is achieved by over-coming the natural tendency to simply reply 'yes' or 'no' to the buyer's demand for information.

'Can you supply a dual feeding system?'

'Can you deliver within 90 days?'

'Can we rent your equipment?'

'Can you carry out the installation?'

To simply say 'yes' or 'no' generates no commitment, whereas responses such as the following advance the salesman toward securing the order:

'Yes, have you decided on a dual feeding system?'

'Yes, do you need delivery in 90 days?'

'Yes, have you decided to take out a rental agreement?'

'Yes, shall we include charges for installation in our proposals?'

Of course, most of the commitments the buyer makes within the sales cycle are initiated by the salesman. One good method of obtaining commitment from questioning is to use a variety of standard beginnings and endings. For example:

'This will . . . won't it?'

'This is . . . isn't it?'

'You will . . . won't you?'

'You do . . . don't you?'

'They are . . . aren't they?'

'This is an accurate statement of your current usage of animal feed isn't it?'

'You do want delivery by October don't you?'

The continual use of questions in order to gain accumulated commitment means that when the right time comes along the salesman can ask for the order with complete confidence. However, questions alone cannot guaran-tee success. As I have said before, and will say again, whatever the stage of the sales negotiation and whichever the technique, there must be con-stant awareness of the need for sensitivity, which in turn relies on the sales-man's ability to listen, as opposed to hear, and see as opposed to look. As I

133

mentioned earlier, the opportunity to close the sale could come at any time, so if the senses are not fully alert, all may be lost. It is what I call the 'You can't give me the order yet, I haven't finished my presentation!' syndrome. However, there is a contrary danger and that is the risk of asking for the order too soon. *The right time to close can only be when the customer is ready to buy.* Unless a positive indication is given that the buyer has as much information as he requires and wishes to buy, it is very unwise to attempt to close without completing the sales story. In those rare circumstances where one is selling a product that is in great demand, it might be possible to get away with it for this is no more than order-taking, but in normal situations premature closing seldom achieves success and such orders are very prone to subsequent cancellation.

The importance of a positive attitude

Many salespeople, it has been said, approach the close with considerable trepidation. There could be many reasons for such apprehension, but the most likely is the potential ignominy of failure. This is a foolish result of negative thinking. The salesman gives his presentation step-by-step—he attracts attention, arouses interest, identifies a need, creates a desire, presents his product and company effectively, overcomes any sales objections. Then, lo and behold, there he is at the close. This is the best time of all; the culmination of all the effort and investment of the selling process; the moment that confirms how well the job was done. It is an end that is but the beginning of a new relationship or the beginning of another selling cycle. That's the beauty of selling—it is a process of continual rebirth.

The fundamental difference between a good salesman and a bad one is that the former always hopes to get the order, and is extremely disappointed when he doesn't, whereas the latter doesn't expect to get the business, and is always surprised when he does. In fact, the accomplished salesman not only assumes a successful close, but also has the close firmly in mind from the start. However, the ability to adopt this attitude very much relies on the security of operating within a structured selling sequence, for whatever distractions may occur, be they objections or buying signals, the salesman has control of the interview. After any distraction, he is able to identify the re-entry point into his sales story, and knows when his presentation is complete. In other words, the security of the selling framework enables him to concentrate from the outset on recognizing those signals from the buyer that mean 'I am ready to buy'.

Having said all of that, I think there is a need for me to explain what I mean by 'positive'. There is a considerable difference between thinking and acting in a positive manner and overt displays of positiveness. Buyers never appreciate salespeople who exhibit artificial enthusiasm, smile excessively, appear over-confident, or are too optimistic. Buyers, and others in a position of authority, are typically intelligent and perceptive people who probably experience a broader cross-section of salespeople than most sales managers, and can spot artificiality a mile away. Their reactions to insincerity are fairly predictable—'Am I being deceived, high-pressured, or both? If so, do I want to buy from this person?' The likely answer is 'no', but even if it is 'yes', the chances are he will ask for time to consider, which will inevitably result in a negative conclusion. The aggressive close, which is but a manifestation of excessive positiveness, is a sterile device, for it tends to create second thoughts. 'Why is this salesman trying so hard if his product is as attractive as he claims? Why is he so anxious for me to sign? Does he know something I don't? The kind of positive attitude that is required prior to, during, and after the close, accommodates mutual agreement through a consultative manner in an atmosphere of relaxed confidence.

Is the decision to buy already made?

Sometimes, but not too often, the buyer has decided to buy long before the salesman has concluded his sales story, or even before the call is made. Of course, he is unlikely to greet the salesman with an admission to that effect, for he will generally feel entitled to the courtesy of a formal presentation, or feel determined to make the salesman work for his living.

There are many ways in which the buyer could have arrived at this pre-sold position. Maybe an acquaintance already has the product, and is very satisfied with it. Perhaps he has been carrying out his own evaluations and has decided that this particular salesman's product is right for him. Like as not, the salesman will have no knowledge of why the buyer is sold; but the reasons are irrelevant, the important thing is the man wants to buy, so all that is needed is simple confirmation of this—'Would you like me to demonstrate the product so that you can witness its capabilities?' 'Shall I go through the description of services again to highlight the major facilities?' If the answer is something like 'No thank you, I have all the details I need', then you are most probably teed-up for an early close. 'That's excellent. Which model would you prefer?' or perhaps 'Well, if that's all the information you need, perhaps you could tell me the most convenient date for us to start the project?'

Speak the man's own language

Chapter 5 deals with communications quite comprehensively, but I would like to restate the importance of ensuring that everything has been understood prior to the application of the close. Do not assume that the buyer fully appreciates the reasons for buying, even though they have been presented to him. Check for understanding before attempting to close, for one can hardly expect the buyer to make a positive decision about something that is wholly or partially still unknown to him. A common failing, particularly with salespeople who are selling technically-orientated products, is to use terms that may be part of everyday conversation to them, but are a complete mystery to the buyer. Technical gobbledegook creates considerable insecurity among the uninitiated, and is not likely to secure a positive sales close. If you use the Queen's English there is far less chance of misunderstanding, and if you can't cope with such technical humility, you shouldn't be in the job!

Buying signals

The privacy of individual thought is often betrayed by spontaneous comments and gestures. The human being is a reactive creature continually responding to external stimuli and expressing feelings vocally or physically. Even those who consciously hide their feelings find it hard to maintain a bland exterior on every occasion. We all make apparent our pleasure, displeasure, anxiety, enthusiasm, and so on, at some time or other. It has been said that 'the eyes are the windows of the mind', and certainly the eyes can often reveal an inner truth that might be contrary to the spoken word.

The interpretation of these emotional signals can indicate to the perceptive salesman the buyer's reactions to each element of the sales negotiation. Yet, this is not simply an intuitive process; it is a skill that can be learned by those aware salespeople who have the eyes to see and the ears to listen. In my opinion this journey into the arena of emotional uncertainty is one of the most fascinating aspects of selling. It is the place where all human relationships reside; where the heavy-footed and insensitive wander at their peril. With practice, the interpretation of these reactions can become an instinctive 'tool of the trade' that could be the shortest route to the close.

Buying signals can be divided into two categories, hidden and overt. The former is usually perceived by way of physical action, whereas the latter is a function of the spoken word. In the case of hidden signals, the salesman must seek to observe any physical movement that might suggest the buyer has arrived at a positive emotional stage. Take, for instance, the situation where the buyer suddenly leans forward attentively. That usually means the salesman has said something that particularly interests him: maybe a solution to a significant problem; a facility the buyer needs and didn't realize was available; the identification of a problem he didn't know he had. Whatever the reason, that kind of physical movement is usually a buying signal which should be taken as an opportunity to attempt a 'full' or 'trial' close, having 'homed in' on the area of interest. The prospect who asks to return to a specific product in the brochure; the one who looks pleasantly surprised when told the trade-in value of his current model; the prospect who attempts to operate the demonstration equipment himself, are all situations where the potential buyer is likely to be considering the product in a positive light, at any stage of emotional commitment, from being mildly interested to absolute possession at any price. It is up to the salesman to find out, by way of whatever closing technique appears to be most appropriate.

What about the buyer who switches from a smile to a frown? At the very least he disagrees with what is being said, but at the other extreme he could be upset, offended, or even insulted. The salesman who does not react to this kind of 'body language' could well be talking himself out of the business. And the buyer who at the end of a sales presentation collects up all the sales literature and puts it into a neat pile on his desk? Is he subconsciously saying 'I now know enough about this product to enable me to buy if I so desire?' Probably! So there's only one thing to do—ask for the order. Then the buyer who is constantly looking out of the window, doodling, or trying to disprove the theory of relativity on his pocket calculator. Something has to be wrong! Apart from the rather obvious conclusion that he is bored to tears, it is essential to discover the reason why. No requirement for the product? Ineffective presentation? Wrong department? There has to be a reason; so ask! The buyer who is constantly looking at his watch. Is he really paying attention? Would it be best to leave now and come back some other time, or is he waiting patiently for the conclusion of the sales story so that he can place the order he has already decided upon. Perhaps he doesn't want to hear all about the benefits. A friend of his already has the product and is delighted with it, so all he wants to do is place the order quickly so as not to be late for lunch! So, be aware, measure the man's reactions, then use an appropriate close:

'I want to be sure you have all the information you need in order to buy this product. The presentation of all the relevant facts will take me a little longer. Would you prefer me to complete the picture, or do you feel you already have sufficient information to make a decision in our favour now?'

Overt signals, as the description implies, are relatively easy to identify because they are usually verbal communications less susceptible to misinterpretation than gestures or mannerisms. This is especially so because more often than not they are accompanied by facial expressions that confirm the inference of whatever statement is being made.

'How quickly can you deliver if I order now?'

'How much could you allow against my existing equipment?'

'What financial terms are available?'

'Do you have this model available with automatic stacking?'

'How do I maintain your product?'

'Is this the best price you can do?'

'I like the quality of the finish'

'Must you have my decision now?'

'Will this thing really stand up to our demands?'

'It seems like good value but. . .'

The salesman's ability to perceive the real significance of such statements, and his sensitivity in interpreting the motivations which created them, must dictate his ultimate chances of sales success.

Many salespeople are afraid of reacting to these kinds of buying signal, fearing they might be attempting to close prematurely—'I musn't ask for the order now, he may not have made up his mind!' As far as I am concerned, there is no such thing as asking for the order too early. Providing a 'trial' or 'final' close is applied in a skilful manner, the chances of an outright 'no' are extremely remote, and even if such a negative response is received, it is more likely to relate only to a part of the proposition rather than the entire transaction. If there is to be a basic guideline for reacting to positive buying signals it must be to attempt a close at every feasible opportunity. After all, as I mentioned earlier, every sales situation offers a number of opportunities to close and no chance should be wasted. The cardinal sin is to lose the opportunity of trying a sales close when it is presented. Unfortunately this is the most sinful area of the sales profession!

Don't accept 'maybe'

People hate making decisions; many are unable to make them at all. It is this aspect of human nature that to some extent justifies the role of the salesman, for it is his job to convert 'maybe' into 'yes', or even 'no'. That, to a great extent, is what closing is about: assisting the potential buyer who has reached the crossroads of 'maybe' to commit himself. Aren't we all the same when it comes to making a choice—'Shall I or shan't I?', This one or that one?' Isn't it so much easier when someone comes along and gives us positive reasons why we should decide on a particular model, colour, or whatever. Buyers, as a breed, are no more decisive than the average citizen, and are just as likely to feel secure in the land of 'maybe' than anyone else.

Striking while the iron is hot is an essential discipline of closing, for, as I have already said, a return visit seldom has as much impact and potential for success as the one where the justifications for buying are first presented. Once the buyer is left to his own devices, while the salesman goes away for more ammunition, he will quickly lose any feeling of commitment towards making a decision of any kind. The chances are he will be reluctant to even speak to the salesman again once he has safely removed himself from the 'pressure' of direct negotiations. In other words, 'maybe' is often a convenient, or even cowardly, way of saying 'no'. It is therefore

138

essential to appreciate the possible emotional dilemma of the buyer, and press for a decision when it is clear that all the factors for making a decision are available. Be confident, be bold! How can the buyer be expected to have the confidence to make a decision to buy when the salesman does not have the confidence to ask for the order?

The danger of trial orders

In many areas of selling, particularly within industrial and commercial markets, trial orders are commonplace. Very often, comparison with other products currently in use or under consideration is desirable or unavoidable. However, there are great dangers involved in trial orders. Salespeople who perhaps lack confidence in their product, or themselves, have a tendency to use the trial order as the basis of their selling strategy rather than the last resort. With such lowly ambitions their eventual success can, at best, be minimal. In other circumstances the trial order may be used by the buyer as a placatory device; the means for ridding himself of the salesman, without feeling guilty for not placing a substantial order when there was every justification for doing so.

In the retail market the trial order is particularly inappropriate. Unless a sufficient quantity is ordered to truly service demands and share the same level of 'stock pressure', and display facilities as other products, then the order is not a proper trial. Part of our heritage of justice and ethics is that the word 'trial' automatically implies 'fair'. Nobody would ever consider that the trial of a product was going to be an unfair one, yet very often that is exactly what a trial is, because the scale and circumstances of the order will not allow anything else. Therefore, any order which by its very nature does not allow a thoroughly fair trial in every respect must be regarded as a pointless gesture that must be refused. If such an order is accepted then the chances are that it will fail its 'trial' and consequently destroy any chances of success in the future. One solution that I recall from my days of selling for *Unilever*, is to ask for a display advantage over other products to compensate for the problem of inadequate stock. This was achieved by erecting a display of the entire trial order adjacent to the cash desk where it could be seen by every customer. In this way the products sold quickly and the ground was laid for a substantial order.

However, this is not the usual practice in industrial or commercial selling. Very often the only way of achieving a maximum order is firstly by proving that the product actually works, or that its performance is superior to existing methods. If the sales objective is to equip every loom in a mill with a device that will automatically stop the machine on the detection of a broken thread, it would be unreasonable to expect the production director to install the equipment throughout his plant. He must first convince himself, by working trials, that the system works and is cost effective. The mistake is to allow the trial order to be seen as a discrete sale. If a trial is unavoidable, then the initial delivery should be accepted by the buyer as an integral part of the entire order, which will be delivered subject to the satisfactory performance of the trial. After all, if he likes what he sees, why should it be necessary to go back and sell the remainder of the order? It should be a formality once the trial is satisfactorily completed.

There is also a particular risk with trials of completely new products. The salesman might well gain acceptance of a completely new technique by way of a trial order, but if he hasn't got the whole requirement sewn up there is always a risk that a competitive salesman might come along and exploit his 'missionary work'.

There is one thing a trial order should never be, and that is the supply of a product of less power, quality, and features than required. Some sales organizations call this 'Lean and Mean' selling. The intention being to gain a foothold, so that by the time the user becomes aware of the limitations of the product it is far easier to order a larger model from the same supplier than replace it with an alternative from another source. I have witnessed this on many occasions in connection with the sale of computer systems, and as far as I am concerned, it is sharp practice. Whether the sales action is deliberate deception, or a desperate attempt to get an order of some kind, selling a product or service which is less than is really needed is likely to destroy future business opportunities, and could also lead to litigation.

Assume a continuing relationship

It is easy to adopt an attitude of finality about the meeting in which the buyer makes his ultimate decision. Whether the response be positive or negative it is easy to forget that the close is a beginning rather than an ending. Even if the order is lost it should still mark the start of a new strategy to secure the business next time. Most sales situations imply a continuing relationship, so the salesman must assume there will be future business. His attitude and behaviour must create an environment within which he has easy access to such opportunities. There may be a future need for the buyer to become a 'reference user' or assist in locating new prospects. Without a meaningful and continuing relationship this kind of support may be difficult to obtain.

This working relationship does not automatically occur once the decision is made. It is rather an understanding that should develop as the sales negotiation progresses, and be assumed without resorting to over familiarity. This can be helped along with the use of such words as 'us' and 'we'.

'Let us review the main benefits and see which will bring the most significant savings.'

'We can solve the problem between us.'

Keep something in reserve

Enthusiasm is a fundamental characteristic of the successful salesman. Sometimes this can lead to problems if the salesman's eagerness to sing the praises of his product results in 'over selling'; highlighting every feature benefit whether relevant or not, or shooting the last bolt before the battle is ended.

A common problem related to closing the sale is to reach the point of decision only to find that any selling points that might swing the balance towards a positive conclusion are but repetitions. As such, they are unlikely to have the effect of tilting the buyer towards an outcome favourable to the salesman. That is why many experienced salespeople always try to keep at least one non-crucial sales benefit in reserve, so that, if need be, a new reason for buying can be introduced which may be decisive:

'By the way, I may have neglected to tell you that our price includes the provision of sufficient supplies to last for the first three months of operation. As this is contrary to the practice of our competitors the relative saving to you will be around £250. That's a considerable saving isn't it?'

He is suitably impressed, but not absolutely convinced. So:

'In addition, delivery and packaging comes free of charge, which should save you a further £100. That makes the direct saving even more significant doesn't it?'

Salespeople often feel uncomfortable about deliberately holding things back. It feels like a kind of deception. 'Surely', they say to themselves, 'the buyer is entitled to know absolutely everything about the product he is buying.' Of course he is—but all in good time! Should the situation occur where the buyer says 'yes' prior to the salesman revealing his 'trump card', then it can be put to equally good effect after the order is received. To briefly deliver an additional benefit after the sale has been made, no matter how small, is a way of saying 'you thought you had a good deal but now you know it is better than you realized' or 'you may still have some doubts about whether or not you have made the right decision, but these supplementry benefits should offset any reservations you may have.'

Give an invitation to buy

A fact, so obvious but sometimes overlooked, is the need to provide the buyer with confirmation that it is appropriate for him to place an order. If a salesman calls, it should be obvious that he wants to sell something. However, how can the buyer be sure that the person in front of him actually is a salesman? It is only when the order is requested that the buyer knows absolutely where he stands.

141

Minimize the options

As previously mentioned, it is important to limit the range of choice, while bearing in mind the buyer's best interests. We have all experienced the confusion of a wide choice range. How many times have you been confronted by a comprehensive restaurant menu and been overwhelmed by the variety of possible choices? You may have been thankful for a waiter's recommendation and possibly even agreed to try a new dish on his advice. This is no different to the situation the buyer can be put into when offered too much choice.

Offer an alternative

This sounds like a contradiction of the previous section, but it is not. When it comes to making a final decision, even a short-list of one gives two options—buy or don't buy. There is consequently much advantage in offering two positive options in addition to the unstated, but obvious, negative alternative. 'Would you prefer this one or that one?' This approach assumes progression towards a favourable conclusion and implies acceptance. Whether the proposal be choice of product or day of appointment, to offer two positive alternatives reduces the chances of getting 'no' for an answer.

Be positive, be bold

It is virtually impossible to conclude a sale successfully if the close is applied without confidence and conviction. To a great degree the buyer reflects the attitude of the salesman. He cannot be expected to commit himself to a proposition that is delivered without authority. Neither does the request for an order come as a surprise to him; after all, he knows he is dealing with a salesman and such people are inclined to indulge in this practice! More to the point, it is the salesman, not the buyer, who is working within the disciplines of selling techniques and the buyer is therefore completely unaware at what moment the order will be requested. It will neither surprise, nor throw the buyer, if the salesman asks for the order in his very first sentence. But what the buyer will regard as abnormal is one where the salesman is apparently uncertain of his case, or where he never actually asks for the order at all. Make no mistake, it is the bold not the meek who shall inherit the business!

Do not invite negative responses

A large proportion of the selling process is devoted to questioning. Great care must be taken to avoid questions that invite a 'no' response. Mistimed ultimatums are most likely to have this effect—'Will this one do?' Negative questions are even worse, as they inevitably generate negative responses— 'You wouldn't like to try a sample order would you?'

Check for agreement

The successful close is seldom a 'one shot' affair. It is more typically an objective that is reached through an accumulation of agreed benefits and selling points that imply commitment. However, when an individual sales benefit is being established it must be agreed with the buyer before it can be regarded as valid. Such verification should, whenever possibly, also be used as the basis of a trial close. The value of this discipline is that a negative response from the buyer does not have the effect of curtailing negotiations. Rejection is a direct response to the check question, rather than the ultimate decision of whether or not to buy. Furthermore, it is an excellent means for the salesman to assess how well he is doing, how the buyer feels, and whether the 'temperature' is right for the final close:

'I guess the increased throughput you could achieve with our system would improve your profitability.'

The client tentatively agrees that the salesman's statement is valid. The salesman immediately responds with a 'trial close' in the form of a check question:

'We could install our equipment by the first week in June. Would that be soon enough for you?'

The response can tell the salesman a lot. If the answer is 'yes' he knows that his proposition is generally acceptable, and, most important of all, that the moment for a full close may well be at hand. If the answer is 'no' it is unlikely to have any significant bearing on the ultimate decision, it is merely a reaction to one isolated question. In other words, June may be too early or too late. In this case the salesman might respond by saying:

'Then, when would be the most suitable time?'

If the answer is once again negative:

'I don't think I'm in a position to discuss delivery at the moment.'

then the salesman has still learned a great deal. The buyer has either not had the opportunity to check on the details and implications of delivery, or has been insufficiently motivated by the salesman to do so. Alternatively, there may be restrictions placed upon him that prevent him from discussing the subject of delivery. Whatever the cause, the salesman knows he has work to do before it will be appropriate to attempt a final close. The salesman must continually check the client's willingness to accept the applicability of sales benefits and in so doing, establish his readiness to buy.

Establish a timetable for decision
Much benefit can be gained from agreeing a schedule of events with the buyer that contains the various stages of the decision-making process:

'Last week we agreed to carry out a feasibility study in order to establish your precise requirements, but today we have to agree the parameters of the system and the help we will need from you. Two weeks from now we should be able to decide upon the appropriate equipment. Then, once we have gained your formal approval, we can proceed with manufacture. This means we could have the whole matter resolved by the end of September. How does that sound to you?'

This approach gives the buyer a better appreciation of the various stages and logistics of the sales negotiation and makes the decision process much easier. The longer the selling cycle the more useful and appropriate this strategy becomes.

Gain step-by-step acceptance
As I have mentioned, the sales close should not be a single momentous occasion, but is rather a step-by-step accumulation of individually accepted elements, so that the difference between the sum of the points agreed and the decision as a whole is relatively small. By breaking down the proposition into its constituent parts the process of presentation and acceptance becomes much easier.

The buyer may find the decision of whether or not to install a computer extremely demanding. What he will find less arduous is whether or not to embark on a 'needs analysis' survey, agree upon the possible areas of application, decide upon the type of configuration, acknowledge an appropriate price, accept a delivery forecast, and so on. Once these affirmative factors are established the effort involved in making a final decision will appear to be relatively small.

Consider the benefits of a trial run
The trial order initiated by the salesman, as opposed to the 'sop' that might be offered by the sympathetic buyer, can often be an effective device for gaining commitment. It is an acceptable form of 'inertia selling', where the salesman is able to exploit the comforts of the status quo as a preferable alternative to outright rejection.

In other words, once the product is with the buyer, providing it lives up to its promises, there is more effort involved in sending it back than in keeping it. This is particularly true of products such as office equipment and domestic appliances. In the case of industrial consumables, like raw materials and components, it would not be logical for the buyer to order any product without first establishing its suitability by trial or demonstration. In such cases the offer of a trial is also a good test of whether or not the buyer is seriously considering the product. However, one serious error of judgement I have witnessed on several occasions, not as a salesman but as a buyer, is the supply of trial equipment for a fixed period where the salesman delivers the product and is not seen again until the trial period is over. On his return he has no real knowledge of whether the equipment has been used or not, and if it has, whether the trials were appropriate. I recall one conversation to the effect:

'We'd better use that typewriter today, the salesman's coming to collect it this afternoon. We don't want him to know we haven't touched it!'

If working trials are to be used as the means for securing an order, it is essential that the validity of the trial is ratified by regular inspections throughout the trial period. This need not necessarily involve only the salesman. Visits by technical or maintenance personnel are likely to fulfil the role perhaps with greater effect. Certainly, the greater proportion of clients who have experienced a successful working trial are simply waiting for the salesman to ask for the order.

Assume a favourable conclusion
I have mentioned the need for taking a positive stance within the sales negotiation, particularly as far as the close is concerned. 'Assuming the order', as a specific closing technique, will be dealt with later. One aspect I would like to touch upon is that of the salesman's attitude towards the close.

To all intents and purposes the salesman's attitude is reflected in the language he uses. Words like 'if', 'maybe', and 'perhaps', imply doubt and uncertainty, whereas 'when' radiates confidence and infers an established, secure relationship. It is much easier for the buyer to say 'yes' when it is made apparent by the salesman's behaviour that it is an apt and reasonable thing to do. Consider the buyer's reaction to the following statements:

'If you try our product. . .'

'Maybe you could go ahead. . .'

'Perhaps we can work together. . .'

They are so tentative that it is an effort to react positively to them. The more instinctive reaction is to be equally negative and think in terms of 'maybe', 'sometime', 'never'. Whereas these same comments sound so much more confident:

'When you try our product. . .'

145

'When you go ahead. . .'

'When we are working together. . .'

Clearly, the manner in which such statements are made is very important, as any suggestion of arrogance or over-assumption can have a worse effect than a negative attitude.

Consider some other words that have positive or negative overtones. 'Could', 'should', 'would', 'might', and 'possibly', are hardly designed to inspire confidence or imply commitment. On the other hand, nothing is more positive than 'will':

'You will enjoy using this product. . .'

'This system will significantly reduce your overdue accounts. . .'

'It will be good working with you. . .'

Talk futures

It is often beneficial to give the buyer relief from the pressure of deciding whether or not to buy by broadening the view to those actions that will come about once a decision has been made to proceed.

'Which application will you want to install first?'

'These should fit in very well with your existing range.'

'It will be a good idea to make deliveries over the next three months rather than taking up warehouse space with one consignment.'

'Our maintenance engineer will install the equipment and also make a mutually convenient schedule for preventive maintenance.'

Again, this is related to 'Assuming the order' which will be dealt with in the 'Closing methods' section. A positive attitude to the sales close cannot be stressed enough. The psychology of leading the client's thoughts towards an affirmative conclusion by anticipating the implications of saying 'yes' is an extremely effective device for putting the buyer into a positive frame of mind. This is particularly true of selling capital goods and high value equipment.

Be prepared to close early

Any formalities related to the structure of the sales call are usually created by the salesman. The buyer is much less hidebound by considerations of when is the right or wrong time to buy, or to be asked to purchase. He may well decide quite early in the proceedings, long before the salesman has concluded his presentation—possibly even before he arrived—that he wishes to buy. If this is the case, the chances are that his wishes will be transmitted by one form of buying signal or another. Such an opportunity to close must never be missed, for it may not be the last chance, but it may well be the best.

Don't take 'no' for an answer

'No' is not necessarily irrevocable. Very often it affects only one aspect of the sales proposition rather than all of it. Even a negative response to a 'full' close is not necessarily the final word, for new factors may be introduced that put an entirely different complexion on the matter. In other words, don't accept the word 'no' until it has been completely qualified. Sometimes the salesman may misjudge the situation, and attempt to close the sale on the strength of features that the buyer sees as being insufficient to justify making a purchase. As a result he says 'No'. What else can he say? Yet that doesn't mean the door is closed to further considerations, it merely means that the appropriate reasons for buying have yet to be presented. This must be a sign for the salesman to review the situation rapidly, and either bring into effect any powerful new selling points, or discover if those feature benefits he thought to be most significant are truly pertinent, and, if so, whether they have been clearly understood by the buyer. There is only one way to find out—ask!

Alternatively, the buyer's 'No' may really be total and irrevocable. If this should be the case, find out why. But be sure to do so in such a way as not to question the buyer's judgement, but rather the applicability of the product, or, preferably, the quality of the sales presentation. To ask this will not only induce the buyer's patronage, but also help to explain past failures and how to avoid them in the future.

Look out for key issues

The chances of closing the sale on a single major issue do not present themselves too often, particularly with high value products. And when they do, 'putting all your eggs in one basket' is a considerable risk. Yet, if this approach is used in the right circumstances, it can be very effective. The essential qualification is that the salesman is completely convinced that the buyer has a specific requirement that is in urgent need of fulfilment. If such a 'hot button' can be clearly identified it is wise to clear all other considerations from the negotiations and concentrate on the major issue, as any other points of the salesman's product, no matter how attractive, will only serve to 'clutter' the main issue. For instance, a business systems salesman might call upon the general manager of a manufacturing company to assess the various areas in which electronic data processing techniques could improve operational efficiency. Once he has identified the areas of need he plans to highlight the relevant features of his product. However, quite early in the interview the client tells him that he is pressed for time, due to serious manufacturing problems. It transpires that this is due to component shortages on the production line through an inadequate stock control system. As a result, production levels are low and delivery dates are regularly broken.

The salesman had planned to discuss accounting, design, and financial management applications, as well as computer aided manufacture. However, he identifies what he believes to be a key issue—stock control, integrated with production scheduling:

'Stock control must be a major headache for you.'

'It certainly is.'

'Would you say that these same problems also relate to production?'

'Not really. We can schedule the manufacturing plant okay, it's holding up production for stock shortages or holding back production for shortages that don't exist that is costing us money. The men on the shopfloor aren't too happy either; they're on piece-work so it's costing *them* money too!'

'I see. So what it gets down to is a need for an accurate, flexible, and fast responding stock control system that is aways right up-to-date and can integrate with your production scheduling!'

'Yes, if there was such a thing.'

'If there was I guess you would want to install one right away, assuming the price was significantly less than the current cost of lost production?'

'That's true, but I have to deal in realities, and the most profound truth of the moment is that my production line has ground to a halt while we send a truck to Birmingham to collect half a dozen locking pins!'

'Look, if I can take you to a manufacturing company much the same as your own where we have a computer system fully operational, that not only gives completely accurate control over all stock issues and receipts, but also re-orders all commodities automatically according to manufacturing demands, will you authorize me to proceed with a feasibility study into your needs with a view to installing such a system for you—assuming, of course, we can justify the cost involved and identify the benefits that will transpire for your customers, workers, management, and, not least, yourself?'

The answer is likely to be a qualified, rather than an absolute, 'yes'. But, even if the answer is 'no' the opportunity still remains to find out the reason why, and possibly to discuss other applications, though granted, a degree of fluency may be lost. I believe it's worth the risk! If a positive need for buying is demonstrated it should be 'grabbed with both hands', whatever stage of the proceedings it comes to light.

Keep the initiative

The salesman cannot afford a passive attitude. Whether the chances of a successful close are looking positive or negative it is extremely unwise to lose control of the selling process. Once the responsibility for action is left to the buyer it is almost certain that the sense of urgency will diminish.

This is particularly true when the buyer decides that he cannot make a decision without reference to other persons or departments. Firstly, the salesman needs to establish whether this is valid consultation or subterfuge. If the latter, he must press for positive action from the buyer. If the former, he must avoid all attempts to put him into 'limbo' by excluding him from any such discussions, for the result must be at least a partial loss of his control over the sales negotiation. There are several actions that can be taken to maintain a strong influence over such a situation. The obvious course is for the salesman to convince the buyer that there are benefits to be gained from the salesman's participation. There are normally a variety of justifications available—direct response to demands for additional information, further demonstrations, provision of technical literature, sample products, etc. The offer of a special presentation on the sales proposal is sometimes well received. Whatever the course, the salesman's objective must be to maintain control of the negotiations. 'Closing by proxy' does not work!

For much the same reasons, follow-up actions must not be left to the buyer. Promises to '. . . let you know after I have had time to review the matter' should be politely declined, and the reasons why discovered. If a sales call is concluded with the onus of action upon the buyer, it is still essential for the salesman to maintain control by agreeing a time or date when he will gather whatever information has been promised.

Even if the order is lost, it is still important for the salesman to maintain the initiative.

'I'm very disappointed that your decision has not been in our favour, but I'm convinced there's considerable benefit to be gained from our working together. I'll call and see you in a few weeks' time to see how you are getting along. What's the best day of the week for you, Thursday or Friday?'

Don't extend the call

In consumer goods selling, the best time for closing is usually during the initial call, for that is the time when interest and desire is likely to be at its highest. The situation is different with high-value goods and services, as it is usually necessary to study the requirement in detail, demonstrate the product, configure an appropriate system, etc., before the client has sufficient information to make a decision.

However, many sales calls and periods of negotiation are unnecessarily extended. This not only results in wasted selling time but also other consequences that can prove to be very costly indeed. Sometimes the call is unduly extended because the salesman lacks confidence to go for the close, and hopes instead that the buyer will interrupt him with an order. This is not only a vain hope, but, more to the point, once the buyer has all the information he needs, the chances of a successful outcome begin to decline at an ever increasing rate. As I mentioned earlier in this chapter (see 'Timing'), there is a great risk if the salesman unnecessarily extends an interview beyond the moment when he has gained the order. It is certainly easier to talk oneself out of an order than into one.

Check for unanswered objections

A buyer may hesitate about making a final decision for various reasons: he may need authority from elsewhere in his organization; he may consider that a particular aspect of the proposition is unsatisfactory or even unacceptable. Alternatively, he may not even know the reason himself. The fact remains that the salesman has come to an obstacle that needs to be indentified, before it can be removed. There is only one way to identify the reason—ask! Invite the buyer to reveal any outstanding objections preventing him from making a positive decision, and consider his answer most carefully. Is it a subterfuge? If so, is it an attempt to hide a negative decision that has already been made, or is it a cover for some other less-reasonable objection? Again, the salesman must ask, and direct the conversation towards pinpointing the truth.

'I see. And what considerations other than this one are also affecting your conclusions?'

Valid uncertainties need to be handled with care. If the buyer insists on referring to third parties, he has clearly not been properly motivated by the salesman, has insufficient confidence in the proposition as a whole, or may not even be the actual decision-maker. The appropriate questions need to be asked.

If the remaining objection is specific, then it has to be faced and overcome. Very often it will be the result of a failure on the salesman's part to have adequately dealt with the problem earlier in the sales negotiation. This demands, not so much a reiteration of previous statements, but more a different approach to the same areas.

The least acceptable form of outstanding objection is where the potential buyer confesses that he is not sure why he is unable to decide. This implies failure on the salesman's part to convince and motivate, perhaps because of a weak sales presentation, or not asking for the order convincingly enough. That is a bad situation, but what would be worse is not to be aware of such a shortfall at all. If the buyer is not invited to declare any unanswered objections, the cause of failure will virtually remain unknown.

'What doubts or uncertainties are likely to prevent you from making a positive decision?'

Avoid the multi-person close
It is wise to avoid a closing situation that involves more than one buyer. Once there are several people involved in the final decision, conflict and indecisiveness are immediately increased. From the salesman's point of view, it is much easier to tune into the motivations of one individual and keep his attention, than to achieve the same control over a group. On the buyer's side there is always a risk of conflict in personality, politics, opinion, etc., that makes it difficult to even agree on what is actually required.

Cut your losses
There are times when it becomes clear that an opportunity to close the sale does not exist. Yet, on such occasions there is often an inclination to struggle on to the bitter end as if the sales presentation were a theatrical performance, where walking out in the interval is too impolite and embarrassing to contemplate, to say nothing of the implications of personal failure.

If the build-up to the close reveals completely justifiable reasons why the buyer should not proceed, then there is every reason for curtailing the proceedings there and then. Time is precious for buyer and salesman alike. So, leave with dignity and seek more fruitful pastures elsewhere. This will surely earn the respect of the buyer—and your sales manager too!

Closing methods
The close is an exciting moment, and the justification of all the effort that has gone before. Both trainee and established professional always feel immense satisfaction and relief when the buyer says 'yes', and always that pang of disappointment and regret when he says 'no'. Whatever the buyer's reaction, the salesman must not be thrown. He should maintain a calm exterior that suggests success is an everyday event, and failure such a rarity as to be unworthy of negative reaction.

There are many well-tried closing techniques and no salesperson can sell effectively without knowledge of all of them. Clearly, some techniques are more relevant to particular types of selling than others. Those which are used regularly in direct selling to the general public are usually less appropriate in a capital goods environment. However, it is reasonable to say that in any area of selling every established closing technique will be called upon at some time. It is therefore essential to become familiar with them all and absolutely fluent in those most suited to one's own personality, marketplace, and product. This is not something that can be learned 'parrot fashion', for, whatever the chosen technique, it is important to adapt it freely to fit the style of the individual.

The application of closing techniques is very much controlled by circumstances. Very often the appropriate one is chosen and is effective. On other occasions a combination of techniques may be used successfully. There again, the initial choice may fail and alternatives used until success has been achieved. There are no firm rules about which, when, and how, closing techniques should be put into effect.

No list of closing methods can be complete. There are always those which are unique to companies or individuals, and those which are a variation on what might be termed 'classic' methods. The list in the following section, includes those I have come across, and contains most of the 'bread and butter', closing methods. Certainly, it represents a substantial basis on which to build a personal portfolio of closing tactics and techniques.

Tactics and techniques: a summary

I think it is important to divide the commonly-accepted closing methods into two categories: tactics and techniques. For instance, the 'continuing affirmation' method is often categorized as a closing technique. In reality its purpose is to condition the attitude of the buyer and the spirit of the negotiations. It is a way to, rather than a means of, closing.

Tactics
Continuing affirmation.
Assuming the order.
Setting up barriers.

Techniques
Reducing the options
The 'either/or' close.
Closing on a minor issue.
Offering special inducements.
Converting an objection.
Exploiting scarcity.
Using impending events.
Summarization.
The 'balance sheet' method.
Using impending events.
Assessing the cost of delay.
Stressing emotional needs.
Altering the proposition.

Continuing affirmation

The strategy of this method is to encourage the buyer to recurrently answer 'yes' within a totally positive sales environment created by the salesman. This is designed to develop a positive frame of mind on the part of the buyer, so that by 'force of habit' he ultimately finds conflict in considering the possibility of a 'no', that is, if he is agreeable to the various elements of the proposition, is it not a contradiction to reject the whole? The final 'yes' should be seen as but one more favourable decision among many made during the course of the sales negotiation. The process of continuing affirmation is a conditioning device rather than a specific closing method.

The statements made by the salesman must establish a positive atmosphere for negotiation, and his questions must be geared for a positive response. This is best achieved by starting the 'yes, yes, yes' process (as it is sometimes called!) with minor questions which demand little commitment from the buyer. The number of positive answers can be increased by re-phrasing and repeating of points already agreed by the buyer. For example:

'You did say you would prefer the compound in glass as opposed to plastic containers, didn't you?'

As the buyer had already said he preferred glass, this can only result in another 'yes' to add to the positive side of the scales.

Most questions can be phrased to emphasize their positive aspects. For example:

'How about an immediate delivery of 20 tons?'

The risk of 'No, thank you' is quite apparent here, whereas the following qualifies and provides justification for saying 'yes':

'An immediate delivery of 20 tons would not only cover all your winter needs, but also protect you from any supply difficulties or price increases during the coming months.'

In a more extreme example, when the sales atmosphere is negative:

'Do you agree?'

'No.'

Such an emphatic response makes it difficult to proceed any further, whereas:

'Am I right in thinking you are unlikely to agree to the proposition as it stands?'

'Yes.'

not only gains an affirmative response but also leaves the salesman with the possible opportunity of introducing alternatives.

Consider the kind of dialogue one might expect within a situation of continuing affirmation:

'I am sure we both agree that the protection of life is a very important consideration.'

'Yes.'

'I imagine the local fire department regulations will have to be adhered to?'

'Yes.'

'This must demand completely reliable and relevant equipment?'

'Yes.'

'I believe you said your new offices will require ten water-based and two carbon dioxide extinguishers?' (Repeat of buyer's previous statement!)

'Yes'.

'Which means you will need to have them installed before your staff move in at the end of the month?'

'Yes.'

'Well, we have already agreed the benefits that the installation of our equipment will bring to your company. May I write out the order for the 12 extinguishers now?'

With a bit of luck, the buyer will continue to say 'yes', but this conditioning process is primarily intended to establish attitudes, as opposed to demanding commitment. In this example the actual 'technique' was ultimately the basic process of 'asking for the order'. The process of continuing affirmation is designed to build up a much stronger psychological value for the sum of the individual elements than could be claimed for the whole, had no commitment been gained before the final request for the order.

Assuming the order

While one can assume nothing in selling, it is nonetheless advantageous for the salesman to adopt an extremely positive stance, implying that the mutual benefits of the sales proposition, and the ease of relationship between buyer and seller, are such that doing business together is a pleasing inevitability. It is, in essence, a harnessing of the power of positive suggestion, as a vehicle for enhancing the confidence of both parties concerned.

Another aspect of assuming the order is that it transfers the onus of decision from the effort of deciding to buy to the effort of deciding not to buy. This exploits the natural inertia of the buyer.

There is, however, considerable risk of doing more harm than good by assuming an order. It is a method that must be applied with extreme sensitivity without the slightest hint of arrogance or complacency. It is not a blatant 'When we get the business. . .!' approach, but rather 'I am assuming you will give me the order, because you have made no reaction to my positive statements that leads me to believe otherwise.'

Assuming the order has two functions. Firstly, it is an attitude of mind designed to create a positive selling atmosphere. Secondly, it can be a form of contrived 'closing by default'. In other words, the salesman is not passively having the order 'thrust down his throat'. He is, instead, evolving a situation where asking for the order is an unnecessary effort as the matter is presumed to be already settled. This device is applicable to any selling situation, from the 'one call close' to the extended selling cycle of capital equipment.

The importance of a positive stance throughout the sales negotiation cannot be overstressed, as the salesman who appears to be unsure or even negative about his product, his company, or even himself, has usually forfeited the business early on in the negotiations.

Assuming the order is but a modification of emphasis that implies agreement. Strong, assumptive words—'will' and 'when', in particular—are used:

'We will give your job absolute priority when we get started.'

'I understand you close early on Wednesdays, so I'll arrange delivery for Tuesday.'

'I know our technical people will enjoy working with you.'

'To whom shall I send the invoice?'

'Let's aim for the first "live run" by the end of April.'

'I think it will be best to deliver at your present consumption rate of 100 units per month.'

'Will two dozen be sufficient'.

'Will you arrange the shipping, or shall I deal with it?'

'This will solve a lot of your problems once it is installed.'

'When can you be ready for the first consignment?'

'I will keep in contact even when the system is up and running.'

These are not leading, aggressive statements, but comments designed to demonstrate the salesman's enthusiasm to work with the potential user, and also to confirm with the buyer what has already been proposed.

Actions can be taken to develop the effects of this technique into a closing device, usually by some kind of physical move. There are many possibilities:

Start to wrap the goods.

Ask to use the buyer's telephone to confirm delivery or availability.

Hand over the keys to the buyer.

Take out the order pad, write out the anticipated requirement and hand it to the buyer. 'There you are Mr Customer. Do I have your requirement correct?'

But, as I have said before, such bold actions demand extreme sensitivity, for it is unwise blindly to assume anything in selling. Do not assume the client understands, accepts, refutes, or believes anything. Above all, don't assume you have the order until the invoice has been paid!

Setting up barriers

Very often the salesman finds a significant proportion of buyers giving the same reason for not buying—the price may be higher than the competition's; certain features may not be available; delivery may be extended; etc. In other cases the situation may be quite the opposite—the price may be particularly low; special features may be unique to this product; delivery may be particularly fast; etc. In such cases the creation of artificial barriers can offset objections that may be expected at the close, and increase the impact of significant benefits and give flight to indecisiveness.

When a lack of funds is suspected, the buyer's position can be tested early in the proceedings:

'It's a pity that only those companies able to invest over £25 000 can enjoy the benefits of our system. Do you envisage your company spending that kind of money on the right solution?'

If the product is more expensive than competitive alternatives:

'Our new design incorporates a unique diagnostic facility for input errors. The ability to identify mistakes before they can corrupt production would be very beneficial to your plant wouldn't it? Yet the cost above competitive products is a mere fragment of the potential savings.'

In the first case, the buyer has the budget barrier to overcome. Either he has the funds, or he hasn't, and knowing one way or the other will ultimately save a lot of time. In the second case, the barrier is a matter of whether or not special facilities can offset extra cost. It's better to know early on than find out at the close.

Then we have the reverse situation, where the salesman knows he has an unquestionable advantage and wishes to increase its impact to the full by helping the buyer to put up an artificial barrier which he knows he can very easily overcome:

'You have a lot of experience of this kind of product. What is the best price you would expect to get at the present time?'

When a significantly higher price is quoted (as it should be if the salesman has his facts right!), the salesman's announcement will not only have increased impact but also have an established and indisputable selling advantage.

Artificial barriers can also be created for special situations. The committed procrastinator may be inclined to dither less if presented with an appropriate barrier early in the proceedings.

'This brief opportunity to double the usual profit margin is quite unique. I know you will wish to act quickly and decisively in order to take fullest advantage of this.'

Such a statement is unlikely to bring about a character transformation, but it creates barriers, which, if left intact by the buyer, will establish a stigma he would prefer to be without.

Another use of artificial barriers is to avoid a disadvantage assumed by the buyer until the very close. It is a barrier created by the buyer's own assumption—'As this particular aspect of the product is extremely significant, the fact that the salesman has failed to mention it must imply a disadvantage!' 'No other product has this particular facility that I need, so why should this one be any different?'

'I guess it would be great to have a machine which automatically diagnosed errors at the input stage and prevented the serious hold-ups in production.'

'Yes, it really would.'

'Well. . .'

The scene is now set for positive closing action!

Then, as in the following example, the removal of an artificial barrier can be integrated with a positive closing device:

'Five hundred units is our minimum order quantity. Will that be sufficient?'

'I don't see how we can handle that many.'

'Tell you what I'll do. If I can use your telephone I will see if I can split the order into two equal batches, or, alternatively, reduce the normal minimum to 400 units. Which would you prefer?'

Artificial barriers may be used to good effect throughout the sales negotiation, but can be particularly effective in the context of the close.

Reducing the options

Making choices is an everyday event for most people. It may be a gross generalization, but in my experience, setting aside individual human characteristics, difficulty to choose is usually directly related to the number of choices available. Shopping in a supermarket can be a long and perplexing affair. There are so many choices to consider—size, brand, price, flavour. . . Life would be so much easier if someone of experience and good taste was available to recommend a few items and prompt a choice from these. The pressure would be off.

The reduction of options encourages the selection process and induces involvement, perhaps even feelings of commitment. Preferences are revealed which ultimately pin-point the product(s) on which the close is to be concentrated. Too much choice impairs the power of selection introducing fear and insecurity into the selling process at the worst possible time, as fear of making the wrong choice can easily lead to making no choice at all—'Better to avoid a decision than to do the wrong thing and lose face!'

It is often a good selling strategy to deliberately withhold products, options, or features from the selection process. It should be easier for the salesman than the buyer to qualify the relevance of a product to a particular requirement. Therefore, there is little point in confusing the issue by including those items that, after perhaps lengthy deliberation, will inevitably be rejected by the buyer. Strict relevance to need is, in effect, the first phase of reducing the options. But this should not be left to the mercy of the buyer's whims. The salesman's task is to overlay the proceedings with objectivity and commitment. Having evaluated the situation and presented what the buyer assumes to be the full scope of choice, the objective is to further reduce the options by the use of well-directed questions that substantiate needs and preferences.

'Do you prefer plain or coloured?'

'Do you expect light or heavy usage?'

'Do you require metric or imperial?'

'Is your requirement for indoor or outdoor use?'

'Is it to be used for business or pleasure?'

The effect of such questions is to generate answers that serve to remove the options and move the buyer towards the most suitable item.

Narrowing the options can apply to almost any aspect of selling. While it is a process that normally precedes the close and relates to considerations such as, which product feature, price, quantity, style, etc., it can also apply to other situations where an attempt is being made to gain commitment.

'Which will be the best day to call—Wednesday or Thursday?'

'Will you say "yes" now, or back at my place?'

Clearly, the primary objective is to unclutter the decision-making process, by reducing the available options to the lowest possible number that is greater than one—ideally two. To reduce the choice to one can be dangerous, for the psychological emphasis is switched from 'which?' to 'yes' or 'no'. In effect, 'which?' implies 'yes', whichever way the buyer chooses. To reduce the choice down to one is a form of dictate that many buyers will find unacceptable. It is as if no choice has been offered and seems to imply the exclusion of a basic entitlement.

The 'either/or' close
Reducing the scope of selection to two possibilities also enables the salesman to use a simple either/or close:

'Both will do the job efficiently. Which design do you prefer?'

'Your competitors tend to use this one, but either will be completely effective. Which do you think is the most appropriate?'

'This one will be the most economical but the power is inferior to that one. Which is more important to you, economy or acceleration?'

'Will you take the large one, or two small ones?'

'They both suit you, but the red one seems to match your eyes better!'

I recall a selling story that embraces both the either/or close and 'closing on a minor issue' (see following Section), as well as the tactic of assuming the order. Apparently the owner of a transport cafe inadvertently and rather drastically over ordered on his supply of sausages. He was not around when the delivery man came, and so found himself up to the gunnels with 'bangers'. The following day was Sunday and the cafe was closed for business. He didn't have refrigerator space either, so he had a real problem on

159

his hands. Soon after the delivery was made a salesman called in for breakfast, and by way of passing conversation the owner mentioned his dilemma. The salesman was both sympathetic and constructive and as he left suggested a way to solve the problem. Soon after, the first of the day's lorry drivers arrived and ordered the traditional English breakfast:

'Bacon and egg please.'

'Certainly sir. Would you prefer one sausage or two?'

'Oh! Well! One will be enough thank you!'

By lunchtime he had sold out. As far as I know, he is still using that same closing technique to this day!

Reducing the options in tandem with the either/or close not only represents a very powerful closing mechanism, but—let's face it—more often than not renders the buyer a time-saving service that is greatly appreciated.

Closing on a minor issue

Decision-making is a very difficult process for many people, particularly as far as buying is concerned. The higher the product value, the greater the dilemma. Similarly, some salespeople, perhaps due to some form of deep-rooted sympathy, find themselves increasingly reluctant to ask the prospect to make a buying decision as the value of the product increases. They may have no hesitation in asking for a decision about the purchase of a typewriter, but are somehow unable to apply the same approach to, say, the purchase of a house or a tractor.

Any purchase implies commitment, and it is certainly easier to make a small decision than a large one. In other words, it is easier to select the design of a house than it is to actually make the decision to buy one. Deciding upon the method of payment certainly involves less psychological pressure than agreeing to proceed with the purchase. This reality can be used most effectively for helping the buyer to reach a positive conclusion. Every product has its minor considerations and side issues—delivery, type, features, colour, quantities, method of payment, etc. By using the tactic of assumption, it is relatively simple to direct the mind of the buyer away from the decision of whether or not to buy towards the relatively less demanding issues of peripheral considerations—a swing of emphasis away from 'if' towards 'which?'

'Will five tons be sufficient, or would you prefer three tons now and the balance in four weeks' time?'

'Would you prefer to pay cash or shall I charge it?'

'Do you want it with or without the all-weather feature?'

'Do you want it with or without the communications inter-face?'

Closing on a minor issue is an approach that most buyers find completely acceptable for it has the effect of relieving them from the pressure of saying 'yes' or 'no' to a major issue. It is also a technique that is relevant to all types of selling, but particularly popular among salespeople who are involved with high-value products. The either/or close and the tactic of assuming the order are integral parts of this particular method.

Offering special inducements
Closing the sale by means of offering a transient inducement is a method one would normally expect of a company-wide promotion of consumer products. While it has become almost a way of life within the retail environment, it is unlikely to be encountered with products outside the realms of fast-moving consumer goods. (Having said that, I have certainly experienced this kind of close with products such as typewriters and photocopiers.)

Special inducements are a positive means of encouragement to buy now by offering savings or special rewards that will be unobtainable later. When I was selling in the soaps and detergents industry, my company's selling methods were substantially devoted to this approach. Every month one item from the product range would be subject to a special deal. A number of free-of-charge cases would be given if the right quantity was ordered, or buyers could qualify for certain material rewards by booking the appropriate amount. I'm sure this approach is no longer in use, but it did create a very interesting phenomenon. Because sales calls were on a four-weekly basis, and every offer strictly terminated at the end of each cycle, the buyers quickly adjusted to the routine of making an immediate decision by the opening statement 'What's the special offer this month?' Salesmen in my company seldom had the need to prod their clients into making an immediate decision.

The use of a special inducement is not an attempt to deceive, it is a trade-off against the buyer's commitment to make an immediate decision. It is also a device for giving potency to the close; a positive 'hook' for gaining the buyer's attention and limiting the scope of indecision.

'I know you would not normally require further supplies for a few weeks yet, but if I can take your order now you will qualify for a ten per cent discount on the entire order.'

The inference is that failure to order now will mean the irrecoverable loss of savings.

161

'This special order closes on Saturday. If you can give me the go-ahead now you will receive ten free cases for every hundred you order.'

'The offer actually closed yesterday, but if I can use your telephone I can talk to my head office and have them make a special exception in your case, provided I have your order now.'

For the right kind of product the special inducement can be a powerful device for directing the buyer towards a more decisive frame of mind where he feels obliged to take positive action.

Sometimes the act of closing on a special inducement is but a repeat of a feature/benefit mentioned earlier in the proceedings. This is nothing to worry about. People seldom absorb everything that is said to them in a presentation, and even if they have heard it before, the repeated offer of a special concession is unlikely to cause offence. However, one situation must be avoided at all costs, and that is the oversight or deliberate act of offering the same deal to a buyer on more than one occasion, for it could easily give the impression that he was misled on the previous occasion. With some products it is possible to call back on substantial buyers who ordered at the beginning of the offer period to see if they will take more before the offer finally closes. But this is a situation which is not available to most salespeople.

As I suggested earlier, the special inducement is not a technique that easily lends itself to products outside of the large scale promotions of the consumer products market. The use of financial incentives for capital items and other high-value purchases can have several undesirable implications:

What will be the effect on other clients who have paid the full price if this situation is revealed to them?

Could this so-called incentive be construed as bribery?

The client who starts out his business relationship with a special deal may well expect the same treatment ever after!

Converting an objection

As I have already mentioned, one of the very best times to ask for the order is immediately after successfully overcoming a significant sales objection. Indeed, as a rule of practice, the salesman should ask for the order every time such a situation occurs, for in doing so he has probably removed the obstacle that is barring the way to closing the sale. Of course, there is always the possibility of further barriers, but in most cases there is seldom more than one significant objection.

Cost related sales objections are the most common of all. Sometimes they question not so much the price, as the relative value for money:

'Your machine is too expensive!'

'Yes, it does cost more than the other devices you are considering, but it has twice the output of the fastest competitive equipment and is much more economical in its use of raw materials. This machine will increase your production, yet reduce your running costs considerably—as you will see for yourself if you give me your approval to proceed with your order now.'

In other circumstances the sales objection may relate to the more basic question of whether or not the buyer can afford the offer:

'I can't afford it!'

'Okay. If I can persuade my manager to reduce the price by five per cent, will you place the order with me now?'

You will notice in this example that the offer to reduce the price is subject to a prior commitment on the buyer's part to proceed with the order if the reduction is given. It is essential to gain a commitment to buy before actually agreeing a price reduction, for if this is not done many buyers will regard the offer as an interim measure and use it to gain even more concessions before agreeing to place the order.

Using an apparent concession to overcome a final sales objection is not limited to price. Very often the buyer's resistance may be due to considerations such as delivery, performance, appearance, etc.:

'Your delivery is too long to satisfy our requirements.'

'If I can make arrangements to meet your delivery needs, will you give me the order now?'

Two aspects of this particular example are worthy of note. Firstly, it shows how the use of the close can make the sales rebuttal more emphatic and puts the onus of decision firmly upon the buyer. Secondly, it highlights—as did the previous example—a very useful form of phrase for use in the process of converting an objection into an order—'If I can . . . will you give me the order now?'

'If I can get it in the colour you require. . .?'

'If I can arrange to provide the special adaptor you require. . .?'

'If I can arrange separate deliveries to each of your branches. . .?'

'. . . will you give me the order now?'

Some salespeople make a practice of holding back their convincing rebuttal to a significant sales objection, so that they can use it as a powerful closing device at the right moment. I have never used this approach myself, but it clearly has some merit provided it is clearly established that it is the only meaningful question yet to be answered:

> 'It appears you are completely happy with every aspect of my proposition other than your requirement for printing this range of mathematical symbols.'

If the answer is 'no' then there is obviously still a need to identify other objections. If the reply is 'yes' then the salesman is safe to proceed with the close:

> 'Then can I assume you will give me the order if I can provide a daisy-wheel that contains all the mathematical characters you have listed?'

If the answer is 'no' there is still qualification to be done. If the reply is 'yes' then the sale is already made, assuming the requirement can be completely satisfied.

Exploiting scarcity

It is the nature of people to be loath to miss an opportunity or be excluded from something that they consider attractive. It is, perhaps, a fear of being missed out—to want what others want—'We only want it 'cause we haven't got it', goes the old song. Certainly many people appear to get a 'buzz' out of obtaining things when, or so that, others can't get it. It is the appeal of the 'limited edition'; the challenge of the 'last chance' on the assumption that freedom of choice will not be available later. This is a reality that can work to the benefit of the salesman when his products are in short supply, or impending change is likely to increase the price or reduce availability. It provides the means for prompting decisive action by using the attraction, or even threat, of short-lived opportunity.

> 'I only have two left and expect to sell them both today.'

> 'This product will revert to the normal price tomorrow.'

> 'This promotion has gone so well that we are unlikely to have sufficient stocks to satisfy the demands of all our clients.'

> 'We can only appoint one agent for this region, and I would like to give you the opportunity before I visit any of your competitors.'

Clearly, this type of close depends very much upon the type of product and the kind of situation in which the sale is being conducted. It is not usually applicable to fast-moving consumer goods except special promotions and major price increases. This is due to the continuity of buying and the usual multiplicity of suppliers that provide the buyer with alternatives. However, this type of close must be based on completely truthful circumstances and the salesman's proposition must be presented with sincerity and sensitivity. Any deception or contrivance is usually apparent to any intelligent buyer, and the result can only be a loss of orders and personal credibility.

All products get into short supply from time to time and prices increase or fluctuate. If such circumstances coincide with healthy demand it is up to the salesman to keep his clients informed of the implications of ignoring the situation.

I can think of no phrase more likely to enhance the attractiveness of a product than: 'Sorry, you can't have that, it's already sold!'

Using impending events
This type of close is a near relative of the previous item, for it also uses the 'threat' of impending events to motivate the buyer into decisive action.

There are often forthcoming events which are likely to have a significant effect upon price and availability: increases in the cost of raw materials, labour, or taxation; impending strikes involving the workforce of either the buyer or the supplier; strikes at national level affecting transportation or communications; changes of design; surges in business activity; changes of government legislation. All of these, like the exploitation of scarcity, can be used most effectively to increase the volume of sales and motivate the indecisive buyer:

'Next week's rail strike could go on for some time, it might be a good idea to double the usual order on this occasion.'

'We are expecting a significant increase in the rate of tax on this item, so there is bound to be heavy public demand during the next few weeks. It makes sense to order the largest possible quantity now.'

'There is still a considerable demand for this model which will not be completely eroded by our new, but more costly, replacement product. Better order as many as you can now while supplies are still available.'

These should not be profound or significant declarations. They should be 'low key', passing comments made during the sales presentation, that 'prime' the buyer for the close and then may be reiterated should there be any uncertainty or sales resistance. Nothing makes the buyer more agitated than the prospect of a personal error, or force of circumstances contriving to put him out of essential stock. This is an understandable fear, that the salesman can resolve to the advantage of both the buyer and himself.

Summary

The sale of multi-faceted products such as complex machinery, scientific equipment, or technical services, always involves a broad array of considerations. The buyer cannot be expected to remember every feature presented to him during the course of the sales presentation, nor can he be expected to recall all of those aspects that are particularly relevant to his needs. Consequently, as the presentation draws towards its conclusion it is necessary for the salesman to summarize what has been said in order to emphasize, not only those features to which the buyer has reacted favourably, but also to restate any relevant objections in the context of the overriding benefits and advantages. This has the effect of focusing the process of evaluation by highlighting the key factors on which the ultimate decision will be based:

> 'We have agreed that this word-processor will halve the time normally taken to produce your tenders and will also reduce your staffing requirement. As you have seen for yourself, our unique printing process produces a much superior quality of impression than other machines in its class, which is surprising when you consider our extremely competitive price. Your requirement for special mathematical symbols can be satisfied by the use of interchangeable print-heads and your requirements for both immediate and future deliveries is well within our capability. I think that is a fair summary of the pertinent considerations.'

Obviously this process usually has the effect of generating questions that need to be answered and objections that need to be overcome. Once these have been resolved it is necessary to check the buyer's understanding of the proposition:

> 'I have described and demonstrated our product, and highlighted its benefits to your company. Is there any aspect of it that you are unsure about?'

If the reply is 'yes' then obviously the query has to be cleared. If the answer is 'no' then the natural reaction must be to ask for the order:

> 'Good. Then if you are quite clear about the implications of the proposition, would you like me to leave this machine with you, or would you prefer me to deliver one in the alternative colour tomorrow?'

Like any other type of close, the summary must be delivered in a relaxed, pleasant, and professional manner, free of any suggestion of pressure, excitement or desperation. It must be perceived by the buyer as a consolidation of his own considerations, rather than those of the salesman.

The 'balance sheet' method

This method of closing involves the creation of a simple statement of account. It is a declaration of the pros and cons of the decision-making process, well suited to industrial and commercial selling where there are usually many considerations to take into account.

Let us consider the final stages of the selling process with the assumption that the buyer's needs have been clearly identified and the pertinent feature/benefits established. If the salesman is dealing with a reasonably effective buyer, and if he has the presence of mind to ask, the chances are he will get the business. Of course, it is not always as easy as that. Very often the buyer, for many reasons, may find himself unable to make a firm decision one way or the other. Lack of information, too much information, complexity of product, external influences, personal insecurity, and so on, may all contribute to this. Such uncertainty could relate to one or more of the following areas:

1. Which is the most appropriate type of solution from any source?

2. Which, if any, of this salesman's products should I choose?

3. Should I choose this salesman's product, or a competitive alternative?

In each of these cases the listing of all the reasons for and against can help the buyer to gain a better perspective of the critical considerations. If he is not willing to participate in such an exercise, the chances are he is not as uncertain as he makes out, and is probably playing for time in order to gain some kind of advantage.

In the first case, a line down the middle of a piece of paper is used to separate the benefits and shortcomings of each type of available solution, including those from competitive sources. The salient features of each alternative are listed in the appropriate column according to whether or not they are suitable and desirable.

The buyer should be left to highlight the relevant advantages from other sources, and similarly to generate any disadvantages related to solutions proposed by the salesman. Clearly, the salesman should be better equipped than the buyer to generate the advantages of his own products and the disadvantages of others. Once this process is completed it is then a matter of summarizing the main considerations of the various solutions, side by side. This will not only provide the buyer with a good overview of the situation, but also, bearing in mind the concentration of the salesman's efforts, highlight the benefits of the salesman's solutions. An ideal moment for asking for the order! If this is not the case, then either the salesman has insufficient knowledge of his own product, or he is making the wrong proposition. Either way, he needs to consult his sales manager double quick, as everybody loses if the buyer is sold the wrong solution.

The second case is much easier to deal with—there is no competition involved, and the choice is limited simply to deciding whether or not to buy the salesman's product. Again, an account is drawn up, with the salesman identifying the benefits for the positive side and the buyer declaring the disadvantages for the other. If the salesman really knows his product, he should be able to fill his side with meaningful reasons for buying, whereas it would be most unusual if the buyer could think of more than one or two reasons against. With this clear imbalance in his favour, the salesman is then well placed to gain the buyer's acknowledgement that there are more reasons for accepting the proposition than rejecting it—a positive closing statement follows. It is worth bearing in mind that if there were any real reasons for not going ahead, the buyer would have no uncertainty in the first place. Again, the absence of an imbalance in the salesman's favour should sound a clear warning note.

In the third case, the same technique is invaluable, but it demands both a comprehensive knowledge of competitive products and absolute confidence that one's own product is at least equal to its competitors. Once again the exercise starts with the salesman listing the benefits and advantages of his products. Obviously the buyer will use the list as an *aide mémoire* for competitive features, and some benefits will be repeated in other products. No problem! These are merely self-cancelling benefits. The main objective is to highlight the **U**nique **S**elling **A**dvantages of one's own product. As this approach enables the buyer to identify them for himself it has much greater credibility than direct claims made by the salesman. Having established this position, the only remaining task is to ask for the order.

The 'balance sheet' method is unlikely to prove successful if it merely consists of a crude list inflicted upon the buyer. It must be a consultative document that is written in the language of the buyer. It must reflect a real understanding of the buyer's needs, and form a synopsis of what is going on in his mind—an aid to positive thinking. If the salesman can become involved in the buyer's thought process, he is much more likely to influence the decision towards his own product.

Assessing the cost of delay

It is often necessary to persuade the buyer to consider the implications of delay, in terms of gain and loss. Usually there is no gain at all, but much to be lost. With some products the loss is simply a matter of having to do without. For example, suspending the purchase of a motor car, stereo equipment, office furniture, etc., merely deprives the buyer of the pleasure of using the products. However, delay in the delivery of some products can have a much more significant effect, particularly within industry and commerce. Few buyers can afford to take the risk of failing to secure the direct or intangible savings gained by increasing efficiency—a more efficient lubricating fluid, a more durable plastic container, a better working environment, a more efficient security system, the computerization of a manual function or industrial process. The buyer may accept a nominal valuation of the anticipated savings, but even if he does not, he must accept the existence of continuing benefit, otherwise there would be no point in the negotiations. Whatever the real value of the product to the buyer, it cannot be enjoyed until the order is placed.

The value to the buyer of some products can be measured specifically: a machine that operates at twice the speed of existing equipment, a better price for the supply of a commodity already in use, a word-processor that reduces the number of staff required. All of these involve a return that can be defined in hard cash and declared as an indirect cost to the buyer if he should delay implementation:

'Our system will enable you to reduce your staffing requirements by three persons, whereas the cost of implementation is the equivalent of one person. This means that any delay will involve the loss of totally irrecoverable savings worth around £1000 per month. Surely this is sufficient justification for proceeding with our proposals right away?'

There is no fundamental difference between losing money and failing to make achievable savings. This is a fact that many buyers lose sight of, and to use it as a means for closing the sale is useful to both buyer and salesman alike.

Stressing emotional needs

Most purchases involve two stages of consideration. Firstly, there is the 'technical' stage, where the buyer decides which products are able to satisfy his requirements. Then comes the 'emotional' stage, where he selects from those that have passed the initial 'technical' test, the one that appeals to him most within prevailing circumstances. He may choose a particular colour, the one with an appealing but unnecessary gadget, one exactly the same as his main competitor, the one that will have most appeal to his wife, or the one the salesman made to appear the most attractive. Whatever the choice, it could be totally different in other circumstances.

It is most important for the salesman to identify these emotional overtones, particularly in a retail environment, for they very often contain the means for closing the sale. To do so he must appeal to the emotional implications of ownership, rather than the performance of the product, by using the basic words that imply satisfaction, pleasure, relaxation, prestige, security, etc.:

'You certainly won't need to worry about intruders once our security system is installed You must be looking forward to peace of mind.'

169

'This new car will really put you among the élite.'

People do not always buy the best, the strongest, the fastest, or the cheapest. There is a considerable tendency to buy whatever satisfies their emotional needs at the time. The salesman who loses sight of the fact that choice is often impulsive and irrational is operating under a severe handicap, for having the best product at the cheapest price on the fastest delivery does not guarantee sales success.

Altering the proposition
Some salespeople have more scope than others for modifying their product and terms of business, but in many circumstances a willingness to amend the proposition can be the difference between losing and winning the sale. Certainly it can be a useful device for directing the reluctant buyer into decisiveness.

The possibilities are unlimited—perhaps the modification of a component or specification, a willingness to post-date the invoice, the amendment of delivery arrangements, booking ahead to exploit forthcoming special promotions, an initial supply of related consumables free of charge, etc. Obviously, by modifying the proposition the salesman is likely to increase his chances of getting the order. In some circumstances he may also increase its value by giving a concession in exchange for one from the buyer:

'If you can give me the order for a complete container load I will throw in the dispensers free of charge!'

Products are usually offered on 'standard' terms, but a total absence of flexibility is a handicap few companies are prepared to accept. However, the salesman should observe the paramount rule of never allowing such alterations to exceed the formally agreed confines of his authority. Any deviations from this, or areas of doubt, must always be checked out with a direct manager before agreement is given to the buyer.

Ask for the order
It may sound rather obvious to mention the need for asking for the order, but it is like so many other aspects of life that we take for granted or completely overlook simply because they are so obvious and fundamental. We often assume events will happen without our initiation, simply because that is our conception of the way things ought to be. Our simple logic tells us that if there is a requirement, a desire to purchase, and the right product, a sale will result, without our becoming involved in unnecessary dialogue. This is a very naïve and dangerous assumption, for the business is never secured until the buyer acknowledges agreement. This is unlikely to

come in the form of an emphatic 'yes' to the question 'May I have the order?' The range of possible closing statements and positive responses is virtually unlimited, as this chapter has tried to show. Nevertheless, there must be a point in the sales negotiation when, either by direct request or by implication, the buyer is asked for his agreement and in turn gives it in whatever terms are most appropriate.

If there was to be a survey of buyers in order to discover the most common failure among salespeople, most prominent would be: *Failure to ask for the order*. Perhaps, as I mentioned at the beginning of this chapter, it may be due to fear of personal rejection, but I have a feeling that in many cases the salesman simply forgets! It is important to remember that whatever closing technique is being applied it must conclude with a request for the order, either stated or implied:

'May I send you ten boxes?'

'Shall I write out the order for your signature?'

'Is this the one you want me to supply?'

'Can I go ahead with the delivery arrangements?'

The real meaning of such statements is: 'Will you give me the order?' Without them the chances of sales success are virtually nil.

Having suggested that a blunt and direct 'Will you buy?' is seldom appropriate, there are times when the forthright approach can be beneficial. Direct questions usually get direct answers, and sometimes it is necessary to discover whether or not the buyer is really serious. On some occasions there is no better way of getting things out into the open than asking if the buyer is prepared to place an order. If the answer is 'no' then the obvious rejoinder is 'Why not?' This does at least point the way to any unstated 'objections', although it demands considerable sensitivity of approach.

Undoubtedly, the most important objective of asking for the order is to help the buyer make a decision. This is surely of considerable value to both sides of the negotiation. As I said before: 'If you don't ask, you don't get!'

After the close

Obtain written confirmation

Written confirmation of the order is essential in most sales negotiations. It ensures, absolutely, that the buyer knows what he has ordered and the salesman understands exactly what has to be delivered. It is also important that this formal acknowledgement is given at the very time the order is secured, for any delay gives the buyer time to change his mind. Many salespeople are reluctant to follow this discipline, and also actively avoid

171

discussing price and product details during and immediately after the 'close', fearing that the buyer might change his mind if he fully appreciates the implications of the transaction. This is an extremely dangerous and shortsighted attitude, for it is a form of mutual deception, if not by intent, certainly by default. There is always a next time and the salesman must always ensure that his return will be welcomed by behaving in a sensible, ethical, and thoroughly professional manner. There is no point in winning an order if it ultimately results in the loss of a customer. The conclusion of the sales negotiation must be free from misunderstandings and ambiguities, and the buyer must always receive exactly what he believes he has ordered.

Avoid post mortems

The formal acceptance of the sales propositions must absolutely terminate all further discussion on the decision-making process and the merits of the transaction. Under no circumstances should the salesman be drawn in to a post mortem on the wisdom of the decision, as once the buyer develops the slightest reservation about his actions, the chances of a completely satisfactory sale decline rapidly.

Show appreciation

It is most important to let the buyer know that his custom is appreciated. However, this must not be overdone, otherwise he may begin to suspect he has been duped—'Why is the salesman being so nice?' 'Could I have bought cheaper?' 'Have I bought a product no one else will buy?' Such questions inevitably lead to thoughts of whether or not to suspend or even cancel the order. All the buyer really wants to hear is an undemonstrative acknowledgement of his favour and assurance that he has done the right thing, particularly if the decision-making process has been a finely-balanced affair. A 'parting shot' such as:

'You'll be really pleased with this product. We have hundreds of users and they all swear by it.'

'This product has been a big success for our company. I really appreciate you giving us the chance to prove its merits.'

gives that touch of confidence that settles the buyer's mind and removes all suggestion of second thoughts.

Solicit other prospects

Existing clients, particularly those of brief duration, are often an excellent source of sales leads. There is some appeal for those who have newly ordered a product to feel the emotional security of having others 'in the same boat' and to confirm their own wisdom by virtue of some third party repeating the same process of evaluation. However, it is important to be sure of one's ground before taking such a step. If there is the slightest doubt about the buyer's willingness to recommend other prospective clients, the strategy is best forgotten.

Always leave the door open

The salesman must always 'leave the door open' for the next sale by making absolutely sure that he will be welcome to call again. An obvious way of addressing this situation, as well as giving the buyer the confidence of an implied continuing relationship, is to make a declaration of intent concerning the next visit. If the salesman's personal telephone number can be provided in case of unforeseen events in the interim, so much the better:

'Here are my home and office telephone numbers. Please feel free to contact me at any time if you have a problem. In the meantime, I shall be planning to visit you again. Of course, I will let you know the scheduled date well in advance.'

Don't talk yourself out of the order!

So many orders are won, only to be lost within a matter of minutes, simply because the salesman does not know when to stop talking and leave.

While I have already stressed the wisdom of leaving as soon as possible after securing the order, it follows that a successful close should not be followed by unnecessary conversation. Superfluous banter only introduces diversions that may give the buyer reasons for reconsidering his verdict. This kind of idle chat often happens because the salesman finds it difficult, almost discourteous, to break up the proceedings immediately after the buyer has made a judgement in his favour. Make no mistake, the buyer's decision is seldom an act of personal affection. He selects a particular product because he believes it is in the best interests of his company and himself to do so. There is no need to edge towards the door on a tide of banal prattle. Nothing could be simpler than a courteous, decisive, and speedy departure:

'Many thanks for the order. I know you will be very pleased with the performance of this system. I'll call back next week to discuss details for maintenance, training and other installation details. Will the 24th be okay, or would you prefer the 25th?'

Once the real business is over, be on your way. There are other sales to be made!

10.
Final stages of the sale

'The man who makes no mistakes does not usually make anything.'
Edward John Phelps 1822–1900

Throughout the selling process there is a perpetual risk that whenever things appear to be going right, some apparently unforeseen event will occur to dissolve all the effort that went before into a disillusioned heap of frustration and disappointment. It is so easy for the salesman to believe that if he plays everything according to the book all will be well. Sadly, hard work and integrity are not guarantees of success, and nothing should ever be taken for granted. Logic, reason and fairness often have little bearing on the outcome of a sales negotiation; uninvited forces are waiting in the wings to destroy, sometimes totally, any delusions of optimism or complacency. What is more, the later in the selling cycle it occurs, the greater the damage. An early disaster does at least waste less time and effort than one which aborts at the very conclusion of negotiations. It is obviously impossible to anticipate the unexpected consistently, but, with consideration and forethought, many apparent surprises can be foreseen.

However, having dealt with the process of 'situation evaluation' in Chapter 7, there is no point in dwelling on the subject, other than to focus on the final stages of the sale and some areas in which things, for reasons of neglect or ill fortune, can oft go awry.

Attempting to close the wrong person

The salesman cannot be expected to get it right every time! There is bound to be a time when, despite taking all the basic precautions, he suddenly discovers that the person he believes to be the decision-maker has to consult another source for final approval. This might involve a parent company board, a select committee, a direct superior, or even a union.

This type of situation calls for bold and speedy action. The salesman must try to make immediate contact with the real decision-maker, and only direct questions can make it happen:

'Who is the final decision-maker?'

174

'Can you make contact with him and see if it is convenient for us to meet briefly while I'm here?'

If the response is negative, it is absolutely reasonable to seek an alternative:

'Will it be best if you arrange an appointment for me now, or shall I contact his secretary on my way out?'

Often the buyer will tell the salesman to leave everything to him. This must be resisted, otherwise control of the sales negotiation will be lost. Effective selling cannot be achieved through third parties! The salesman must view the situation through the eyes of the newly revealed decision-maker(s). It is obvious that no decision is going to be made in favour of his product unless those directly involved know all about it. The existence of a sales proposal can be a considerable asset here, whether or not direct personal contact with the actual decision-maker is an achievable objective. More bold questions need to be asked:

'When will the decision be made?'

'How many people are on the board?'

Then, when the relevant facts are known:

'Right, I'll prepare a copy of our proposal for each of them and make sure they are delivered right away.'

Maybe the buyer will ask the salesman not to trouble. In that case, there can only be one appropriate response:

'It's no trouble!'

An individual covering letter should accompany each copy, giving a synopsis of negotiations to date and indicating the section of the proposal which highlights the reasons for buying.

This is certainly a difficult selling situation requiring great sensitivity. The buyer may not be the actual decision-maker, but he is likely to have a considerable influence on the proceedings. Alienate him at your peril! On the other hand, it is not a problem easily resolved by handing over a bunch of technical leaflets in the hope that they will be conveyed to the right person. This is a predicament indeed! The chances of getting the order without an established face-to-face relationship with the actual decision-maker are very slim. Yet, this problem need never have occurred if the salesman had asked the most important question at the initial sales call:

'Who makes the decisions around here?'

—or words to that effect!

No order is ever absolutely secure

A colleague of mine recently asked me out for a drink to celebrate his first order for a completely new product. I refused his offer—not the drink you understand, just the celebration! I merely suggested that we left the celebration until the money was in the bank. The very same day I had interviewed a potential sales recruit. When I asked him what he considered to be his most significant selling achievement in recent months his response was immediate: 'Making the sale against the "XYZ Computer Company" after they had already received the official order!' Nice one! Yet, this was far from being a unique coup, for I have myself won and lost one or two orders like that in my time.

It all seems so straightforward. Once you have got the order all you have to do is deliver. Doesn't your sales manager keep telling you closing is what it's all about? You ask the buyer to give you the business; he agrees and gives you a letter of intent or even signs an order. Fantastic! Surely the salesman has then done all that can be expected of him and can go home to calculate his commission entitlement. Don't you believe it! Getting the order can be relatively easy. Afterwards is the time for increased vigilance, as nasty little things can happen to flush the salesman's hard-earned success into oblivion. Just consider a few of the things that can go wrong:

1. Your company finds it cannot meet the delivery date.

2. Your product does not come up to specification.

3. The competition launches or pre-releases a new product that makes yours look virtually Medieval.

4. The client cannot fund the project, has its government grant withdrawn, or goes bankrupt.

5. The client's related contract is cancelled.

6. Some beastly competitive salesman persuades the client he has ordered the wrong product.

7. The client does not get what he thought he had ordered and refuses to accept delivery, or simply won't pay.

8. The buyer leaves in the meantime and his replacement simply does not like the salesman and/or his company.

9. The buyer is replaced by someone who has hitherto been a dedicated user of a competitive product. Maybe he even used to work for them!

10. The client is taken over by a company which is a major user of competitive equipment.

11. The salesman's company withdraws the product.

12. Having heard nothing from the salesman, since giving the order, the buyer suspects he is being taken for granted, cheated, or will be disappointed one way or the other. So he cancels.

13. The buyer does not have the authority to place the order.

14. Having had time to consider, the buyer changes his mind. He doesn't switch to competition, he simply decides he can manage without it.

15. Someone discovers that a zero accidentally got stuck on the end of the volumes on which the proposals were based and consequently the job is now too small to justify the product.

16. The client cannot get planning permission for the premises to contain the ordered equipment.

17. The salesman's company cannot provide the resources to deliver the product they promised.

18. The salesman promised the impossible.

19. The salesman's company makes a mess of the job due to bad luck or sheer incompetence.

20. A third party cannot provide on time, or even at all, the service on which the salesman's product depends.

Are you worried yet? You really ought to be, because these examples represent just a few of the possible occurrences which can convert the joy of sales success into the gloom of total failure. Getting the order is no time for the salesman to relax, but rather a time for evaluating all the possible ways in which the situation might revert into disaster. He cannot afford to be complacent for a moment, at least not until the client's cheque is cleared through the bank. Then celebrate!

Proposal follow-up

During the course of any month I meet quite a few people who want to move from a technical role, typically pre- or post-sales support, into a selling job. After evaluating the human characteristics and career potential of the individual, we usually manage to point them in the right direction, which is not necessarily into direct sales. Sometimes our judgement is wrong. When we do make a mistake it usually relates to one or both of two simple factors: a reluctance to get involved in cold canvassing; the inability to ask for the order.

One of the hallmarks of a salesman who is hesitant to ask for the order is a collection of unsettled sales proposals. In most areas of technical selling one of the final stages of the process is the creation of a sales proposal which typically states what the client needs, what the supplier is proposing in order to satisfy that requirement, the cost of the product or service, and the related feature/benefits. For the reluctant order closer this is psychologically the end of the selling process—a statement of capability and price has been made, it's up to the client to choose.

I know this rejection of responsibility sounds rather naïve, but believe me, it happens all the time! The delivery of a proposal is where the hard selling really begins. Of course, the sales proposal should only be a confirmation of points already agreed, but it is still subject to misinterpretation. The proposition needs to be kept alive, for it can still be influenced by hitherto unknown and apparently disinterested parties. More to the point, a situation where there is little to choose between the short-listed suppliers can easily be tipped in the favour of competition merely because, since the delivery of their proposals, they have sustained or enhanced their personal relationship with the client, confirmed their continuing interest, or even discovered the prime criteria for decision which may have revealed itself through the very proposals themselves.

Proposal follow-up is a key element of the selling process. Failure to do so is a kind of self-vandalism, which creates something only to destroy it by neglect at the very time when the justification for its existence might come to fruition. Apart from all that, it's such an awful waste of time!

Proposal follow-up is an essential act that requires enthusiasm and efficient organization. There is obviously a variety of methods for checking out the status of a proposal and attempting to close the sale—personal visit, telephone, letter, etc. This is the province of good personal organization. For my own purposes I have always kept a 'proposal league table', which qualifies all outstanding sales proposals within my territory or sales operation. Predominant factors include total value, percentage chance of success, date of origination, decision date, etc. This provides a continuing, at-a-glance, order of priorities, so that all appropriate action is clear to my peers, my subordinates, and myself. It's the only way of gauging where and when the next sales close can best be achieved. Would-be salesmen must fully appreciate that selling is all about getting the order; not simply a means for giving clients the opportunity to buy, but the process of persuading them to buy one's own product.

Contracts and agreements

Most people are very casual about signing contracts and agreements. I suppose the emotional implications are quite considerable. One assumes that the supplier is honest and therefore to check out every syllable is an unnecessary nuisance and brings the integrity of the supplier into question. Clearly, there is always a considerable reluctance to do that, so the typical inclination is to sign and hope for the best. From the average salesman's point of view the attitude is not usually very different. His company has gone to the trouble of producing a standard contract which has been used for many other clients, so why bother about checking out the fine print on the off chance something may not be applicable?

This reminds me of a conversation I once had with a colleague about his annual income review. It was all very straightforward, no problems from either of us. Some days after the discussion took place he mentioned in passing that he was rather surprised, and a little hurt, that I had asked him to sign a formal document confirming in detail the arrangements we had agreed. 'After all,' he thought, 'we had a good relationship. Has he begun to distrust me after all these years? His word was good enough for me, wasn't mine good enough for him? Why this sudden obsession for paperwork?' These were the kinds of question going through his mind. My response was simple: 'How secure would your entitlement be if I fall under a bus?' In other words, the agreement was absolutely secure until such time as:

1. Either party was temporarily or permanently removed from his part of the bargain for circumstances beyond his control.

2. Our relationship declined, due to the influence of emotional factors.

3. External pressures such as politics, lack of personal success, third-party interference, etc., came between us.

4. The company was taken over.

And so on!

I must confess that during my career as a salesman I have needed to have some lessons drummed into me. The one that has taken the longest to learn, and has caused me most pain and anguish, is the simple truth that the closer the human relationship, the greater the need for formality in business agreements. The subject could be anything from a commercial contract to a social arrangement with a friend. There has to be some positive reference point which can be used to clarify any future possible misunderstandings. The stronger the human relationship within a business arrangement, the higher the cost of failure, for when such a contract goes irretrievably wrong, you not only lose the business, you also lose a friend. I have both personally experienced and witnessed, among friends and business acquaintances, many instances of anger and distress due to the lack of formal agreement. This is not necessarily the result of a misunderstanding of the original arrangement, but more minor modifications or imperceptible changes in the factors involved which slowly accumulate into a significant problem that suddenly erupts into an irrational and emotional mess.

Let's view the sales contract with these considerations in mind. The details of an agreement to supply a service or product typically consist of a number of standard factors—volumes, capacity, size, model, etc. In addition, there may be some modifications of normal terms—early delivery, special discounts, etc. Then there could be special facilities—extra capacity, modification to cater for foreign specifications, non-standard means of use, and the like. The trouble is, both the salesman and the buyer believe they know what was understood at the time the business was closed. Yet, without absolute detailed confirmation in written form, both parties can fall into the trap of what might be called 'specification semantics'. Do both parties mean the same thing when they use such terms as early, fast, extra? Does the buyer really understand the delivery implications related to a product being produced for the first time? The only way the salesman can prevent, or at least minimize, such potential conflict is to, (a) document every aspect of the client's situation and requirements plus his own company's capability and commitment, and (b) obtain written confirmation from all parties concerned (within the client's company as well as his own) that the agreement to be signed represents a true picture of all that is required and all that is being promised.

Most salesmen say they hate paperwork, but under pressure will admit they hate unnecessary paperwork and will tolerate the rest. Believe me, the documentation of formal business agreements is the most important paperwork of all.

In conclusion, the acid test is:

'Irrespective of my good terms with this person, will the agreement between us still operate effectively should our relationship decline or be terminated for whatever reason?'

If the answer on both sides is 'yes', then the agreement has a reasonable chance of working. Conversely, when it comes to doing business with friends, even if it involves something as apparently simple as selling a second-hand car or doing a plumbing job, it is still important to ask yourself the question. 'If this arrangement does not work, will my good relationship with this person be impaired?' The answer is usually 'yes'.

So, don't forget to write it all down to confirm that all parties understand the same thing. Then, keep well away from buses!

Delivery promises

There is probably more unnecessary client dissatisfaction related to broken delivery promises than any other aspect of selling. Very often the failure to deliver on time is beyond the salesman's control. However, it's no good him standing on the side lines bemoaning the inadequacies of the production, despatch, or whatever department. Even overdue deliveries can be acceptable to the customer if the salesman handles the situation intelligently. Most delivery problems are actually created at the time of the sale. In most circumstances the client asks the salesman for a delivery quotation, and the salesman quotes the lead time he believes to be currently applicable. This 'guideline' from the salesman invariably becomes the buyer's delivery promise. Time can easily distort what was actually said on the occasion! So, the only way to avoid this is to complete a formal company order and a formal company acceptance. Notice, by the way, I say 'company' order and acceptance. What might be acceptable to the representatives of both parties may not necessarily represent the wishes of their respective employers. Innocent misunderstandings can quickly lead to total disasters.

A common mistake of salesmen at the order stage is to fail to discover the amount of delivery flexibility existing within his own company and that of the client. If the standard delivery period of the salesman's company is quoted as ten weeks, and the salesman conveys this blindly to the client, then what was intended as a loose guideline can become an unbearable strait-jacket, as everyone is on the hook for ten weeks. The salesman commits his team and the buyer does the same within his own organization. Potential problems are created, all for the want of a few simple questions:

'When do you require this product?'

'How much earlier could you take it?'

'What is the very latest acceptable delivery?'

'What could be the implications of later or earlier delivery?'

'With what other schedules, operations, deliveries, etc., will our product have to interface?'

Whether or not the client has already thought about these points, he will quickly recognize the benefits of discussing them. One thing is for sure, the answers will provide essential information for those people who have the task of delivering the goods at a time which is acceptable to the buyer.

This kind of questioning also brings about two additional benefits. Firstly, it establishes a delivery 'zone', which gives much greater flexibility to the salesman's production and despatch departments. Secondly, it can often overcome the sales advantage of competitors able to offer a quicker delivery. For example, what is the benefit of a six week delivery when ten weeks is acceptable?

The logic of agreeing a delivery date should be the same as negotiating a sales target. Whatever number is agreed you have to accept that one per cent improvement makes you a hero, and a one per cent shortfall means total failure, whatever the retrospective logic of the number first thought of.

One of the realities of selling is that occasionally some unforeseen event occurs and prevents the delivery promise from being fulfilled—strikes, embargoes, licences, transportation failure, raw material shortages, a wrong address, etc. One paramount rule must apply in any such circumstance. Tell the client—*now!* The implications of expecting a delivery which will never arrive can be disastrous. No matter how momentarily annoyed a client might be when told that a delivery, for whatever reason, cannot be met, you can be sure he is going to be far more enraged to discover the same facts for himself on the crucial day when people, equipment, and other suppliers, are standing by. It isn't the easiest thing to do, but it is a duty the salesman must accept as an inevitable part of his job. However, it isn't only salespeople who sometimes try to arrange unfeasible delivery periods. Buyers will often attempt to cover themselves against late delivery by asking for a shorter period than they actually require. This gives the salesman the apparent choice of committing his company to an impossible delivery period, or losing the business. There is only one response the salesman can afford to give. 'Sorry Mr Prospect, I can only commit my company to promises it is able to keep. I don't want to run the risk of letting you down.' Subsequent enquiries back at the office might enable some improvement to be made, and going back to the client with a 'special favour' does no harm at all. However, if the ultimate option lies between quoting an unachievable delivery and forgoing the order, the latter is the only honourable course. Choosing the former is likely to lead to the same conclusion.

The lost sale post-mortem

Successful selling is the antithesis of the Olympic spirit. There is no glory in simply taking part. It is a game where only the winner is acclaimed. Of course, you are unlikely to win them all, so what do you do when you fail? Pretend you never really wanted the business anyway, or try and discover how you came to lose? One thing is for sure, if you don't analyse your losses (and your wins) you will never really know what happened and consequently the same mistakes will be made again. Having lost, there are two things you must always do:

1. Leave the door open. That is, maintain the integrity of your product, your company, and yourself in order to ensure a future business relationship with the prospect.

2. Learn from your mistakes. That is, analyse the outcome in depth with someone who really understands the situation and has the experience to provide objective criticism, preferably your sales manager.

Perhaps the best approach to a post-mortem of this kind is to have a checklist. You may notice that some of the questions that need to be asked are ones that should have been raised right at the beginning of the sales negotiation:

1. Were you simply supplying the prospect with a check on current market prices?

2. If so, why was your product unable to show better cost/performance, i.e., superior feature/benefits to those of other suppliers?

3. Was he really a potential client for your kind of product?

4. Were you selling to the right person? Is he the real decision-maker?

5. How did you make contact with him in the first place? Did you start at the top, i.e., the managing director, or was your point of entry too low?

6. Was he a first-time user? If not, who got the business last time and why?

7. Who got the order on this occasion and what did they have that the prospect needed and was unavailable from your company?

8. Was there a requirement you failed to recognize?

9. Did you put in your quotation because you really had something the prospect needed, or did he simply let you get on with it in order to placate you?

10. Are you absolutely certain that funds were available for the proposals you were making?

11. Did your proposals reflect the prospect's stated requirements, or your opinion of what he ought to have?

12. What information on the outcome have you been able to obtain from the people you met while you were preparing your proposals?

13. Was your final proposal handed over as part of a formal presentation to the prospect's senior management, or was it sent through the post?

14. When you went through your detailed proposals with the prospect, did you emphasize the benefits and advantages in absolute terms, or did you simply discuss the specification and price?

15. When your proposals were discussed, did you really listen to everything that was said by the prospect?

16. Did you really understand the prospect's desired mode of acquisition, e.g., lease, rental, purchase?

17. Did you allow the continuity of the sales negotiation to lapse so that it became too 'cold' to resurrect?

18. Did you really answer all the objections that were raised during the course of the negotiations?

19. Did you fully use the total resources of your company in the context of both expertise and rank?

20. Were the political obstacles insurmountable? If not, did you really overcome them all?

21. Was the decision actually made before your negotiations started?

22. Did you ever discover the prospect's formal decision criteria?

23. Did you really appreciate the buyer's personal motivation and its effect upon the decision-making process?

24. Would you have chosen the solution proposed by you if you had been in the prospect's situation?

25. Did you ask the prospect why he did not give you the business and why the product of a particular competitor was chosen?

26. Was there any conflict between the prospect's staff and your own, as far as the specification of the product was concerned?

If you can obtain valid answers to these question, then your chances of a gold medal in the next event will be greatly enhanced.

'No' does not always mean 'goodbye'

'You can't win 'em all' is a reassuring expression with many implications. One thing emphatically implied is that the event or negotiation in question has been taken to its absolute conclusion. This, however, is not always the case. It is essential that the salesman establishes the fact beyond a reasonable shadow of doubt before drawing the sales negotiation to a final close. The familiar '80/20' rule is very applicable to the selling process. Eighty per cent of the haggling typically occurs in the last twenty per cent of the sales negotiation. Within this framework one also has the 'long-list/short-list' syndrome. This means that some suppliers are being told 'no' when those remaining have not yet been told 'yes'. That is, sometimes to be told 'no' means you have not been short-listed, not, as the salesman might assume, that the business has irretrievably been given to someone else.

To be told 'no thank you' is, to some salesmen, a *fait accompli* to be greeted with resignation. To the better salesman it is a challenge to be assailed with sensitivity and commitment. Whether rejection is received verbally or by formal letter, the salesman must quickly establish from the buyer whether or not the decision is irrevocable:

1. Has the business irretrievably gone to another supplier and, if so, whom?

184

2. If the salesman could persuade his company to improve its offer by way of a different product, price, delivery, or whatever, is there still room for manoeuvre?

Obviously the latter question needs to be be handled with considerable sensitivity, as it could imply deliberate over-quoting or proposal of the wrong product. It should therefore be made clear to the buyer that the question is strictly personal to the salesman, rather than company originated, and is unlikely to result in any further action. If this type of questioning makes it absolutely clear that the business is finally lost, then the salesman should accept the situation as it is and commit himself to two further actions:

1. Leave the door open for future negotiations.

2. Carry out a post-mortem evaluation of the situation with his manager. Maybe he will do better next time.

There are two extremes to be avoided at all costs:

1. Surrendering before the battle is lost.

2. Fighting a lost cause.

The latter is often personified by the 'management visit'. I'm sure you know the one I mean. The salesman either lost it fair and square, or completely mishandled it. Either way, it is an established fact that the business is lost. Nevertheless, salesman and manager troop in solemn procession to retrieve the irretrievable in the guise of a 'rescue operation'. My manager back in the IBM days called it 'peeing on the ashes'. It is a procedure that gives rise to two very obvious questions:

1. Surely the management effort should have been made before, rather than after the event—possibly at the 'hot prospect' stage.

2. Such time could be better spent on other live situations rather than attempting to resurrect the dead!

So, in conclusion: make sure that the order has definitely gone elsewhere; ensure that no kind of alternative proposal can change the decision; make sure you do nothing to destroy the company's professional credibility in defeat; know why you lost. Then, go somewhere else and win!

Handling mistakes

'Everybody makes mistakes.' This expression rolls easily off the tongue. Yet when errors occur they are always a source of much anguish and frustration.

185

The salesman often finds himself in a difficult situation which results from his own, his colleague's, or even a client's error of judgement. The nature of mistakes is that they almost always come as a surprise. Areas of possible error can be anticipated, but not individual events, otherwise they would never occur in the first place. Certainly, problem areas which are anticipated tend to generate items of lesser impact than those ignored. However, when the salesman is hit with the reality of a mistake, he is usually caught unawares, particularly if the situation is revealed by the client rather than his own company. In such circumstances the instinctive reaction of many a salesman is to lay the blame elsewhere. He needs to sustain a good relationship with his client, and wants to avoid anything which might impair it. After all, making a mistake is really letting someone down, and the client needs to know the salesman can be relied upon.

Client
'We specially ordered imperial gauge and you've delivered metric.'
Salesman
'It must be the factory. We're always having that kind of problem.'

Client
'I didn't receive the literature you promised to send me.'
Salesman
'I shall have some strong words with my secretary.'

Client
'I'm sorry, but I gave you the wrong specification.
Salesman
'Oh dear. That's going to create some problems I can tell you!'

These kinds of response from salesmen are common whenever mistakes occur, yet their effect can be very damaging to the client's regard for his supplier as a total entity. The inevitable conclusion from this type of cover up is that the salesman is trying his best, but the company is inherently unreliable.

The fact is, we all make mistakes, and, what is more, we all know we all make mistakes. So, that is obviously the basis on which the salesman must handle the client's reaction to mistakes, if he is to reduce the impact of their effect. The salesman handles this by always blaming himself, or at least stating that he could have made some contribution to the mistake being avoided. This applies whether the mistake has been made by a colleague, the client, or, of course, the salesman himself. The field of mistakes consists of two main factors: the practical and the emotional. The former is self-explanatory and has to be dealt with accordingly, whereas the latter can soon be exaggerated out of all proportion and become more difficult to handle than the actual problem itself. By blaming himself the salesman tends to 'defuse' the emotional aspect of the matter. So, to the client who received the wrong gauge:

'If I had double checked before it was dispatched, it probably would not have happened. I'm sorry.

I'll give the matter absolute priority.'

To the one who didn't receive the literature:

'I'm sorry. I should have delivered it personally.'

But, in the case of the client who supplied the wrong specification, the salesman obviously cannot take the blame. If work has been done and has to be paid for, he can at least be sympathetic and reassuring, by relating himself to the situation:

'It's easily done, I might have made the same mistake myself. Don't worry, I'll do my best to rectify the situation.'

This type of attitude and response can only enhance the relationship between a salesman and his client.

It is often said that we learn from our mistakes. I don't accept that philosophy at all, but believe that we really learn from putting mistakes right. Many errors are made and left to fester—'putting it down to experience' is a handy evasion of responsibility. If a salesman is involved in a mistake, whether he caused it or not, it is his responsibility to discover why it happened, to seek alternatives, and ensure it doesn't happen again. That way he learns something, and there can be no greater embarrassment than making the same mistake twice.

11.

Political and emotional forces

'Nearly all men can withstand adversity, but if you want to test a man's character, give him power.'

Abraham Lincoln 1809–65

Selling is never a straightforward matter. There are always forces lurking around to confound unwary salespeople. Very often, despite having done the most thorough job and having the best product, price, and delivery, and a good relationship with the buyer, the salesman finds he has lost the business due to apparently unreasonable, unfair, or even unethical causes. When this occurs, the salesman, more often than not, blames politics or irrational behaviour. Company politics, emotional reactions, and uncontrollable external influences are often presented as reasons for inaction or negative decisions; but these are excuses rather than justifications. The possibility of political or emotional influences is present in every sales situation, and therefore their effects must always be anticipated.

Selling in times of economic recession

One of the realities of the Western economy is its periodic fluctuations from stability to the extremes of expansion or recession. Such conditions are then tempered by the effects of inflation or reflation as individual governments attempt to solve whatever problems may prevail and in doing so invariably create a monetary 'domino effect' that leaves no country unscathed. The 'eighties began disastrously with the severe contraction of traditional industries and high unemployment throughout Europe and North America. This has affected almost every business sector, killing off many companies and demanding more efficient operation of the survivors. This kind of selling environment creates a lot of problems for the salesman.

From my layman's point of view, I have always thought that there is nothing more likely to create an economic recession than politicians and financial pundits forecasting that we are likely to have one! I believe that to a great extent, economic collapse is simply a sudden lack of confidence brought about by negative propaganda. But, to the subject of selling, and how these apparently adverse trading conditions affect the selling process.

Winning an order very often relies on the ability of the salesman to sus-

188

tain a positive stance, rather than become involved in the introspective justifications of why failure is unavoidable. The superiority of those salesmen whose attitude is 'I will win, but. . .' over those who are resigned to 'I will lose, but. . .' may appear to be marginal, but in my experience ultimate achievement is always considerably in favour of the former. In periods of impending or existing economic decline, the buyer is given the best excuse in the book for not buying, and for many salespeople such circumstances provide an ideal excuse, not only for failure, but also for not getting out into the street and even trying.

What actually happens to the buying process during a recession? Clearly luxury goods are hit more severely than essentials. However, it is fair to say that almost no market dries up altogether. It is in this kind of environment that those salespeople who have the determination to spread their nets wider and win are able to shrug off the apparent limitations of economic recession, while others sit in their offices thumbing tired copies of *The Financial Times*. In fact, one can argue quite convincingly that any service or equipment designed to promote efficiency or increase product exposure must have greater justification in times of industrial restraint than during economic boom. If savings are to be made they can only be achieved by increased productivity, not by putting up the shutters and hoping the problem will go away. If revenues are to be increased, promotional activities must be enhanced not cut back in order to generate short-term economies. These are arguments that need a resolute and determined mind, for without them sellers of office equipment and advertising, for instance, are doomed to failure. It is the salesman's responsibility not only to justify the purchase of his product in cost/benefit terms, but also in the context of prevailing economic circumstances. Often, the promise of recession can provide an ideal opportunity for the salesman to close:

'Now that there are positive indications of economic recession that could affect your industry, it must be important for companies such as yours to take every possible step to raise efficiency to the highest level, in order to ensure survival in what is likely to be an increasingly competitive marketplace. A decision to proceed now, while funds can still be made available, may avoid a possible situation where you are in urgent need of increasing productivity without the ability to fund it.'

Whatever the product, the argument is still the same.

In the case of selling any non-luxury product (I will leave the interpretation to you), if the buyer's words suggest 'I can't make a decision, because of prevailing economic circumstances', he is not usually giving a reason but making an excuse.

Company politics

Every company has to suffer the idiosyncrasies of internal politics. It is a

189

sad commentary on human nature that chauvinism, egocentricity, auto-
cracy, corruption, megalomania, and so on, constantly penetrate all
aspects of business life. Key personnel move to other companies to escape
or are unhappy in their job because of it; irrational and harmful decisions
are made; profitable opportunities are lost; salesmen fail to secure orders
because of it. Politics is a sterile phenomenon that can grow from a conflict
involving only two people into open warfare between entire company divi-
sions and departments. So, how can the salesman pull business out of such
a morass without getting his hands dirty? The inevitable answer is: with
extreme sensitivity and caution!

A familiar clash is between the purchasing department and a user
department. A photocopier salesman may be making good progress in his
negotiations with say, the manager of the finance department, when, out
of a clear blue sky, the manager of the purchasing department gets
involved—'No department has the authority to order any equipment without a purchase order generated with my formal approval.' Or even a cry
from the general office manager—'We already have a significant photo-
copying capability in the general office which was specifically installed for
the use of all departments.'

There is no easy and guaranteed solution to this kind of problem, but the
action most likely to succeed is to get all the protagonists together. It's
amazing how attitudes change when such people are face-to-face as
opposed to delivering proclamations from their ivory towers. The venue
could perhaps be a working lunch or a formal meeting on the client's premises. The salesman's contribution to such a meeting is simply:

> 'I want to put to your organization the best possible proposition my com-
> pany is able to offer, but I am not sure how I can do so and also satisfy all
> your individual requirements. Please tell me what I should do.'

If this doesn't work there is only one effective alternative for discovering
the real decision-maker. Approach the situation via a non-political source.

There are usually only two areas of a company which are relatively free
from personal politics: the very top or the very bottom of the hierarchical
pyramid. If the salesman has started the sales negotiation at the very top,
as he should, he avoids the problem. If he hasn't, then he can arrange for
his sales manager to make contact with the managing director on his
behalf. At the other end of the scale one usually discovers that the shopfloor intelligence network is reliable and a consensus of opinion at that
level will be a valuable guide to where the majority of sales effort should be
made. Whatever happens, the salesman must always be an apolitical
animal in the eyes of the client.

Always get the story right

To say 'Always get the story right' suggests a cover-up of a deliberate lie, or even a 'snow job' for multi-person subterfuge. What I have in mind is not conscious deception carried out with premeditation and malice, but rather that which comes with the innocence of incompetence and insensitivity.

It is possible to misunderstand technical details or make groundless assumptions and then, with absolute confidence and conviction, present such information to the prospective buyer as absolute fact. This possibility is compounded, and the chances of contradiction greatly increased, when several people are dealing with the same client. This can become even more complicated when dealing with a number of contacts within the same company. And if you are selling for an international supplier to a multinational organization the situation can get very messy indeed. Let me give you a true example of the kind of situation that can occur.

In 1981 a large US-based international company decided to add yet another computer to the six or so that it already had installed in the UK. So, contact was made with the local salesman responsible for the account and with whom the company had a very good relationship. The negotiations proceeded very smoothly and it was only a matter of days before the configuration was established and a tentative price and delivery date decided upon. Value of the order: about one million pounds.

In the meantime, the managing director of the client company attended a regular business review with his boss, the international vice president, who was located in the USA. The anticipated expenditure of a million pounds was obviously high on the agenda. During the course of conversation the price, delivery, model, etc., were discussed and it soon became apparent that there were some significant discrepancies in comparison with similar equipment recently purchased in the USA. As a result, the vice president decided to make some investigations of his own. He made high level contact with the stateside head office of the computer manufacturer and queried the situation. They admitted to knowing very little about the transaction (which probably meant this was the first they had heard of it!) and assured the vice president that, despite the fact that the basic price in the UK would be higher than in the USA, it would be subject to a discount which reflected the supplier's appreciation of their custom. Furthermore, delivery could be made at short notice and would be the very latest version of their equipment. In real terms this meant a more advanced system at a lesser price than had been quoted in the UK. Having achieved this concession, the situation was then dropped back into the lap of the UK managing director. The local salesman was completely taken aback when he was informed that the previous order was cancelled. All he could say was that he would consult his local management to see what could be done. He soon discovered that he was able to do nothing. The matter became incredibly political, with the UK supplier stating that it could not make the kinds of concession that had been declared by its parent company because of the impact on other client situations. As far as the machine itself was

191

concerned, the version mentioned by their corporate executive could not be supplied, particularly on rapid delivery, because that particular release was not yet launched in Europe. There were other complications as well, and the final outcome, of what became a very traumatic situation, was a decision by the UK client to buy direct from the USA.

The salesman was obviously very upset, having lost a large order in a non-competitive situation because it had become a competitive exercise involving two elements of his own organization. I am sure the word that sprang most easily to mind was 'political'—he had lost the order due to political forces beyond his control. Not true! He lost the order because he did not go to the trouble to ensure that all possible areas of influence were covered and under control. It should have been obvious that there was some risk of the two US parent companies, between whom there was continual business activity, discussing such a large transaction. Therefore, conflicting or even wrong information might be put forward at that level if the salesman failed to put them (or indeed any other interested parties) completely in the picture. Some might argue that it was the job of senior management in the UK to keep head office informed about international developments, as they are the ones in day-to-day contact with the corporate entity. To some extent this is true, but it is the salesman's task to monitor every aspect of the sales negotiation, and this must include continual verification of whether or not senior management is fulfilling its obligations, be they to the client or within the company. It can never be taken for granted that people will always fulfil their role within the scheme of things. This applies as much to one's own management as it does to the prospective buyer or existing client. Make no mistake, no manager worth his salt will take exception to being reminded about actions that have to be taken; quite the contrary. He is likely to be favourably impressed by any salesman who is able to show such a high level of sales awareness.

Never assume anything in selling, and be sure to cover every possible source of influence upon the sale. If you don't, you can be sure that fate will step in with its usual aplomb and pull out the plug!

Always locate the actual decision-maker

I recall a conversation with a salesman who was rather distressed and disappointed at losing a major sale which he had been absolutely confident of securing. It appeared to be a ridiculous situation. He had a very high level of personal credibility with the principal executives of the company. He had a particularly clear understanding of that organization and its needs, as he was a past employee and knew that his product had a variety of meaningful advantages over his competitors—yet he lost the business!

Virtually all the books and training courses that deal with the process of selling capital goods and services, either state, or imply, that the ultimate decision-maker is the managing director. Therefore, he is the one to whom the sale must be made. This is a very misleading assumption which is not true in many circumstances. The chances of the managing director being the absolute decision-maker increase in parallel with the value of the proposition, and decline the larger the size of organization he is controlling. For instance, the managing director of a small services company buying a new photocopier is likely to decide personally upon the actual machine to be purchased. The managing director of a major corporation will merely 'rubber stamp' the decision of a subsidiary or division to invest several hundred thousand pounds in a new computer. However, it would be a serious mistake to exclude the managing director from the selling strategy of any prospective sale of significant value, for in most cases he is likely to have a considerable influence upon the decision-making process, as, indeed, have other of his fellow directors and senior executives. The important distinction to make is that between the influencer and the decision-maker.

Within the sales training scenario one often comes across the expression 'the ultimate decision-maker'. I would prefer to use the term 'actual decision-maker', for the former virtually implies that the final commitment will always come from the top of the company pyramid, which is not usually the case. There is no question that a reference from the managing director to a subordinate can usually strengthen the salesman's position, however, this is an approach that demands sensitivity, as some people react badly to 'pressure' from their peers, which they consider questions their own ability to make a decision, and attempt to prove their worth and independence by fighting against it.

If sales success is to be achieved, it is essential to identify the actual decision-maker and to view the situation through the eyes of his direct superiors. Very rarely will a manager of any worth inflict a decision upon a subordinate, for to do so effectively absolves him of any responsibility for a bad choice. If the managing director says to the buyer 'You will purchase an "XYZ" drinks dispenser' and it turns out to be a 'can of worms', the buyer is 'out from under'. Whereas, 'Purchase a drinks dispenser of your own choice within this range of price and performance' leaves the ball of responsibility firmly in the buyer's court. Only when the person responsible for making the decision is obviously making a foolish choice, will a worthy managing director wade in and overrule all parties concerned. Influence the influencers by all means, but be sure you are selling to the actual, as opposed to the assumed, decision-maker.

The organization within the organization

There is another idiosyncratic element of the decision-making process that can also be overlooked: the unofficial company organization that exists within the official one. In many companies and institutions, particularly larger concerns, there can be an interaction between individuals and/or

193

groups of people, which is in reality more powerful than the official 'family tree'. This can be a subtle trap for the unwary salesman, who does not realize that the organization chart which the managing director was so happy to give him, is more of a camouflage than a selling aid.

The salespeople most affected by these 'hidden organizations' are those involved in products which, by their very nature (usually high value capital goods), demand many levels of contact over a substantial period. Such complex negotiations demand a comprehensive and enlightened selling strategy accounting for both declared and undisclosed factors. The reason why so many salespeople fall foul is that they only approach the prospective company from one direction, usually the top. Clearly, top management is unlikely to acknowledge the existence of influential pressure groups or individuals, for to do so gives them credence and demeans and even jeopardizes the management's own position. Without doubt, the best way to penetrate the 'hidden organization' is from beneath. In some cases, middle management may know 'who calls the tune', in others the answer may best be found on the shopfloor.

The 'hidden organization' can have many manifestations, and is not limited to one form within a single organization. Let's examine some of the possibilities.

One of the most common forms of hidden influence upon the decision-making process is introspective pressure groups, whose primary interest lies, not within what is best for their company at large, but for their own limited sphere of influence. One of the 'classic' examples is where a company is deciding upon a computer both to process accounts and handle production. Probably the computer installed some years ago was for accounting purposes only. Consequently, it was controlled by the chief accountant, as were subsequent machines that also catered for production needs. The production department feels left out, and believes that its requirements are always given bottom priority, when they should really have top. So this time they are determined it will be different, and they have had a long time to think about what to do. There is little chance of them taking over control of the existing computer operation, so their only real alternative is to secure independent processing facilities. Consequently they create practical justification and explore all lines of political influence in order to rally support for their cause. Good timing is essential, so they are most likely to play their cards towards the end of the selling cycle.

Meanwhile, back at the top of the company pyramid, the salesman believes he is competing with just one or two other manufacturers for a centralized computer system. In reality, he is also competing with a number of small system manufacturers for part of what may be a solution based on two separate computers. Unwittingly, he is fighting the organization within the organization, and, depending upon its strength, may be pro-

194

posing a solution without alternatives that may ultimately become politically untenable. The wary salesman will identify all pressure groups, take their insular needs into account, and propose alternative solutions that keep him in the running whatever the outcome of power group activities.

Other forces to reckon with
There are lots of other hidden factors that are not declared within the official company structure, the 'lightweight general', for example. On paper, he may be the top man, but the people who really make the decisions for his 'rubber stamp' approval are his lieutenants. More often than not, the influence will stem from one person who, in turn, will have friends and allies within the organization who are likely to get preference.

Then there are the 'shooting stars'. These are the up-and-coming wonder boys who are already earmarked for stardom. Such people may, apparently, have a relatively low status in the context of the organizational chart, but, very often, an assistant production manager could also be the chairman's favourite grandson. Ignore him at your peril!

Sometimes, a company will have an informal reorganization to divert business activity away from an individual who officially has a fairly senior postion. This is usually due to his incompetence or he has become a political alien. The salesman must have a real understanding of how much influence each senior executive really has.

There are often managers working 'under the influence'. You must have heard expressions like 'He's a Ponselby-Smythe man', which means he does whatever a particular individual tells him or is subservient to a particular lobby. Sources of powerful influence are often outside the scope of the formal pyramid.

Then there are 'favourites'. Chief executives, usually of low competence, have people for whom they have a strong personal liking whom they allow to cloud their judgement. The fact that a particular decision is outside their sphere of competence or authority appears to be of no consequence. They state a preference and it is firmly taken into account.

In summary, no organization is what it appears to be, and it is the salesman's job to discover the reality of its hierarchical structure and all sources of undisclosed influence.

Types of buyer

I frequently use the word 'buyer'. As far as I am concerned it does not necessarily refer to someone within a buying department, but rather to any person who buys, i.e., makes the decision to purchase.

Buyers and salesmen are not only of various age, experience and seniority, but also have a wide range of individual moods and attitudes. If a satisfactory, lasting business relationship is to exist between these two parties, then it must be a well-balanced interaction. It is therefore the salesman's responsibility to measure his approach for each buyer to ensure that a balanced relationship is established. If he becomes subdominant he will lose respect; if he becomes dominant he will be regarded as insensitive to the buyer's needs; if he does not exhibit due deference to any gap in age, status, or experience between the buyer and himself, he may be considered disrespectful. This is where sales sensitivity really counts.

Here are seven examples of buyer attitudes, most of which I am sure you will recognize, together with some brief comments on how the salesman might handle them.

1. The busy buyer

I don't mean the familar 'Something just cropped up. I can only spare you a few moments'. In that case the salesman should just make another appointment and leave. No, I mean the buyer who is prepared to hear the whole story, while having too much else on his mind—telephones ringing constantly, heads around the door, etc. In this situation the salesman must be brief and to the point. It is also a good idea for him to let the buyer know that he is sympathetic towards his situation and get to the point quickly. The buyer will greatly appreciate such a gesture. An early close is essential.

2. The matey buyer

A good relationship between the salesman and the buyer is conducive to good business, but one that is too familiar becomes an obstacle. There are two approaches that can add discipline to this situation: a constant awareness of the need to keep the conversation on the business topic, and using the trial close at every opportunity as a constant reminder of the salesman's primary intention.

3. The hesitant buyer

This type of buyer is usually both indecisive and insecure, which means he needs help without being patronized or being submerged in over enthusiasm. The salesman should make his points simply, clearly, and positively, by declaring all the advantages and benefits pertinent to the buyer, omitting all peripheral and intangible claims.

4. The aggressive buyer

The prevailing message is, keep cool. The salesman should view this kind of buyer with the calm detachment of a bystander and avoid any direct involvement in the source of aggression. Why should the buyer be aggressive, even angry? Maybe the salesman offended him? So, he should ask and apologize in advance. That usually results in an immediate softening of attitude to a more tolerant level, whatever the actual reason for his manner. Too many salesmen match aggression with aggression, which inevitably leads to an artificial confrontation inconsistent with possible sales success.

196

5. The disorganized buyer

Judging the best time to call is usually the most effective way of handling this type of buyer. First thing in the morning is usually the best time, before he gets immersed in the problems of the day, or in the evening after the telephone stops ringing. From the selling angle the salesman needs to take whatever steps are necessary to hold the buyer's attention constantly. Summarize step-by-step and trial close at every stage of the negotiation. Written confirmation of all items agreed is essential.

6. The autocratic buyer

As with 'the aggressive buyer', a calm detachment is essential. A totalitarian usually despises subdominance as much as he hates opposition. Therefore, the salesman is obliged to show respect for the buyer's status, but at the same time to handle himself with confidence and authority. The biggest mistake the salesman can make with this kind of buyer is to create conflict, or attempt to embarrass him or reveal his shortcomings, as this will destroy all possibility of sales success.

7. The 'know all' buyer

One sure way to lose business from this buyer is to contradict him. On the other hand, I believe it is the salesman's responsibility to provide the means whereby the arrogant buyer informs himself of his own ignorance— 'I'm sure you're right. I'll get our technical department to send you some details so you can confirm it for yourself!' Above all, the salesman must know his product and be well prepared for such a meeting. His presentation should be planned and fluent. He should avoid verbosity and listen carefully, making notes where appropriate. All follow-up action, either written or verbal, should be precise, well considered and verified.

Maybe there are other types of buyer who come to mind. When dealing with them you could do worse than consider the reasons why they adopt their particular attitudes and how best to handle them.

Steering committees

Sometime ago I was discussing a lost sale with a salesman, who was bitterly upset about the whole thing. He believed he had done everything right throughout a prolonged negotiation, which had included initial proposals, presentations, short-lists, and a multitude of meetings and discussions. He had even been told, unofficially, that his equipment had been selected and required only the mere formality of 'rubber stamping' by the board. It was a big order worth a lot of commission. Imagine his bewilderment when he was subsequently informed by a sincerely apologetic steering committee chairman that a competitor had secured the order by 'going over the head' of the steering committe. The salesman was furious! It wasn't so much the fact that he had lost, it was more the way in which the competition had won. He considered it to be immoral—'That's the kind of extreme some unprofessional companies will go to,' he said, as a token of absolute despair, 'fancy nobbling the group chairman!'

'I've often heard this kind of statement from salesmen. Surprisingly, it is always presented as a criticism of competition rather than self-condemnation. In the case of my associate, he was not the victim of some sinister marketing strategy, he had simply lost to a better salesman. I suppose one could say he had fallen into the 'steering committee trap'.

The power of steering committees ranges from absolute power to total impotence. Mostly they are at one extreme or the other depending on whether or not the real decision-maker is included in its ranks. The steering committee is an excellent device for promoting a democratic myth within a totalitarian environment. They typically recommend rather than decide. For this reason it is essential that the salesman knows with absolute certainty who really makes the final decision and ensures his case is clearly stated at the source. In addition, he must also be certain that all other interested parties who may have some influence on the decision-making process are equally well informed on the benefits/advantages of his product. In the case of the salesman I mentioned, he had 'locked' himself into the steering committee of a group subsidiary, which included the company managing director, but not the group chairman, who turned out to be the real power in the organization and also a formidable autocrat. The business was not lost to unfair practice, a superior product, or a more powerful company, it was simply lost to a better salesman who had thoroughly evaluated the prospect's decision-making process and set his selling strategy accordingly.

12.

Some financial aspects of selling

'There are few ways in which a man can be more innocently employed than in getting money.'

Samuel Johnson 1709–84

The ultimate purpose of any business is the supply of goods or services in exchange for money—the days of barter are all but gone. The role of the salesman is to facilitate this interchange; to locate areas of need and construct a bridge between such requirements and his company's ability to supply. The outcome of this process is inevitably the payment of money for the commodity that has been provided. However, the total implications of business finance are somewhat more complex than this. There are many factors that can have a considerable bearing on the financial success of a business organization. International exchange rates, inflation, economic policy, bank rate, money supply, cash flow, are but a few of the forces that can enhance, confuse, or even destroy the viability of a company. While it may appear that matters of this kind are outside the salesman's interest and responsibility, there are many ways in which his activities and awareness can have a profound effect on the fortunes of his company and himself. Financial awareness, in terms of product pricing and the various ways in which payment can be made, is a most important part of the salesman's responsibility. It can mean the difference between success and failure, both for himself and for his company.

Prospecting and company cashflow

One of the biggest problems of running a business is maintaining a balanced and positive flow of cash, so that sufficient liquid assets are available to cover all immediate debts, particularly those regarding supplies, rent, and payroll. Every company has continually to be aware of the financial problems that can be brought about by the vagaries of the marketplace, production and sales fluctuations, and the tardiness of its debtors. It is therefore quite remarkable that so many salesmen believe (and their companies don't dispute) that the flow rate of orders and money into the company is not their problem. As long as they reach their targets by selling at a competitive price and the company eventually gets paid, they believe they

199

are fulfilling their obligations. The possible implications of such an attitude can be horrendous.

Consider the matter from a production point of view. One thing guaranteed to create absolute chaos for those people producing the end product is a violent and unpredictable fluctuation in demand. The ensuing problems in terms of labour and materials can be considerable, if not disastrous. Such an inconsistency of demand is often created by an unpredictable flow of orders, which in turn, typically comes from an erratic selling pattern due to haphazard sales prospecting. Meanwhile, someone has to cope with late deliveries and turning away business because of a sudden over capacity, or salaries and rent still need to be paid when the production line grinds to a halt. For many salesmen, sales prospecting is an activity which takes place when one runs out of prospects. The implications of this inconsistent approach on the frequency of incoming orders, compared with the consistent effect of regular prospecting, should be self-evident. One can reasonably argue that the importance of continuing sales prospecting becomes less as the sales cycle increases, but, by and large, the salesman who sees prospecting as a spasmodic and transient activity, makes a valid contribution towards the demise of his employer.

The implications of discounts

For many people, a reasonable price is that which remains after the subtraction of a discount. There are two significant factors related to discount. Firstly, the point is reached quickly where the job requirement is for an order taker rather than a salesman. Secondly, if a company cannot consistently maintain its profit levels, it is likely to go out of business. Too many salesmen are convinced that price is the paramount consideration of the decision-making process, when in fact there are many other elements, such as company viability, delivery, related experience, reference clients, support services, product reliability, capability, quality, performance, etc., which are at least as important. Yet, as essential as these factors are, their quality must decline relative to the reduction in the profits which fund them. If discounts are relevant and necessary, they should be the last item on the agenda of sales negotiation, not the first. Starting out by offering a discount is probably the best means of destroying one's professional credibility.

It is unfortunate that the salesman has, for the most part, little control over the profitability of his company other than maintaining standard prices. Otherwise it would make a lot of sense for sales targets to be based on profit rather than revenue. However, a sliding scale of reduction in the rate of sales commission might be a reasonable incentive for not giving away the company's money! That, of course, assumes the discount was the salesman's idea and not his manager's.

Overdue accounts

Discounts are of course effectively academic when it comes to the critical factor of payment. A sale is not a sale until the goods are paid for. I am always surprised when I hear people ask: 'Who is responsible for getting the money in?' It seems to me to be a contrived dilemma, a buck-passing exercise, so that no one gets the nasty job of asking people for money. Make no mistake, it is the salesman's responsibility to ensure that payment is ultimately made, because agreeing a price and a time of payment must be part of his initial sales presentation and subsequent contract. Only in circumstances where his company (rather than he!) fails to fully satisfy its part of the bargain can he have the possible excuse of getting 'out from under'. Even then, it is still the salesman who has the face-to-face contact with the client, and is therefore most likely to obtain payment.

The question of debt collection also raises the problem of whether commission should be paid before the client pays the bill. To a degree, it very much depends on the delivery lead time. It would be unfair for the salesman who is selling large value capital products on extended delivery lead times to have no credit for securing the order. On the other hand, maybe this type of salesman should be on such a high proportion of basic salary to commission, that payment of commission on settlement of the bill might not be too much of an imposition.

From an accounting and administrative point of view, payment of commission is more easily done at the billing stage, although bad debts are usually deducted when they are confirmed. Consequently, few companies actually hold the commission of payment until the money comes in from the client. Nevertheless, it is both unreasonable and inefficient to leave bad debt collection to continual letter-writing and telephone pleas of the accounts department. A quick face-to-face approach by the salesman who sold the goods is usually the best way of getting the money.

One way in which the salesman can promote subsequent prompt payment and sometimes also help the client, is to offer hire purchase or leasing terms when actually making the sale. You would be surprised at how many people withold payment, not because of that small technical fault or that slight departure from specification, but simply because they can't afford to pay. Could that mean they were over-sold in the first place?

Profitable selling

Getting what you pay for isn't always as easy as it should be. To a great extent, this is a function of the eternal triangle of buyer, supplier and salesman. The buyer is entitled to receive what he was promised for the price he agreed to pay. He cannot be expected to concern himself with such factors as: 'He only bought a small one'; 'It represents excellent value for money'; 'It was a special offer'; 'It's a discontinued line'; 'He got it cheap'; and so on.

The supplier's fundamental interest is to provide his product or service in order to make a profit. Even 'loss leaders' represent a device inextricably linked to a profitable business scenario.

The salesman's role, is to create a situation where the demands of both the buyer and the supplier are met in full. This is not always as easy as it seems.

Post-sales support

The implications of price cutting and similar policies which directly affect profitability and professional credibility are clear. One less apparent, yet more common area in which the needs of the buyer and supplier often run awry is within post-sales support. Any product which involves after-sales service, guarantees, technical support, etc., must have the related costs included in the selling price or contained within a scale of additional charges declared prior to the sale being made. The purchaser must be absolutely certain of what it is he wishes the product to do—both immediately and in the future—and be absolutely clear of the implications of making it happen. Despite these obvious business considerations, many transactions result in disaster due to either or both parties having insufficient consideration for the consequences of the sale/purchase. For instance: the buyer underestimates the time and resources required for installing the product or using the service he has ordered; the supplier discovers that the cost of providing the additional support the client now requires is in excess of the profit on the transaction.

The salesman may believe he has absolved himself from the matter, having closed the sale and moved on to some other prospect elsewhere. Alternatively, he may still be involved, but firmly convinced that the client is demanding too much, or, alternatively, that his company has insufficient resources or an inept pricing/costing system. Whether or not he is right, the fact remains that responsibility is his, by virtue of failing to make clear to the buyer from the start the amount of support that could be provided for the price, or, alternatively, informing his company of the likely support requirements of the client concerned. One of the biggest failings, particularly in the pricing of most high technology products, is the implied belief that a client buying a product for £5000 needs ten times less support than one who spends £50 000. Often the reverse is nearer the truth.

Many situations where a buyer is dissatisfied through lack of after-sales support, or the prohibitive cost of it, can be avoided if the right actions are taken prior to the sale being made. Often through enthusiasm or determination to get the business, salesmen fail to give 'chapter and verse' details about what will happen after their product is delivered, for fear that such information, especially if it involves additional costs, might tip the sale in the favour of their competitors. This is an extremely short-sighted attitude which can only generate unnecessary problems, as the installed product must contain no surprises! Many salesmen lose a considerable amount of prime selling time because they have to become involved in 'propping up' existing clients who believe they are not getting what they paid for. This unsatisfactory investment of time can often cost the salesman more than the commission he gained from making that sale in the first place, and highlights the constant need for truth in selling.

If the salesman has told the buyer precisely what he will get for his money in terms of product and subsequent support, and the delivered/ installed product is exactly as promised, yet the buyer is still dissatisfied, it is the salesman's job to be 'the company to the client' and tell him firmly and constructively that his requirement, as stated, has been honoured and he will get no more without the negotiation of additional charges for additional services.

On the other hand, the buyer may have a just grievance. If so, the salesman in the role of 'the client to the company' must ensure that his management provides what has been promised. Lack of facilities or manpower are not his problem. While he can be expected to be sensible about transient company problems, particularly related to the availability of technicians, he should not condone deliberate under-manning or over-selling. If his company, as a matter of policy, is, (a) prepared to minimize its technical support, while appearing to provide an effective after-sales service, (b) foolish enough to offer a 'tailor-made' product beneath a price level at which only a standard package can show a predictable profit, (c) prepared to sell a product which is not totally proven without informing the potential user, (d) cannot afford or recruit the right level of technical staff, (e) maintains a pricing structure of the product, which does not cater for the 'open ended' support demanded by the nature of the product, then the salesman has only two alternatives: inform his manager in detail about the implications of the situation as he sees it, and suggest ways in which the problems might be alleviated while protecting the company's profitability. If his company cannot, or will not, solve the problem, he should find a company that already has!

Is the price too high?

Inevitably, every salesman is occasionally unable to close the order because the client believes, or says, the product is too expensive. In these circumstances the salesman's first priority must be to establish that price is the real reason, rather than camouflage designed to hide less justifiable and more easily refuted objections. Having reached a point where it is absolutely established that cost, in terms of budget rather than competitive alternatives, is the prime obstacle, there are three types of sales argument which need exploring to ensure that the client (and the salesman) has fully understood all the financial implications of both costs and savings. Sometimes, potential buyers fail to take into account the financial contribution which the salesman's product could make to reducing stocks, increasing service, reducing costs, improving earnings, providing greater management control, etc., because such factors are usually difficult to identify in finite, and that means financial, terms. However, features of this kind cannot be written off as intangible and therefore to be disregarded. Arbitrary values need to be established for all benefits and set against the cost of the proposed system or equipment. These in turn can be compared with the costs of the salesman's proposals and also with the costs and relative efficiency of the potential user's existing methods. In addition, it is essential that the client gives close consideration to the cost implications of not going ahead. This includes the unrecoverable 'loss' of any savings that might be made, increased prices at a later date, and the risk of falling behind their competitors.

Often, the total cost of large-scale equipment, particularly to a first-time user, comes as a profound shock. Even when compared with the related savings and benefits, the amount involved can often lead to considerable insecurity on the part of the decision-maker. In this kind of situation the salesman can sometimes help the buyer to take a more objective view of the financial implications by breaking down the total cost into units which are more easily identifiable. An assessment of cost per manufactured item, person, period, copy, unit of weight, customer, etc., can give the potential client a different, and perhaps more realistic view, of the overall financial implications.

There are occasions when the client simply does not have the capital available to pay for the equipment proposed by the salesman, no matter how attractive the ensuing benefits might be. In such circumstances the salesman is unlikely to be asked for 'easy terms', although this does not necessarily mean that methods of payment other than purchase would be unattractive. It is, therefore, important that the salesman is prepared for the proposition of alternative methods of payment and fully understands the financial implications in company terms of rental, leasing, purchasing, and other methods of payment. Fluency in such methods can greatly enhance the credibility of both the salesman and his company.

Finally, price is seldom the ultimate deciding factor in the decision-making process, as potential buyers often view the lowest price with a degree of insecurity and not a little suspicion. Buying is, by and large, a process with considerable emotional bias, where final decisions are not typically technical or financial ones, but rather more political, intuitive, or impulsive. In my experience, the salesman who believes all he has to do is get the price right, has probably misjudged the real basis of decision-making.

13.

Personal disciplines

Personal appearance

My first selling job within the computer industry, was with *IBM*. Despite five years of previous sales experience I had to undergo almost eighteen months of training in systems analysis, programming, and sales before they let me out selling on my own. During this period I was inevitably subjected to a degree of company indoctrination. I am not acquainted with the working environment of *IBM* today but, in those days, two of the basic rules were that alcoholic drink was never consumed on company premises, and all salesmen were expected to wear white shirts. I must confess, the ruling on dress was a source of considerable irritation to me at the time and my reaction was predictable—'If I needed a company edict to compensate for any lack of dress-sense, I would ask for it!' I never actually got round to wearing a black shirt but, my multi-coloured rebellion was not the greatest success of my career.

Like many an unmade fortune, retrospective wisdom usually provides a better informed view of past events. I can now see much more clearly the inherent benefits of the 'white shirt philosophy'. In fact, my interest in dress and personal presentation was reawakened when I became involved in the recruitment business. Continual exposure to salesmen and the process of personal evaluation makes one much more aware of the elements which make up the individual, and appearance is certainly significant. Usually, the initial judgement of an individual is based on appearance. So, the man who arrives in T-shirt and jeans is likely to have less immediate credibility than someone wearing a smart suit, collar, and tie, etc., although it would be unwise to assume this to constitute a guaranteed formula for smartness. It is easy to completely destroy the effect of acceptable dress by untidiness and lack of attention to detail—uncombed hair, dirty finger nails, crumpled suit, and unpolished shoes, etc. I have always believed that many, if not most men, have a less than adequate dress-sense. In any office there are always some who are better presented than

205

the rest, and some, who on a good day, look like they have just been pulled through a hedge. On the other hand, there are some who always wear clean, new, well-pressed, even expensive, clothes, yet never look well dressed because of an imbalance of colours, materials, styles, textures, and patterns. In most business circles, it is necessary to take a 'Jekyll and Hyde' approach to dress. If you want to project individuality through your clothes, it needs to be done away from the business environment. Within the working environment it is better to view your appearance through the eyes of the typical business onlooker, and decide what mode of apparel will give a positive impression of efficiency, stability, confidence, and reliability. This is where the white shirt comes in!

The jacket, shirt, and tie are those items of a businessman's dress which usually first meet the eye. The shirt serves the function of visually linking the tie and jacket together. White, being a tone rather than a colour can never clash, whereas a colour might, and a pattern invariably will. If the white is bordered by a dark colour then its properties are highlighted. So, a white shirt with a dark suit gives maximum impact, and an impression of smartness and efficiency. While this is an illusion, and, possibly an untrendy one at that, it does have the desired effect. Personal appearance and its effect upon personal credibility within the selling environment must be a constant consideration. After all, a scruffy appearance must be some reflection of the individual's attitude, general efficiency, and reliability.

Mental and physical fitness

Despite the life of luxury hotels and fast cars, often imagined by those on the outside of selling looking in, being a successful salesman is a direct result of hard work and positive thinking, more consistent with coronaries, through continual business pressure, than Bacchanalian revelries.

Most jobs involve either mental or physical demands, but the salesman, certainly in the realms of capital goods and high technology products, has significant exposure to both. His total capability, therefore, needs to be much more than is normally expected of the typical technician or manual worker. However, mental and physical condition cannot really be separated, as mental pressures can quickly lead to psychosomatic symptoms and physical problems, which , in turn, stimulate anxiety and depression—an extremely vicious circle. Conversely, a calm or exhilarated mind can bring about a relaxed and energetic body, and an extremely healthy physical state can offset many of the effects of stress. Unfortunately, many salesmen, particularly those over the age of thirty, appear to be completely unaware of these rather obvious facts. They seem not to appreciate the benefits of being able to approach the sales negotiation with a positive and enthusiastic mind, uncluttered with the garbage of day-to-day self-inflicted trivia. This is a most profound failing, for, unless the salesman can get up early every morning, whatever the weather, and feel physically one step ahead of the game, he will never achieve his true potential.

So, how is this state of fitness and tranquillity achieved? In truth, the answer must be with much determination and effort, yet, never constantly! As I have already said, one's mental and physical metabolisms are interactive; the enhancement of one is usually the improvement of both. Consequently, if the salesman is to make a real effort to improve his overall condition, it is best to start out with either a physical or a mental approach. For one person, it might be yoga or transcendental meditation; for another, squash or jogging.

There are many avenues one can explore for a greater mental awareness and total relaxation. My only suggestion is that individuals should reserve their judgements on the related benefits of a pursuit until after they have really tried it, rather than dismissing it beforehand.

The opportunities for improving one's physical condition are innumerable. However, those starting out should avoid playing dynamic, stop-go, sports like football and hockey. Squash, in particular, is a potential killer. Remember, you don't play squash to get fit, you get fit to play squash. Just take it easy, and aim only to improve on what you did before, no matter how marginal. Forget the next Olympic Games!

Most people in selling find their life far too demanding and unpredictable to be able to commit themselves to being in a given place at a given time. Consequently, court games, let alone team games, run too much risk of having to let other people down. For them, and many others, jogging has become a very attractive and sensible route to physical fitness as it is really non-competitive running, where the individual travels whatever distance at whatever speed is appropriate to his or her capability. Apart from greatly benefiting heart and lungs, it has the added benefit of being totally independent of time, location, equipment, courts, pitches, and other people. However, for some people it may lead to back or joint problems, so be careful! Nevertheless, whatever the level of involvement, most regular joggers will tell you they never felt physically and mentally more able to cope with the rigours of day-to-day living. For salesmen that has to be worth at least an extra couple of calls a week!

There are some people who have tried jogging and find it boring or difficult to pursue in the winter. The primary objective is to exercise the heart and lungs, and to increase the efficiency of the circulation and the oxygenation of the blood. My doctor once advised me that swimming and cycling are superior forms of exercise, as they achieve the essential stimulation of the heart and lungs without jarring the joints and internal organs. This may be so, but whatever physical exercise you may care to pursue, if you are starting out for the first time or after a long lay-off, take it very easy. Exercise is not a competition!

Working in the office

On one occasion I received a letter from a reader of the weekly column on which some of this book is based, describing a situation in which salesmen all too often find themselves immersed. My correspondent worked as a salesman for a computer equipment manufacturer. He was a very conscientious, enthusiastic and hard working salesman, and whenever any of his clients telephoned the office with a problem, he did whatever was necessary to make the caller happy. Unfortunately, when these clients applied for service to other departments with non-sales problems (if there are such things) the quality of response was so poor that his clients would no longer deal directly with them. Instead they telephoned this particular salesman whenever they had a problem. The result of this was obviously a severe loss of selling time, and consequently a loss of commission earnings and a performance against target which was less than it might have been.

What can salesmen do in this kind of situation? As far as I can see it is all a function of what one is employed to do. While a salesman, above all people, needs to be very flexible in his attitudes and actions, he needs a point of reference so that, when all else fails, he can make some kind of demarcation between his responsibilities and those of other people. A salesman is employed to sell, but, in his role of being the 'company to the client' and the 'client to the company', he can become everybody's 'whipping boy' when things go wrong. That is why it is essential for every salesman to have a formal job specification, which precisely states his responsibilities and, if necessary, his non-responsibilities. Assuming the salesman is armed with a formal statement of his role within the company, it should then be a simple matter to discuss the problem with his sales manager. After all, the loss of selling time must also have a direct effect on his manager's performance too, and, consequently, on that of the company as a whole. On the other hand, if the company shows no interest in providing effective client support and product related services, the salesman's best action is to find a company that does.

Having said all of that, my experience of salesmen who spend a lot of time around the office sorting out non-sales problems is that many of them, consciously or unconsciously, prefer such activity as an alternative to getting into the street and knocking on doors. It is very easy for a salesman to get himself deeply involved in a demanding situation, when it would be better for the company and himself to back off. Handling a problem, which is not directly a selling matter, is often a very slippery slope, and, once you are committed, it is very difficult to escape until you get to the bottom. Sometimes the salesman's refusal to become involved can be to the client's detriment. If this happens too often there is something drastically wrong with the salesman's company, and the remedy is in his own hands. One cold fact is that it is the salesman's employer who pays him, not the client, so loyalties must take that firmly into account. In other words, salespeople are employed to sell, and that demands maximum use of the time which can be made available for this activity to take place. If the amount of selling time is being seriously eroded by an unreasonable amount of activity which is ostensibly the province of other people/departments, then it is up to the salesman, to decide whether the fault lies within himself or his company—then act accordingly. The existence of formal terms of reference make subsequent debate rather more rational than it might be otherwise.

Workload priorities

I have always envied people who have a real sense of purpose, those with the strength of character to be single minded whatever the pressure or distractions. How nice it must be to schedule one's work instinctively in a rational way, so that the most important tasks are always given their proper priority. You must be familiar with the usual situation—the desk covered in paper debris, job priority based on last in/first out, efficiency and temper in rapid decline. One might say that this kind of situation falls into the following three categories.

1. Pressure due to personal disorganization
It is difficult to accept that one is fundamentally a badly organized person. However, it is reasonable to suggest that the need for keeping things in their place and dealing with them according to their relative importance is as applicable to the disorderly mind as it is to the meticulous. Some people are very well organized until the pressure is on, when, suddenly, they go under only to re-emerge as their former selves once things have quietened down. Almost always, the originating source of pressure is outside the individual's control.

2. Pressure due to indiscriminate interruption
The worst kind of pressure, in my opinion, is the result of indiscriminate interruptions, which create an artificial workload, that, by its very nature, demands absolute priority, irrespective of the importance of the task in hand. The prime examples are telephone calls and people who 'pop in for a quick word'. Those who are naturally generous, warm-hearted, considerate, helpful, or altruistic, are particularly susceptible to this kind of invasion. There you are, writing the key section of a very important sales proposal that you have faithfully promised to the client that day, when the telephone rings! Nothing is more immediately important to you than completing that document, but, you pick up the telephone and it's the Sales Director's secretary, who has a desperate problem with her rubber plant and could you render immediate assistance? It's a damned nuisance, but you drop everything and rush to her aid. On the other hand, it could be the production manager, popping in to request a copy of a recent order

209

because he's lost the original document. So, cursing as you go, you struggle through your inadequate filing system to find your copy because the guy has problems and he needs your help. I call this the innocent exploitation syndrome. The initiator of the distraction assumes you have no more urgent task on hand, for, had that been the case, you would have said so, wouldn't you? Yet, most times, for reasons of courtesy you don't, and, as a consequence, you allow yourself to be exploited. How short-sighted! Nobody really wants to take advantage of your good nature, as you only have to let them know that you are under pressure and they'll go away—'Sorry everybody, I'd love to help, but right now I'm deeply involved in an extremely urgent report. I'll give you a call as soon as I've finished.' That's not being rude, it's being honest and practical.

3. Pressure due to work overload

Disorganization by overload is bad enough in itself but, exacerbated by interruption, could easily lead to unnecessary stress. There's only one thing to do when totally overloaded—stop and assess! Evaluate the outstanding tasks, separate the non-essential from the essential, and put the former to one side for attention in easier times. Then make a list of the essential tasks in order of importance, and start work again in strict order of practical priority, refusing to see or speak to anyone, unless they can convince you that their problem is more urgent than yours. Be ruthless. It's the only way.

People react to pressure in a wide variety of ways. A 'classic' is the 'Nero syndrome'. This is where the individual becomes so bewildered by an overload of problems, that his mind virtually switches off, yet, by way of a subsconscious smoke screen, he becomes deeply involved in some irrelevant task. Many people find they cannot cope with their job because they are overwhelmed by a confusion of problems which have no apparent beginning or end. In such circumstances, a list of tasks by order of priority is essential. It's a control, a discipline, and a statement of reality. You see, Nero wasn't necessarily being casual as he played his fiddle while Rome burned—he simply couldn't find his job priority list!

The effective use of selling time

Time is the salesman's most valuable asset, so his greatest responsibility is to use it in the most effective manner. This demands a considerable amount of thought, dedication, and, above all, efficient planning. Whatever objectives a salesman may have, the route to success can be described in elements of time, and the effective use of it is as much dependent on attitude, habit and possibility horizons as it is on the speed at which it passes. Take, for example, planning a sales target at the beginning of a new target year. The route to achieving total sales quota can be expressed in terms of

210

an approximate number of orders, based on the typical value of an individual sale. Using the experience of the previous sales year, these can be described as a proportion of the required number of prospects available for conversion, which in turn can be derived from a much larger quantity of 'suspects' which emanate from initial 'pioneering' work. These possible sources of business are then a function of the number of calls which can possibly be made in a working day, and this is clearly derived from the amount of time available.

The effective use of the salesman's working day consists of many elements: journey planning, scheduling of appointments, controlling the duration of sales calls, etc. Above all it is dependent on having a real awareness of the amount of time actually available for selling.

Positive thinking

I don't intend to get locked into a heavy discussion on the powers of positive thinking. My interest in the topic concerns personal attitudes rather than the ultimate power of the mind. My idea of positive thinking is a personal or group commitment to: 'We will succeed, but these are the problems we will have to overcome' rather than 'What if we fail, even though there are some areas in which success might be possible?' That is, confidence in the ability to succeed, without over-optimism or arrogance, rather than concentrating one's efforts on the avoidance of failure.

I was once told a story of two salesmen who were sent to Central Africa to sell shoes. After a few days the sales director received a cable from the first salesman to the effect 'Forget it—nobody wears shoes in this part of the world!' This communication was closely followed by a telegram from the other salesman, which declared 'Great opportunity. No one has shoes. Unlimited potential!' Maybe this is not a practical example of positive thinking, but it serves to illustrate how easy it is to see a situation as a problem when it could just as easily be a golden opportunity. Nothing motivates more than success, and, by the same virtue, one can only produce the level of enthusiasm and confidence necessary for success if everyone truly believes they will win.

Public conversations

Travelling and dining with colleagues and clients often presents an excellent opportunity for discussing important business matters—perhaps the implications of the new equipment you are about to install; the opening of a new branch office; the highlights of your prospect portfolio. Unfortunately, whether travelling first or second class, dining at the 'Ritz' or 'Joe's Cafe', there is no way of assessing whether you are in the company of disinterested bystanders or fascinated competitors.

The implications of having business conversations overheard are fairly obvious, yet people continue to chatter in public, even though such carelessness could easily result in the loss of a forthcoming sale or an existing client. Of course, it is essential to prepare for every sales call, whether one is accompanied or not, but there is a proper time and place for everything. So, if you must discuss your business publicly, keep it quiet, don't use proper names of companies, products or personalities, and make it brief. Conversely, if you are travelling or dining alone, just listen to the world around you. The loose talk of other people is fair game. And the next time you visit the pub with the lads from the office, just think about all those clients, competitors, journalists, or government officials who might be in there with you.

Routine calls

I recall a sales call once made on me by an office equipment salesman—'Just a routine call', he announced, and I knew just what to expect. I've heard that expression so many times before, particularly from salesmen making appointments by telephone:

'I'd like to visit you next week.'

'Oh really, why?'

'Just a routine call.'

'Well, alright, I suppose so.'

or alternatively:

'I see. Well why don't you leave it until you have some real justification for calling?'

Either way, the client cannot be very impressed. Whether he gives the first response, or the second, he has the problem of deciding whether 'Just a routine call' is a cover for a crafty selling ploy or merely a waste of time. Whatever the conclusion, his respect for the salesman must be diminished. Having said that, there are always clients who appear to have plenty of time to discuss anything from football to Freud, the only notable exception being business. The 'routine call' is an attitude of mind—it is casual and has no objective; it is unprepared and is negative; it requires no greater effort than making the journey to the client's front door:

'Morning Fred. How's the wife? Looks like the summer's over. You don't want anything today do you?'

I know it sounds silly, but it happens all the time.

What is a sales call? As far as I am concerned it is the application of a pre-conceived plan, devised to achieve one or more predetermined sales objectives which will result in advancement of profitable business between the client and the salesman's employer. The sales objectives can be wide and varied, but whether the need to call is brought about by client complaint, sales prospecting, or whatever, most of these objectives must have one thing in common: a potential for being converted into additional business. I admit there are times when a speculative call can be useful; the salesman can often benefit from dropping in to see a client without a formal appointment. However, the same rule still applies. The salesman must spend time reflecting on his reason for calling before he enters the client's premises:

1. What is my reason for calling, and what do I tell the client if he asks me?

2. What can be achieved now that could not be achieved easier and better at a later date?

3. What are the benefits to my company and the prospective buyer?

4. Am I really prepared to handle any situation which may arise?

As far as I am concerned there is no such thing as a routine call, only conscience salve and time filling.

Anyway, to get back to my original story, it turned out the salesman had a new 'best-ever-in-the-whole-world' photocopier at a 'price-we-couldn't-refuse'—but we did! We were busy and his interruption was an imposition but we were far too polite to tell him to clear off; we didn't really listen too much because we were trying to keep mentally attuned to the problem we were processing when he arrived. We didn't want to spend money with him anyway because 'Just a routine call' meant he didn't want to sell us anything—or so we thought. So when he did, we felt he was trying to 'pull a fast one', and we pulled down the shutters. Otherwise it was quite a reasonable call—I suppose.

Consequential thinking

Plan ahead! I am sure these often unheeded words of wisdom are familiar to you—one might call it 'consequential thinking.' Unfortunately, like many other declarations of commonsense the impact is transient, and, once acknowledged as being right and desirable, they quickly dissolve into apathy and complacency. One of the many aspects of non-consequential thinking is the use of double standards in the context of social and business behaviour. I have known many salespeople at all levels, but particularly managers, who make great demands on their subordinates, yet themselves have an apparently limitless appetite for Friday afternoon golf and extended lunches. Such people are often oblivious of the implications of their behaviour and the damaging effect upon the respect and motivation of those for whom they are responsible. Consequential thinking is about ensuring that no action is taken in isolation, that positive account is taken of what went before and what might come after. Of course, such a discipline is not limited to selling, or even the business world. Every significant business, or even social, process should be accompanied by questions like:

1. Is this the correct action, time, place?
2. Why am I taking this action?
3. Why have I been asked to do it?
4. Is the action acceptable, reasonable?
5. Have I checked to ensure my understanding is correct?
6. What are the implications of the action I am contemplating?
7. What will be the effect on other parties?
8. What are the alternatives?
9. Will the action fall within the rules of acceptable behaviour?
10. Has the action I have taken had the expected effect?
11. Is the action feasible/possible?
12. Have I informed interested parties about the outcome of my action?
13. What have I learned from this experience?

I know that sounds like an awful lot to take into account, but just try out this checklist the next time you are thinking of writing an angry memo, bending the product specification, making a rash claim, or contemplating a romantic affair. It will certainly reduce your chances of being caught in a compromising situation!

Familiarity breeds contempt

A feature of new and high technology industries, in comparison with other longer-established businesses, is the predominant use of Christian names, regardless of rank or duration of relationship. While this practice may be commonplace in some countries, it is still the exception rather than the rule in Europe, and contains many pitfalls for the naïve and insensitive salesman. 'Familiarity breeds contempt' is an old saying well known to all of us, but it has a particular significance for salesmen, as 'familiarity' and its close relative 'flippancy' are seldom endearing qualities. On the contrary, they are perhaps two of the better devices for destroying empathy between negotiating parties. What might appear to the salesman to be an attitude of friendliness and enthusiasm, could be seen by his client as casual and disrespectful.

Don't ever be the first to use Christian names; that should always be the prerogative of the buyer. What is more important, make it clear that you have respect for him, his company and its product, simply by your manner and the words you use. 'Hi Fred' may seem to be a cheery first time greeting to the president of an international corporation. A man of that stature will certainly be too smart to let you know his real reaction, but rest assured you will have created an instant barrier which will subsequently have to be taken down again, brick by brick.

One might expect this failing to be limited to the young and inexperienced salesman, but not necessarily so. It is more a function of self-awareness and sensitivity, and unfortunately there are many so-called experienced salesmen whose personal objectivity and sales sensitivity is no more developed than it was when they started out!

Many years ago I was on a sales training course, and during a role playing exercise I had to make a call on a well-established client. In order to demonstrate the good relationship that existed between my client and myself, and also hoping to throw the instructor, I started the call by casually saying 'Good morning Mr Smith. I had a super time with your daughter last night.' Without any sign of reaction at all he looked me straight in the eye and said 'Then you will be sad to learn that she died this morning!' Get out of that!

Consistency

By and large every individual has a manner, an attitude towards other people and situations which gives an outward impression of the kind of person he is. This generates a corresponding reaction from others, who either consciously or subconsciously make a judgement of what they see and use it as the basis for categorizing the person concerned, tempered by their own self-conceived standards. This is likely to result in convenient 'pigeon holing' such as 'like', 'don't like' and 'take or leave'.

One of the most difficult aspects of human coexistence is the unwillingness of most people to attempt a penetration of this façade in order to ascertain the truth. The justifications for avoiding this precarious adventure range, unfortunately, from insecurity to apathy. 'What's this got to do with selling?' You might ask. Quite a lot really. Any person-to-person interaction inevitably has to overcome the instinctive poses and affectations we wrap around ourselves in order to hide our fears and vulnerability. This is as applicable to a buyer/salesman relationship as it is to a husband and wife. The important thing is to use truth to discover truth. The more pretentious the approach of one party, the more exaggerated the likely reaction of the other. The only way to have a chance of discovering the reality of another person is first to make an honest statement of oneself. In the selling process, a clear and truthful statement of one's product, company, personal attitudes, and intentions is the only viable basis for establishing empathy and an effective buyer/salesman relationship.

Achieving this level of trust and understanding isn't easy, but having got there it would be foolish to assume that the process is complete and invulnerable. Like marriage, which after all is just one of a multitude of human relationships, one has to continually strive to make it work. If you take it for granted, it inevitably goes sour. Certainly, one of the best devices for destroying a human relationship is inconsistency, and this relates as much to attitudes as actions. Salesmen can easily destroy years of effort in establishing personal credibility by a single instance of uncharacteristic behaviour.

A good example of this is the fluctuating manner some salesmen employ depending on the apparent level of influence of the person they are addressing—subdominant to some, rude and offhand to others. This is a rather unintelligent and puerile attitude, for it assumes that the parties concerned never interact. An example is when a caller gives the telephonist/receptionist a bad time because she can't locate the person he wants, or is rude to a secretary who fails to provide the information he requires, yet the very next moment is courteous, helpful, and charming to the chief executive. Managing directors do speak to telephonists and secretaries, and the inconsistency that such conversations reveal can destroy a salesman's credibility, and, even worse, without him realising that his cover has been blown.

New Year resolutions

At the beginning of each year, no matter how well he performed in the previous twelve months, the salesman usually has the challenge of proving his capability over again. This is the occupational treadmill that differentiates selling from most other jobs, and demands a special assortment of human characteristics for coping with its perpetual challenge.

New Year is the right psychological time for new beginnings in the shape of traditional New Year resolutions. Invariably, these promises of self-improvement imply the application of greater personal discipline—stop smoking, more exercise, less eating, etc. So, next New Year's Eve, why don't you make a serious personal commitment to apply one or more selling disciplines throughout the coming year which you know you have not effectively applied hitherto? Here is a short summary of some of the topics included in this book, from which you might care to choose a resolution that you feel is appropriate.

Throughout the coming year I will definitely:

1. Pre-plan all my sales calls.

2. Write my call reports immediately after each call.

3. Not discuss company business in public.

4. Include Monday morning and Friday afternoon in my working week, particularly as far as face-to-face selling calls are concerned.

5. Apply 'vertical marketing' discipline to sales activity within my territory.

6. Invest some of my time in self-education as well as urging my company to provide continual sales training.

7. Identify sales benefits and sell sales advantages.

8. Always be sure I have identified the client's problems and agreed them with him.

9. Make sure my sales proposals contain no surprises, but confirm all sales benefits and advantages already agreed.

10. Apply the 'so what?' test to all sales benefits before I present them to clients.

11. Qualify all prospects thoroughly before committing my company's resources.

12. Analyse all completed sales negotiations, whether won or lost, to discover why.

13. Make sure I know the real decision-maker at the very beginning of every sales negotiation.

14. Make my initial sales contact at managing director level.

15. Keep my appearance smart and business-like at all times.

16. Never make derogatory remarks about my company or its employees in order to avoid personal responsibility for mistakes, even when it isn't my fault.

17. Ask for the order as soon and as often as is appropriate.

18. Never directly belittle the products of my competitors.

19. Listen and talk in accordance with nature's ratio of two ears to one mouth.

20. Make no assumptions about the best time to close.

Happy New Year!

Company cars

The supply of company cars for the use of salesmen has always been an emotive subject. Most selling jobs in the UK today involve the provision of a motor car, although many companies still prefer to operate a car allowance scheme typically based on mileage. Which is most financially beneficial generally depends on the generosity of the scheme and the nature of the individual sales territory. As a crude generalization, the individual salesman is financially better off having a company car if he has a city territory, and better off with mileage allowance if he works in 'sheep country'.

It is essential that salesmen have the right attitude towards company cars. They should remember that their vehicle is merely a container on wheels, representing the most efficient way of being transported from one place of business to another. If there was a more effective way they wouldn't get one at all. Yet to some salesmen the company car is not only a divine right, it is a profound statement of his success within a materialistic society, and a status symbol within an 'executive estate' mentality.

One of the best ways for the salesman to irritate his manager is to keep moaning about company cars. Except for those rare occasions when car schemes are modified to the salesman's detriment, most situations which are thought unsatisfactory by the salesman operate on a basis that was in existence from the moment he was first employed. So, why did he join if he didn't like the terms of employment? The company car, no matter how unreliable or unsuitable, is still only a marginal factor within the selling process. If it is allowed to take up an unreasonable proportion of the salesman's attention, he is soon seen as a negative individual where selling is a peripheral activity to his interest in motor cars. If the salesman believes he has a real grievance and it is affecting his sales success, he should state it positively to his manager. If this does not result in satisfaction, the only options are to accept the situation as it is or move to a company where the problem does not exist. What he should not do is moan continually about how unfairly he is being treated. So, please:

1. Don't keep moaning about the company supplying cars when it is committed to a mileage allowance scheme.

2. Don't fit accessories which cannot be easily removed to leave the vehicle in its original state.

3. Don't use the car for holidays, touring caravans, horse trailers, etc., without formal company approval.

4. Don't keep complaining that the car is too old, too large, too small, beneath the status of the job, tatty, difficult to park, etc.

5. Don't play out 'grand prix' fantasies in the vehicle that's meant to be a

consistently reliable means of business transportation. (Those with company Ferraris are excused!)

6. Do remember that, despite the typical salesman's absolute dependence on the car to perform a selling function effectively, it is nonetheless a perk and that private use is a privilege, not a divine right. There is no real social justification for the salesman to have a car at weekends when the neighbours in less mobile occupations are having to struggle along with second-hand cars and the exorbitant cost of petrol, depreciation, and maintenance. The provision of a company car helps the salesman avoid most of the financial pressures of supplying reliable transportation as well as providing a little social kudos. In other words, it's a special privilege and should be treated as such.

Usage and abusage of a company car

For most salespeople outside inner-city territories, the motor car is an essential tool for efficient performance, and in many cases territorial coverage would be impossible by any other means. However, there is a danger that motor vehicles, like family and other everyday familiar things, can be taken for granted and therefore abused. The outcome of the thoughtless user is, at least, a reduction of efficiency, and potentially total disaster.

There are a number of disciplines, directly and indirectly related to the motor car, which salespeople must accept as absolute essentials. Some obvious, some maybe less so, but all falling into the category of 'I know you know it, but do you do it?' Let's take basic care of the car.

Most motorists stop at a garage simply to buy petrol. No consideration is given at all to other essential aspects of their vehicles' mechanism from one service to another, assuming that such servicing is carried out at the specified intervals. 'Management by disaster' appears to be the basic convention—tyres are only inflated when seen to be flat, oil considered only when 'the little red light' comes on, etc. Salesmen are no exception to this kind of neglect. Regular servicing of a company car is imperative and a stop for petrol should automatically involve the consideration of oil, battery, and tyres—and getting a receipt of course! As for the car's presentation, there is no better reflection of a salesman's attitude and personal organization than the condition in which he keeps his car. Show me a dirty and unkempt company car and I'll show you a disorganized and uncommitted salesman.

Every morning, salesmen all over the world ease themselves into their vehicles and then ask themselves two questions: 'Right, now where am I going today' and 'How do I get there?' The first question, I admit, may serve as a reminder, rather than an instant journey plan, but the second is a consideration being made for the first time, too late to cater for any external influences like road accidents, snow drifts, and major roadworks along the motorways. Always plan a sales journey the day before, particularly if it is a long one. A quick call to your motoring organization is often a good way of avoiding or coping with adverse road conditions and traffic problems. Simply relying on the car radio, having already made a commitment to a particular route, is not really a very satisfactory means of arriving on time for an appointment. Having planned the route and estimated the journey time, add a further time allowance of 25 per cent or 15 minutes, whichever is the greater. Far better to arrive early and relaxed than late and agitated.

A top quality road map is an absolute essential for any salesman. This is not simply an asset for planning a journey, but also a great help when looking for a way out of a traffic jam by whatever byways are at hand. In the latter case a complete set of ordnance survey maps for the whole sales territory (depending on area, of course) can be even better.

Driving disciplines

Assuming a well-maintained and prepared car, and a sensible journey plan which caters for unforeseen delays, there are several aspects of the driving process which need to be taken into account.

Motor car travel involves considerable psychological stress which is not always apparent to the driver. It is very easy for the effects to result in less effective selling on arrival, and the distinct possibility of a road accident *en route*. Particularly in the case of long journeys, there is a great temptation to 'get the journey over' and keep pressing on despite tiredness or even boredom. This is a rather foolish attitude that can have dire results. It is most important to make a stop for refreshment and relaxation, for this not only contributes to more efficient driving, but also helps the salesman to reduce the risk of arriving over-tired or even in a distraught condition. Then, at the end of the journey, no matter how brief, it is essential to spend at least five minutes regaining maximum composure and reconsidering the strategy and objectives of the call. This is so much preferable to the not uncommon habit of arriving late, abandoning the car in an anti-social manner, rushing into the client's premises in a dishevelled state, oblivious of the client's situation and your selling intentions, and starting out on the defensive by having the discourtesy to arrive late for a client who was prepared to allow you some of his precious time.

A problem I have often suffered on long distance journeys is falling a sleep at the wheel. This is a fairly common affliction, which only becomes a real hazard when one attempts to fight it off while still continuing the journey. Don't ever run the risk of overestimating the strength of your willpower in this way. If you feel yourself getting drowsy, don't rely on winding down the window and directing the air-vents on to your face. Leave the road and take a ten minute nap. It is quite amazing how refreshed one can feel after such a brief interlude.

Another common problem among salespeople is back trouble, brought on by bad driving posture and/or stress. Clearly people with this kind of affliction must ensure that the car provides a comfortable driving position, even if they have to go to the extreme of replacing the original seat. Driving for extended periods every day of the week, in a strained posture and with a back susceptible to anything from disc rupture to sciatica, can lead to painful and irrecoverable spinal damage. The principal hazard of motor cars for back sufferers is that the normal vertical posture of the spine while driving exposes it to maximum impact from road vibration, plus gravitational and inertial forces. A remedy I have found very helpful is to recline the back of the seat to whatever feels to be the most comfortable angle. This not only serves to alter the more demanding vertical position of the spine, but also makes for greater freedom for getting in and out of the car in times of really bad attacks. Finally, don't make the mistake of assuming that only the elderly get bad backs; I had my first attack when I was eighteen. An unfortunate aspect of this kind of problem is that once you've 'joined the club', you never really get out of it.

If it is at all practical, for long journeys, travel by train or aeroplane. This provides an opportunity for relaxation, time to consider the sales situation in depth, getting on with other work, and arriving fresh.

Many salesmen, particularly those who work from home and cover large geographic territories, spending several days at a time away from home, derive much benefit from constructing their own mobile office. This lies either in the car boot or at home, and consists of an accessible box with partitions to cater for such things as client record cards, call report forms, sales literature, product specifications, samples, directories, and so on. Not the range or number of items one would wish, or be able, to carry around in a briefcase. It soon becomes second nature to 'top up the office' before a trip, and can make a significant contribution to selling efficiency.

A code of practice for professional salespeople

There is an assumed code of practice among professional salespeople which is based on common sense, integrity, and the laws of the land. Like any other rules, written or otherwise, they are broken occasionally, and such offenders are justly labelled as acting unprofessionally. Of course, it is rather difficult to work to a set of rules that have not been formally declared, even though they may be entirely based on good citizenship. Here are my thoughts on a code of practice for professional salespeople.

Professional salespeople always:

1. Endeavour to achieve the immediate and continuing satisfaction of their clients on a basis of mutual trust and good faith.

2. Ensure that any contract is explicit, unambiguous, and complete, to such an extent that it could continue to operate without any problems

should the involvement of either party who instigated the original agreement be removed from the operational process.

3. Ensure that the client is aware of any additional work or expense that will be incurred by using the product concerned.

4. Make the client fully aware of any risks implicit in the purchase and use of the product and any ways in which it might adversely affect his plans.

5. Inform the client of any intention to sub-contract part of the responsibility for supplying the product and state precisely what control their company will have over quality and reliability.

6. Ensure that formal references to an existing user as a statement of product credibility and suitability are entirely relevant to the needs of the prospect, and are made with the expressed authority of the client concerned.

7. Inform the client of any product modifications prior to delivery, and secure his agreement to such changes.

8. Ensure that the client has a total understanding of exactly what he will be getting for the price he is being charged, and any impending price changes.

9. Respect and protect the confidentiality of client and employer alike.

10. Ensure that they accept commitments for supplying only those products their company is able to provide and has authorized them to sell, as opposed to those which might be anticipated or assumed.

11. Pursue only that business which they truly believe will be profitable to their employer.

12. Process the clerical and administrative aspects of their job diligently, honestly, and promptly, subject to the reasonable demands of their employer.

13. Gain fluency in product specification and application, and continually apply their best endeavours to keep abreast with new developments by way of company training and self-education. This also includes comprehensive knowledge of competitive products.

14. Act in a loyal and honest manner, and openly declare their job function and intentions.

15. Present themselves as the 'company to the client' and the 'client to the company'.

16. Do everything in their power to preserve the integrity of both their own industry and the sales profession.

Professional salespeople do not:

1. Agree to any changes, modifications, or additions to any product or service after the order has been placed, without the expressed authority of their employer, and without immediately informing the client of any resulting change in price, delivery, specification, performance, etc.

2. Sub-contract any part of their selling responsibility to any agent or third party, without the expressed authority of their employer.

3. Promise or give away any part of their commission earnings in order to solicit business, nor do they give or accept bribes of any kind.

4. Involve themselves in sharp practice or the use of any selling technique which will serve to mislead or take advantage of the client.

5. Become involved in price fixing or similar deceptions. This includes market sharing, falsifying tenders, under-quoting, and the omission of additional costs, such as related supplies, labour, electricity, construction, installation, licences, delivery, maintenance, environmental control, fuel, packaging, etc.

6. Become party to any form of practice that could lead to corruption.

7. Denigrate the character of their company, their competitors, or any fellow professional.

8. Make exaggerated claims concerning the benefits and advantages which might be achieved by the use of their product.

9. Exploit the special freedom of their occupation by devoting less time and effort to their job than can reasonably be expected by their employer.

I do not expect this list to be complete. Indeed, it is nothing more than rather obvious statements of integrity and common sense. Nonetheless, for people new to selling, it is a reasonable basis from which to develop a personal code of practice. For those already established in the profession, it stands as a reminder of disciplines and principles that have particular significance when the pressures of selling suggest the possibility of ethical compromise.

Index

Accounts, overdue, 201
Advantages, sales, 81–84
    qualification of, 82–84
Appointments, by 'phone, 29

Benefits, sales, 81–84
    qualification of, 82–84
Buyer, types of, 195–197
Buying signals, 136–138

Call reports, 53
Cars, use of company, 218–221
Cash flow, 199–200
Categorization of clients, 46–47
Checklists, 53–55
Christian names, use of, 214–215
Client records, 50–53
Close, the:
    disciplines and objectives, 131–151
    failure to, 125–127
    psychology of, 128
    techniques (see Closing)
    timing of, 129
Closing:
    altering the proposition, 170
    ask for the order, 170–171
    assessing the cost of delay, 168–169
    assuming the order, 154–156
    'balance sheet' method, 167–168
    concentrating on a minor issue,
        160–161
    continuing affirmation, 152–154
    converting an objection, 162–164
    'either/or', 159–160
    exploiting scarcity, 164–165
    multi-person, 151
    offering special inducements, 161–162

post close disciplines, 171–173
    reducing the options, 158–159
    setting up barriers, 156–158
    stressing emotional needs, 169–170
    summary, 166
    tactics and techniques, 152
    using impending events, 165–166
    wrong person, the, 174–176
Colleagues, business, for prospective
    business, 28
Committees, steering, 197–198
Conduct, code of, 221–223
Courtesy calls, 74
Customer, as source of knowledge,
    23–24

Decision-maker, the actual, 192–193
Decision timetable, 144
Direct mailing, 27
Discounts, 200
Door-to-door canvassing, 28
Dress, 205–206
Duration of sale (see Selling cycle)

Early start, importance of, 47–48
Economic recession, selling in, 188–189
Emotional reasons for buying, 7–8
Enquiries, 38–39
Evaluation:
    competition, 88–90
    sales situation, 87–88
Existing clients, as prospects, 26

Film shows, 67
Fitness, mental and physical, 206–207
Flip charts, 66
'Flogging book', 67
    source of knowledge, 21

Hidden organizations, 193–194

Initiative, keeping the, 149
Interview, opening, 77–79

Knowledge:
applications, 17–18
competition, 18–20
customers, 23–24
'flogging book', 21
industry, 17–18
library, public, 23
pre-call preparation, 74–75
product, 16–17
product manual, 23
sales manager, 22
sales meetings, 21
sales support, 23
sources of, 20
training, internal, 20–21

Letters, not to send, 69–71
Library, public, 23
Listening, importance of, 60–61

Management:
of territory, 44–46
of time, 46–48
Managing directors, dealing with, 35–38
Middle management, hazards of
contacting, 37–38
Mistakes, handling, 185–187
Mobility, importance of, 13

Objections:
overcoming, 99–124
unanswered, 150–151
Opening questions, 68
Organization, personal, 209–210
Outlets, types of, 11

Personal organization, 73
Planned presentation, telephone, 31–33
Planned sales calls, 48–50
Politics, company, 189–190
Post mortems, 172, 182–184
Presentations:
condensed, 80–81
disciplines, 79–80
sales, 79–81
Press, for prospective business, 26
Pressure selling, 127
Price, too high? 203–204
Problems, identifying the real ones, 16
Product manual, 23

Products, types of, 10
Proposals, sales, 93–95
Prospective business:
business colleagues, 28
direct mailing, 27
door-to-door canvassing, 28
existing clients, 26
press, the, 26
salespeople, other, 28
social contacts, 27
trade associations, 26–27
trade directories, 27–28

Qualification:
of advantages, 82–84
of benefits, 82–84
of prospects, 39–43
of the sale, 95
Questionnaires (see Checklists)

Rebuttals types of:
agree and counter, 116–120
blind eye, 121–122
comparison, 123
inapplicability, 122
indirect denial, 114–115
paraphrasing, 116
postponement, 122–123
questioning, 120–121
turnaround, 115–116
Routine calls, 212–213

Sales call:
preparation, 72–75
structure, 75
Sales literature, 66
Sales manager, source of information, 22
Salesmanship, 2–4
Sales meetings, source of information, 21
Sales objections (see Sales resistance)
Sales objectives, 73–74
Salespeople:
for prospective business, 28
types of, 11–13
Sales resistance:
basic types, 103–107
don't contradict, 107
overcoming, 99–124
related disciplines, 109–112
timing, importance of, 108–109
valid and invalid, 102–103

Sales support:
   post, 202–203
   source of information, 23
Sales surveys (*see* Studies, feasibility)
Secretary, the protective, 33–35
Selling cycle, duration of, 11
Selling time, effective use of, 210–211
Sensitivity, sales, 67
Social contacts, for business, 27
Solutions, selling, 85–87
'So what' test, 83–84
Studies, feasibility, 91–93
Suppliers, types of, 10

Telephone:
   disciplines, 32

inappropriate uses, 30
making appointments, 29
operators, 32–33
planned presentation, 31–32
protective secretaries, 33–35
Territories, types, 10
Thinking, positive, 211
Trade associations, 26–27
Trade directories, 27–28
Training, internal, 20–21
Trial orders, 139–140, 144–145

Written confirmation, 171–172